Behavior Modification
for the
Classroom Teacher

Behavior Modification
for the
Classroom Teacher

Saul Axelrod
Temple University

McGraw-Hill Book Company
New York / St. Louis / San Francisco
Auckland / Bogotá / Düsseldorf / Johannesburg / London
Madrid / Mexico / Montreal / New Delhi / Panama / Paris
São Paulo / Singapore / Sydney / Tokyo / Toronto

Library of Congress Cataloging in Publication Data

Axelrod, Saul.
   Behavior modification for the classroom teacher.

   (McGraw-Hill series in special education)
   Includes bibliographical references and index.
   1.   Classroom management.   2.   Behavior
modification.   I.   Title.
LB3013.A93   371.1′02   76-23296
ISBN 0-07-002571-1
ISBN 0-07-002570-3 pbk.

BEHAVIOR MODIFICATION FOR THE CLASSROOM TEACHER

   2 3 4 5 6 7 8 9 0 D O D O 7 8 3 2 1 0 9 8 7

This book was set in Times Roman by Black Dot, Inc. The editors were
Stephen D. Dragin and Phyllis T. Dulan; the cover was designed by
Lana Giganti, A Good Thing, Inc.; the production supervisor was
Thomas J. LoPinto. The drawings were done by Fine Line Illustrations, Inc.
R. R. Donnelley & Sons Company was printer and binder.

Contents

Foreword

Teachers and other school personnel have experienced a great deal of frustration over the years when faced with the management and learning problems of their students. Much of this frustration has been caused by the fact that until recently there has been no objective way for educators and psychologists to approach behavior, and few specific techniques have been available for dealing with problem behaviors.

Although most teachers have taken psychology courses designed to give them a basic understanding of the needs and characteristics of children, many teachers find that once they get into the classroom, they are ill-prepared to deal with many of the problems which arise. Looking back, the teachers realize that their courses in child psychology and teaching methods have been too nebulous and nonspecific to help pupils who disrupt the class or who are having academic difficulties.

Often, a teacher who becomes aware of such problems refers the pupil to the principal, the guidance counselor, or the school psychologist, hoping that with their greater experience and training they may either be able to suggest procedures for dealing with the problem or will remove the child from the classroom. All too often, however, the principal, counselor, and psychologist have been frustrated in their efforts to help the teacher and the child who has been referred. For instance, if a fifth-grader was referred to the principal for being disruptive, the principal might look at the child's permanent record card. It is likely that the principal will find that the child has been a behavior problem for several years. The chances are good that parent conferences were held, that various intelligence tests were given to the child, and that one or more psychological evaluations were made. It is also likely that the principal will have one or more conferences with the child and will try to convey concern about the problem, but at the same time will try to show understanding and will attempt to enlist the child's cooperation. When this approach fails, the principal will probably confer with the parents and seek their cooperation. It is likely that the parents will express their anguish and give permission to have the school psychologist evaluate their youngster. Following the evaluation it is possible that a meeting will be scheduled which will include the principal, the counselor, the psychologist, and perhaps the child's parents. The meeting will focus on the psychologist's report, which will probably confirm the results of previous evaluations. The report usually will suggest a number of possible causes of the child's problems such as a lack of motivation, resentment of adult authority, sibling rivalry, or insecurity. The report might indicate that the child needs a great deal of support and understanding. Counseling may be recommended so that the child's feelings can be expressed and understood. All concerned hope that increased insight into his or her problems will help the child to overcome the difficulties.

After the conference the teacher usually thanks everyone who assisted the child and returns to the classroom determined to continue all-out efforts to help and to understand the child. The teacher probably realizes, however, that nothing new has been learned from the referral. The teacher has made referrals in the past and received similar information that was not translatable into specific procedures which would reduce the disruptions. In all likelihood the student will continue to be a problem until either dropping out of school or graduating, leaving behind frustrated teachers, counselors, principals, and school psychologists—not to mention parents.

One wonders why this pattern has so often been repeated. Why educators so frequently have experienced this sense of frustration at their inability to cope with the problem behaviors of students? Why has it been difficult for successful teachers and supervisory personnel to help teachers who are ineffective?

In seeking to understand why such situations have existed for so long, one can look to several historical factors. One is related to viewing behavior from a psychoanalytic or personality viewpoint. According to this approach, which has long dominated our perceptions of child development, causes of behavior have their roots in the distant past, that is, the early developmental history of a child. Thus, when behavioral problems have arisen, educators and psychologists have looked primarily to the home and the early years of development in their search for causes. The emphasis on the past diverts attention from the ongoing situation and the dynamics of what is occurring in the present environment—the here and now. Another view of behavior is as an indirect manifestation or expression of the inner self and its relation to the basic hierarchy of needs. It has been assumed that there are certain basic psychological needs. If these needs are met, it has been claimed, an individual's energy will be channeled in positive directions and behavioral problems will disappear. This view has tended to focus attention away from the problem behavior itself. Since the behavior of concern has been considered merely a manifestation of an inner-psychic imbalance, attention has been placed on identifying and correcting the psychic imbalance, rather than on working with the observable problem behavior itself.

Another traditional approach to classroom problems is related to the trait theorists and the testing movement. The trait theorists have encouraged educators and psychologists to attempt to classify behaviors or patterns of behavior and thus to identify and label the behaviors of those who exhibited them. There has, therefore, been a powerful legacy handed down which almost compels us to classify children and to apply a label to them. The development of various intelligence, achievement, and projective tests has likewise done a great deal to strengthen the propensity to categorize and label children. These practices exist regardless of the lack of evidence that such categorizing and labeling help a teacher to work with children. In fact, the processes might be harmful. If a child is classified as "very disturbed" or "mildly retarded" a teacher might decide that the child's situation is hopeless and abandon efforts to help the youngster.

Finally, personality and intelligence tests have caused us to further divert our attention from actual behavior in the natural environment. Such tests, attempting to measure something which will get at the underlying causes of behavior, caused us to look away from the overt behavior in the real-life, day-to-day situation. It has also caused teachers and psychologists to regard measurement only in terms of sampling behavior indirectly through tests and surveys, rather than by looking directly at behavior and attempting to measure it as it occurs.

Thus, until very recently, when management or academic problems occurred, solutions to the problems were hampered by: (1) concentrating on the past of the child rather than the present environment; (2) regarding observable behavior merely as a symptom of underlying psychodynamics rather than being important in its own right; (3) categorizing and labeling children; and (4) looking at behavior indirectly through personality and intelligence tests.

In light of all this we can grasp why it has not been easy for us to see clearly the relationships between behavior and its causes and why we have had difficulty in devising specific procedures which have a high probability of meeting with success in dealing with classroom problems. It is also easy to see why teachers have not been adequately prepared to deal with many of the situations they have encountered in their classrooms. The truth of the matter is that we have not known enough about behavior and its causes, and we have not been able to see the relationship between the behavior of pupils and their environment to know what to do when things go wrong.

Fortunately, this situation is rapidly changing. In the past few years it has become possible to deal with management and academic problems more directly and effectively with a new approach called "behavior modification." What is behavior modification? There are many misconceptions among educators and those in other fields about behavior modification. Perhaps it would be well to state first of all what it is not. It is not a process of dispensing M & M's with abandon. It is not rat psychology. It is not altogether new. It is not a panacea which will instantly eliminate all management and academic problems from today's classrooms. It is not a coldly scientific approach which removes all creativity and warmth from the educational process. (In fact, behavior modification, properly used, can lead to greater creativity and warmth on the part of both the teacher and the students.)

More positively, behavior modification, as the name implies, is concerned with changing behavior. Specifically, it is concerned with changing behavior in desirable directions, that is, increasing the strength of appropriate behaviors and decreasing the strength of those that are inappropriate. Behavior modification has its basis in modern learning theory and unlike many previous approaches, it focuses on an individual's ongoing behavior and interaction with the present environment. Primary attention is given to observing as directly and accurately as possible what the individual is doing *now* and how the environment affects what she or he does. Exact procedures are used which are designed to improve behavior as directly and effectively as possible. Little emphasis is placed upon diagnosing causes related to the distant past and early developmental history.

Little or no attempt is made to label the child according to traits or test results. Whenever possible, the procedures used are carried out in the setting where the problem is occurring. Hence, a classroom problem will usually be dealt with in the classroom under the supervision of the teacher rather than in the counselor's office under the supervision of the counselor.

In the chapters which follow, my colleague Saul Axelrod has provided a detailed description of how teachers and other educators may apply behavior modification techniques in classroom settings. In Chapter 1 he describes basic behavioral principles and means of applying the principles in the classroom. In the second chapter less basic but important and useful procedures are discussed. Chapter 3 presents means by which teachers can accurately and conveniently measure student behavior. Axelrod also describes research designs which educators can employ to determine with great certainty which factors cause an improvement in pupil performance. In the fourth chapter the author provides many examples of how teachers and other school personnel have used behavior-modification procedures to solve a variety of classroom problems. In the final chapter, he presents some of the most commonly asked questions about behavior modification and offers some interesting answers to these important questions.

R. Vance Hall
University of Kansas

Behavior Modification
for the
Classroom Teacher

Chapter 1

Basic Processes and Principles

Let's face it. Teaching is really difficult. A teacher who enters the classroom on the first day of school may find thirty-five energetic fourth graders or ten glaring emotionally disturbed children. The teacher hopes, of course, that his or her personality and teaching techniques will be sufficient to motivate the children toward making scholastic progress. Frequently, however, chaos prevails. The children are all over the place, and the teacher considers abandoning the profession and becoming a social worker or real estate broker.

When teachers discuss children's difficulties, some will claim that their problems are due to the unfortunate home environments of their students or will state that their youngsters are good on Mondays but terrors on Fridays. The problem with such explanations is that a teacher has little control over a child's home environment and cannot change a Friday into a Monday. Other teachers will claim that disruptive or speech-deficient children will "outgrow" their problems. They are often wrong. Many children will not outgrow their deficiencies. They need help, and teachers with the required skills can offer their students the necessary assistance.

Helping children is an active process. It is *not* achieved by sitting back and hoping that "everything will turn out all right." Teachers must pursue the means by which they can improve student performance. Fortunately, with the proliferation of behavior modification studies, there are now numerous techniques, of documented success, that teachers can apply in their classrooms. The techniques can be used to alleviate disruptive behavior and to increase academic achievements. They can be used in regular classrooms and in special classrooms. They can be used with students from preschool through secondary school levels.

In order to modify student behavior, teachers will have to modify some of their own behaviors. They will have to keep daily records of their student's performance. They will have to be systematic. They must be willing to fail and to try again. They must be willing to explain their actions to dubious parents and colleagues. Sometimes the process will require a great deal of effort, but teachers who are successful behavior modifiers will acquire one of the greatest rewards of all—the academic and social growth of their students.

In this chapter, the basic procedures and principles that teachers can use to make favorable modifications in their students' behavior are presented. First, however, it is necessary to have an understanding of what behavior is, the types of behaviors there are, and the fundamental principles involved in behavior change. It is also necessary to know how a behavior modifier investigates whether or not a certain procedure is responsible for a change in behavior.

TYPES OF BEHAVIOR, CONDITIONING, AND REVERSAL DESIGN

When behavior modifiers use the term "behavior," they are referring to anything a child does. This is in contrast to the manner in which other educators have used the term. To some educators the term "behavior" refers only to a child's deportment, that is, whether she follows a teacher's directions, whether she talks without permission, and so on. The term as used in this book not only refers to deportment but also includes the whole gamut of students' school activities, such as their reading, writing, and arithmetic performance.

Skinner (1938) pointed out that there are two kinds of behaviors. One type is called a "respondent" and refers to involuntary behaviors. It is said that respondent behaviors are elicited by known stimuli. In other words, a stimulus is presented and the response automatically follows. An example of a respondent behavior is eye pupil dilation when an individual enters a dark room. The pupils spontaneously become larger. Other examples of respondents are shivering in cold weather, sweating in hot weather, and blinking when a cinder enters the eye.

The second kind of behavior is known as an "operant." Operant behaviors are emitted or "voluntary" responses. Examples of operant behaviors include reading a book, completing a homework assignment, running through the hall, arguing with the teacher, and doing arithmetic problems. There are no known stimuli which will automatically elicit these behaviors.

It is a well-established fact that the rate of occurrence of operant behaviors is influenced by events that follow the behavior. These events are called the "consequences" of behavior. The word "consequences" might be confusing to some people because they associate the term with something negative. Actually, consequences can be positive or negative. If the consequences of a behavior are positive, the chances are that the behavior will recur at a high rate. Suppose a teacher consistently smiles at a student who says "Hello" to him. Since most students enjoy their teacher's smiles, it is likely that the child will continue to say "Hello" to the teacher in the future. On the other hand, a teacher might scold a student for something the youngster did wrong each time the student greets him. In this case the consequence is negative, and it is likely that the student will cease saying "Hello" to the teacher in the future. The process by which the consequences of behavior increase or decrease the future rate of that behavior is known as "operant conditioning."

In order for consequences to have their maximum impact on behavior, it is necessary that they be arranged in a "contingent" manner. A "contingent" relationship is one in which the consequence a student receives depends on the behavior he performs. Thus, if a teacher allows a student extra free-play time only after he obeys classroom rules, she has awarded the student free time contingent on his prior behavior, and the student will probably continue to follow classroom rules in the future. If the teacher allows the student extra free time whether he obeys the rules or not, she has awarded the consequence in a "noncontingent" manner and it should *not* be expected that the student will obey classroom rules in the future.

Operant conditioning is but one technique available to the behavior modifier. At the present state of knowledge, however, operant conditioning methods are the most thoroughly investigated and useful techniques which the behavior modifier can offer to educators. This book will therefore concentrate on behavior modification techniques which involve operant conditioning procedures. At times, however, mention will be made of other techniques which are helpful in teaching desirable classroom behavior.

Chapter 3 will describe the research designs which are commonly used in behavior modification studies. For the present section, however, some understanding of research design is necessary. In a behavior modification study, the teacher typically notes the frequency or quality of a student's behavior under normal or baseline conditions. The baseline phase (sometimes called "Baseline$_1$"), is the performance of an individual or a group over a period of time before any special procedures are employed (see Baseline, Figure 1-1). After baseline the teacher applies a procedure which is intended to improve the student's behavior. This stage constitutes Experimental Phase$_1$, but is usually given a label which describes the procedure, for example, "Extra Recess for Assignment Completion," "Ignoring Tantrums," "Reinforcement" (see Reinforcement$_1$, Figure 1-1). If the rate or quality of a student's behavior improves during Experimental Phase$_1$, the teacher will be pleased with the results but may wonder whether the technique he used was really responsible for the change that occurred. It is possible that some other factor, such as student

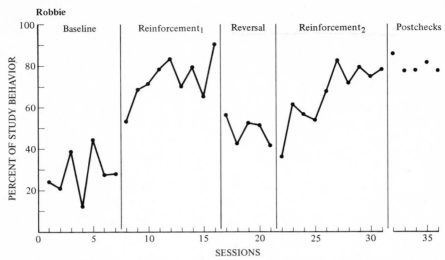

Figure 1-1 The percentage of study behavior by Robbie during each of five experimental phases. *(From R. V. Hall, D. Lund, and D. Jackson, "Effects of Teacher Attention on Study Behavior,"* Journal of Applied Behavior Analysis, **1**, *p. 3, 1968. By permission of the publishers.)*

maturity, for example, may have accounted for the improvement. As a result, the teacher will frequently return the student to baseline conditions in a phase known as "Baseline₂," or "Reversal" (see Reversal, Figure 1-1). If the behavior deteriorates to a level resembling Baseline₁ performance, the teacher will have evidence that the procedure he employed during Experimental Phase₁ really was responsible for the improvement. Once the effect of the Baseline₂ stage is observed, the behavior modification procedure is usually reapplied in Experimental Phase₂ (see Reinforcement₂, Figure 1-1). If improvement again results, there is additional verification that the behavior modification procedure is causing the improvement in behavior. After the formal termination of a study, occasional checks are sometimes made to determine the long-range effectiveness of the procedure. During this period the procedure is still in effect, but measurements are made less often (see Postchecks, Figure 1-1).

Although the rationale behind the reversal design might appear foreign to the reader, its use is a daily occurrence. A popular television advertisement states, for example, "If you don't think Protein 21 helps you to get rid of the frizzies, stop using it and see what happens." The notion is that the shampoo has helped to improve the condition of the user's hair. To verify this, it is suggested that viewers stop using the shampoo and thereby experience a return of their old hair problems. It is implied, of course, that following the reversal period, the viewer will again use the shampoo and reexperience the joy of frizzless hair.

As indicated earlier, the operant conditioning process can bring about an increase or decrease in student behavior. When a desirable behavior does not

occur or when it occurs too seldom, teachers will be concerned with the r.
by which they can bring about increases in behavior. This can ofter
accomplished with the operations discussed in the next section.

MEANS OF INCREASING THE RATE OF BEHAVIOR

Positive Reinforcement

The behavior modification procedure that teachers most commonly use involves rewarding appropriate behavior after it occurs. The reward is called a
"positive reinforcer" and is defined as any consequence of behavior whose
presentation increases the future rate of that behavior. The process by which
the behavior increases in rate is known as "positive reinforcement." Commonly used positive reinforcers include praise, free-play time, candy, and special
privileges. A positive reinforcement procedure might consist of placing a star
on a student's paper whenever he reaches 80 percent accuracy on a weekly
spelling test. If the youngster's spelling accuracy increases over what it was
before stars were used, the stars are considered positive reinforcers for spelling
accuracy. If the student's spelling performance does not improve, the stars
cannot be regarded as positive reinforcers.

In order for a positive reinforcer to have its greatest effect, it should be
delivered immediately after the appropriate behavior occurs. In this manner the
student will quickly associate the behavior with the reinforcer. If a teacher
waits too long to reinforce a desired behavior, it is possible that another
behavior will occur in the meantime and will be reinforced instead. It is,
therefore, better that a teacher walk around the classroom rather than sit at a
desk. As she moves from one student to another, she can quickly attend to each
student's work and compliment youngsters when they are correct. The teacher
who sits at her desk and grades papers at the end of the period might find
herself praising a child's work output when she is pulling a classmate's hair.

There are numerous examples of the successful use of positive reinforcement procedures in classrooms. A study by Tribble and Hall (1972) involved a
student, John, who completed only a small portion of his daily mathematics
assignments. As shown in Figure 1-2, the percentage of problems John
completed each day never exceeded 25 percent, and his average over a
fifteen-day Baseline$_1$ period was only 21 percent.

Following Baseline$_1$, Ms. Tribble told John that if he finished 60 percent of
the assigned problems, she would mark a "+" on his paper; John could take
papers with a "+" to his mother and exchange them for a "surprise." During
the first day of the "Surprise at Home" stage, John completed 100 percent of
his assignment; joy turned to disappointment, however, as John's performance
deteriorated during the remaining days of the phase.

Undaunted, Ms. Tribble tried again, this time with the knowledge that John
could do the work if she could only keep him motivated to try. On day 20, she
announced that if John completed his mathematics problems within twenty
minutes of the beginning of the period, the entire class would go outside to play

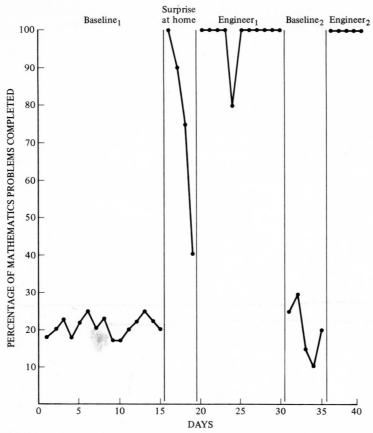

Figure 1-2 The percentage of arithmetic problems John completed on daily assignements. *Adapted from A. Tribble and R. V. Hall, "Effects of Peer Approval on Completion of Arithmetic Assignments," in F. W. Clark, D. R. Evans, and L. A. Hamerlynck (eds.),* Implementing Behavioral Programs for Schools and Clinics: Third Banff International Conference. *Champaign, III.: Research Press, 1972, pp. 139–140. By permission of the publishers.)*

a game, and that John could be the engineer leading the "train" of students to the school playground. For the eleven days of "Engineer₁," John finished his entire assignment on all but one day. On many occasions John's classmates would cheer for him after he completed his assignment.

Following Engineer₁, John returned to baseline conditions. During this period some other child was chosen to be "engineer" and the class had the opportunity to play games whether John completed the problems or not. For the five days of this Baseline₂ phase, John finished an average of only 21 percent of his mathematics problems. Thus it can be seen that the improvement which John showed during the Engineer₁ phase was due to his being chosen the engineer for the free-play time after he completed the assignment. When games were again made contingent on John's finishing his work during Engineer$_2$, John completed 100 percent of the problems each day.

The positive reinforcer for completing assignments in the Tribble and Hall (1972) study was the opportunity to play games. The reinforcer was administered not only to John but to other members of the class. As a result, John's classmates provided additional reinforcement by applauding and praising him after he completed his arithmetic problems.

It should be pointed out that the first procedure that Tribble and Hall used was ineffective in improving John's performance. This is not surprising, since behavior modification techniques, like other techniques, sometimes fail to help a child overcome his difficulties. The important factor is that when one procedure does not work, the teacher should attempt alternative techniques until an effective one is found.

Another study using positive reinforcement was done by Hall, Lund, and Jackson (1968). The authors were interested in increasing the amount of time in which the students were engaged in study behavior. "Study behavior,"[1] however, is an ambiguous term which requires further definition. The investigators observed classroom situations and decided that, in general, study behavior included "orientation toward the appropriate object or person: assigned course materials, lecturing teacher, or reciting classmates, as well as class participation by the student when requested by the teacher [p. 2]." The definition of study behavior varied somewhat for each student depending on the subject matter being taught during the observation period. The critical point, however, is that if a teacher is interested in using behavior modification techniques, he must decide what he means by such terms as "study behavior" and then break these terms down into smaller, observable units.

Six students were involved in the Hall et al. (1968) study. The data for one of the pupils, Robbie, are depicted in Figure 1-1. During baseline, Robbie was engaged in study behavior only 25 percent of the time. It was then decided to use teacher attention as the reinforcer for appropriate behavior. During Reinforcement$_1$, the teacher attended to Robbie at times when he was engaged in study behavior. She would move toward his desk, verbally praise him, smile at him, or give him a pat on the back. Sometimes she poked him in the ribs and joked with him. When Robbie was not engaged in study behavior, the teacher ignored him. For the nine sessions in which this procedure was used, Robbie's study rate increased steadily until it reached a mean of 71 percent. During a five-session reversal period, in which social reinforcement was discontinued, Robbie's study rate quickly decreased to an average of 50 percent; when reinforcement procedures were reinstated, Robbie's proportion of study behavior stabilized at a high rate.

The importance of the Hall et al. (1968) study was not so much the fact that

[1]The terms "study," "attending," and "on-task" behavior are used interchangeably in the behavior modification literature. Throughout most of the book, I have used the same term as the various authors used in their original reports.

pupil study rates increased with behavior modification techniques. Of greater significance was the demonstration that student behavior could be improved with nothing more than the contingent use of teacher warmth and attention. People in our society often talk about the power of tender, loving care, but they should realize that its effectiveness is enhanced if it follows appropriate behavior.

Negative Reinforcement

When a teacher uses a positive reinforcement technique, a student performs an appropriate behavior and the teacher gives him something he likes. A second type of reinforcement procedure is known as "negative reinforcement." This is an operation in which a student performs a behavior and the teacher removes something he dislikes. That which is removed is known as a "negative reinforcer." An example of negative reinforcement would involve students who are working at a furious pace after their teacher states that she will relieve them of homework if they complete a certain assignment. The homework is the negative reinforcer. Another example of negative reinforcement would be a child who cries, "Uncle!" in order to escape the arm twisting of a classmate. In this case the arm twist is a negative reinforcer, since it increases the probability of the child yelling, "Uncle!"

Positive and negative reinforcement are similar in that both procedures result in an increase in the frequency of the target behavior. The difference between the two operations is that when positive reinforcement is programmed, an appropriate behavior will add something desirable (for example, extra recess, toys, or praise) to the environment. With a negative reinforcement procedure, an appropriate behavior will remove something aversive from the environment (for example, detention, scowl, or an arm twist).

Teachers sometimes unknowingly become trapped by negative reinforcement arrangements. Ms. Carlton, for example, might learn that every time she screams at Sandy for talking out, the youngster ceases talking out for a period of time. Since the screaming procedure is somewhat effective, Ms. Carlton continues to scream at Sandy whenever Sandy talks out. The tactic qualifies as negative reinforcement because the teacher's screaming rate increased and something undesirable (talking out) was subtracted from the environment. In spite of the apparent effectiveness of the screaming, the procedure may eventually become self-defeating. It may happen that when other annoying situations arise, Ms. Carlton will again scream at the children until the problem ceases. Thus, the teacher might find herself controlling her entire class through repeated screaming episodes. Such a tactic would not only make the classroom environment aversive to the students, but the teacher's overall effectiveness might be curtailed because many adults find it difficult to function properly following screaming incidents. A better means for reducing Sandy's talking-out behavior would be to positively reinforce her for periods of time in which she refrained from talking out.

Differential Reinforcement and Shaping

Experience has shown that it is relatively easy for behaviorally oriented teachers to increase or decrease the rate of behaviors their students can already perform. Consider a child who raises his hand occasionally but less often than is desirable; it is not too difficult for a teacher to devise a positive reinforcement procedure to motivate the student to raise his hand more often. Similarly, if a student is in her seat at some times but is often out of her seat without permission, it is usually a simple task to program consequences which will decrease her rate of out-of-seat behavior. The solution to such a problem might involve periodically reinforcing a child when she is in her seat and withholding reinforcement at other times.

The procedure of reinforcing only one behavior from a group of behaviors is termed "differential reinforcement." An example of a differential reinforcement tactic was given in the previously mentioned (p. 7) Hall, Lund, and Jackson (1968) study. In this study, the teacher attended to and praised Robbie when he behaved appropriately and ignored him at all other times. The student soon exhibited appropriate behavior at a rate exceeding baseline levels.

It is a more difficult task to teach a behavior which a student has seldom or never performed. Thus, a teacher must be quite skillful in teaching a fourth-grade student to read if the student has no reading vocabulary. A technique which has been useful in teaching new behaviors is termed "shaping" or "the reinforcement of successive approximations." Shaping is a procedure in which a teacher first determines how close a student is to being able to perform a desired behavior, known as the "terminal behavior." Once the initial level of the behavior is determined, the teacher progressively requires the student to perform a series of behaviors which approximate the terminal behavior. Each time the student performs the required approximation, the teacher reinforces the student until he or she is consistently able to perform the terminal behavior. The distinction between differential reinforcement and shaping is that in the case of differential reinforcement, a teacher is attempting to change the rate of a behavior that a student already performs. In the case of shaping, one is attempting to teach a new behavior, or one that rarely occurs.

An important point to note in a shaping procedure, or in any behavior modification program, is that the increases in the difficulty of a task should be made in small steps. The author can recall many sad experiences in which he failed to observe this elementary principle and was forced to restart a behavior modification program after weeks of employing a procedure. Novices who have become enthusiastic about the prospect of using behavior modification techniques sometimes proceed too quickly and, as a result, frustrate themselves and the students whom they wish to assist.

The game of "hot and cold," which many children play, makes use of shaping principles. One child hides an item in some part of the room. When the second child attempts to find the item, the first child tells her if she is getting closer by saying "Hot," or further away by saying "Cold." Whenever the second child hears "hot," she continues to move in the same direction until she is eventually "shaped" into locating the hidden item. Parents sometimes fail to make use of shaping principles when they attempt to motivate their children to eat a new meal. Often, a parent will say, "Eat all of your broccoli, and I will give you a glass of Coke." Many children will still refuse under these conditions. The child would be more likely to eat the broccoli if the parent first required that the child take a small bite of the vegetable for a small amount of soda, and then required that the child eat progressively larger portions for the soda reward.

A classic example of a shaping procedure was conducted by Wolf, Risley, and Mees (1964). Dicky, the subject for the study, was a hospitalized, autistic youngster who had previously had the lenses removed from both of his eyes. Parental efforts to induce the youngster to wear glasses had repeatedly failed. When Dicky reached the age of three, an ophthalmologist predicted that unless Dicky wore his glasses regularly, he would lose his macular vision within six months. The shaping procedure began by placing several pairs of empty glass frames in the hospital room in which the training sessions were held. Initially, Dicky was reinforced with small amounts of food for picking up the frames, holding them, and carrying them with him. Gradually, it was necessary for Dicky to bring the frames closer to his eyes in order to receive the reinforcer. As Dicky mastered each step, the experimenters slowly required closer approximations to the terminal behavior in order for the child to obtain the reinforcer.

When Dicky's behavior improved sufficiently, the corrective lenses were placed in the frames. More advanced steps included his putting the glasses to his face, in any position, and later it was required that the glasses sit on his face in the appropriate position. After wearing the glasses was established in the hospital room, the behavior was extended to other areas by requiring that the glasses be in place before activities such as meals and outdoor play were allowed to take place. Before the child was released from the hospital, it was reported that Dicky was wearing his glasses for an average of twelve hours a day.

A teacher might use a shaping procedure with a student who spends merely a few minutes of each period doing his work and the remainder of the period clowning around. Suppose a reading teacher finds Donald spends only five minutes of a thirty-minute reading period doing his reading assignment. She might set up a program in which Donald can have access to a game area in the back of the room if he works for the first seven minutes of the period. Once Donald consistently works for seven minutes, the teacher could set a ten-minute work criterion in order for Donald to spend the remainder of the period in the play area. Next, the work criterion can be raised to fourteen minutes. Gradually, the teacher can increase the amount of work time required of Donald until the youngster is working for amost the entire period (for example, twenty-five minutes) for a few minutes of play (for example, five minutes).

Programmed instruction materials make use of the shaping process. Typically, a student begins a task at a level at which he is already competent. Next, the program prods the student through the learning process with hints and questions, so that he can proceed along the task. The student answers questions and, if correct, is reinforced by receiving information verifying his accuracy. If a student has difficulties with a certain portion of the program, he is often directed to another section of the program that proceeds in smaller steps. When a student successfully completes a program, he is usually capable of performing a new behavior.

Fading

Shaping procedures are used to teach children behaviors which they cannot perform or have rarely performed. There are some cases, however, in which a student *can* perform a particular behavior but does not do so in certain desirable situations. A child, for example, might wear his eyeglasses at home but not in school; or he might speak fluently to family members but refuse to speak to neighbors and classmates; or he might sit quietly in a library but not in church. For such cases, a "fading" procedure is sometimes useful. This is a process of gradually changing the conditions under which a behavior occurs from one situation to a new situation.

An example of how a fading process can be used to teach a task to a nonhuman might involve a pigeon which has learned that pecking a bar in the presence of a red light will produce a reinforcer. The experimenter may then wish to have the bird peck the bar when a blue light is presented. If he simply presents the blue light, it is unlikely that the pigeon will peck the bar, since the new color differs greatly from the color associated with reinforcement. It has been found, however, that if only a slight amount of blue is mixed with the red light, the bird will continue to peck the bar. Pecking behaviors in the presence of the new light are, of course, reinforced. Then, if the light gradually becomes more blue and less red, the pigeon will eventually peck the bar in the presence of an entirely blue light.

Some outstanding demonstrations of the use of fading procedures were provided in a study by Martin, England, Kaprowy, Kilgour, and Pilek (1968) in a study involving seven seriously emotionally disturbed children. One of the most serious problems of the youngsters was echolalic speech—a language pattern in which a person repeats words that are said to him. Hence, if an echolalic child is asked, "What's your name?" he is likely to respond, "What's your name?" The authors embarked on a fading program designed to train functional speech. An example of the process was provided by having the teacher point to his shirt and ask, "What's this?" Initially, a child would answer "This." The child was capable of saying "Shirt," but did not do so.

The fading process then proceeded as follows: The teacher would point to his shirt and say, "Shirt." If the student also said "Shirt," he received a small amount of food as a reinforcer. The process was repeated several times until the child consistently said the word "shirt." In the second step, the teacher pointed to his shirt and said, "What's this? Shirt." "What's this?" was said in a soft voice and "Shirt" was spoken in a loud voice. When the student regularly answered, "Shirt," he proceeded to the next level. The teacher continued to say, "What's this? Shirt," but gradually said "What's this?" in a louder and louder voice and said "Shirt" in a softer and softer voice. In the final step the teacher asked, "What's this?" in a normal voice and the child consistently answered, "Shirt."

Using the fading procedure, the teacher was able to teach the median child to name 136 of the 200 items to which he was exposed in 65 hours of training. Examples of items included parts of the body, toys, articles of clothing, varieties of food, animal pictures, and household items.

Fading procedures are helpful in teaching a variety of academic skills. In teaching a child to print the letter "A," a workbook might provide students with the following exercises:

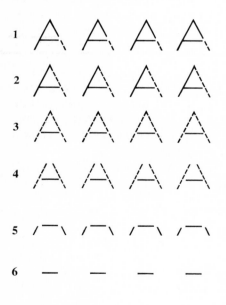

At each step the supporting stimulus is gradually decreased until the child is required to print the entire letter without assistance. Fading can also be used to teach a child to read a word such as "bear" in a reading textbook. The first time the word is presented, a picture of a fuzzy brown bear might appear over the word. The next time the word appears, the bear might be less fuzzy. At a later stage there may be only the outline of the bear, until eventually the student must read the word itself, without support. For an excellent article on the use of fading procedures to teach arithmetic skills, the reader is referred to an article by Haupt, Van Kirk, and Terraciano (1975).

Schedules of Reinforcement

A "continuous reinforcement schedule" is an arrangement in which reinforcement follows every appropriate behavior. Some teachers probably feel that reinforcing each desirable behavior is a difficult, if not impossible, task. Fortunately, it is not necessary that a teacher use a continuous reinforcement schedule in order to teach a student a new behavior or to maintain a desirable behavior that already exists. When reinforcement follows only a portion of the desired behaviors, the arrangement is called an "intermittent" or "partial reinforcement" schedule. Intermittent reinforcement schedules are more representative of real-life situations than continuous reinforcement schedules. A laborer is paid not for each appropriate behavior that he or she performs, but at the end of the week or month for a series of behaviors. Certainly, the behavior of professors, fishermen, and hitchhikers persists in spite of a thin schedule of reinforcement. Since reinforcement is delivered less frequently, intermittent schedules sometimes provide the advantage that students become satiated on the reinforcers more slowly than is the case when they are exposed to a continuous reinforcement schedule.

The four most popular schedules of intermittent reinforcement are: "fixed-interval," "variable-interval," "fixed-ratio," and "variable-ratio." When the two interval schedules are employed, a response is reinforced only after a certain amount of time has passed since the previous reinforced response. The two ratio schedules deliver reinforcement after an individual emits a certain number of responses.

On a "fixed-interval (FI) schedule," reinforcement is accessible at standard intervals of time. If a fixed interval of five minutes (FI5) is in effect, for example, reinforcement becomes available after *exactly* five minutes has elapsed since the last reinforced response. The first response that occurs after five minutes has passed is reinforced. Following this response and reinforcement, a new five-minute cycle is begun. An individual who is exposed to an FI schedule eventually learns that responding before the time cycle has been completed does not lead to reinforcement. Thus, he ceases responding during the initial portion of the FI cycle. The decrease in responding which follows reinforcement on an FI schedule is termed a "fixed-interval scallop" and limits the usefulness of FI schedules.

A situation analogous to the pattern of responding on a FI schedule is the amount of activity exhibited by elected officials at various times of the election cycle. Immediately after the election the victor often seems to have disappeared. A few months before the next election, however, the incumbent reemerges to raid pornographic bookstores, kiss babies, and eat soul food. Another example of FI performance is the flurry of study activity by college students immediately before an examination and the lack of study behaviors immediately after the examination.

An interval schedule which results in higher and more steady rates of behavior than the FI schedule is the "variable-interval (VI) schedule." With a variable-interval schedule, the first response to occur after a period of time, which varies from one reinforcement to the next, is reinforced. If a variable-interval schedule of one minute (VI1) is in effect, for example, a reinforcer is available on the *average* of once a minute since the previous reinforced response. A VI1 schedule might consist of a sequence of reinforcers delivered for the first responses to occur after 100, 2, 40, 60, 118, 20, and 80 seconds. (Note that the average interval is 60 seconds, or one minute.)

That is, the first reinforcer is available after 100 seconds has elapsed. The first time an individual responds after this period of time, he receives a reinforcer. The second reinforcer is available 2 seconds after the first reinforcer is delivered. The first response to occur after 2 seconds has elapsed will be reinforced. The third reinforcer is available 40 seconds after the second reinforcer is delivered. Responses made before 40 seconds has elapsed will *not* result in reinforcement, nor will they delay the availability of reinforcement; they will merely provide the individual with some exercise.

Since at least some responses are reinforced shortly after the previous reinforcement on a VI schedule, the pauses in responding associated with FI schedules are usually eliminated, and higher and steadier rates of responding generally develop. The game of musical chairs is played according to a VI schedule. Since a player is uncertain when the music will stop (making the reinforcer, in the form of an empty chair, available), he stays alert at all times. One can speculate as to the degree of increased activity on the part of politicians if elections were held on a VI schedule. Similarly, the study patterns of college students would probably change radically if their professors gave "pop" quizzes (a VI schedule), rather than announcing the dates of midterm and final examinations (FI scheduling). In areas of the country in which the time of mail delivery varies from one day to the next, individuals who find mail reinforcing can sometimes be seen checking their mailboxes ten to fifteen times a day.

When the ratio schedules of reinforcement are used, an individual is reinforced for the number of responses he makes. A "fixed-ratio (FR) schedule" specifies the exact number of responses a person must perform to receive reinforcement. This number stays the same from one reinforcement to the next. With an FR15 schedule, for example, an individual is reinforced for every fifteen responses made. This is similar to the practice of piecework in which a farm worker receives a certain amount of money each time he or she fills a basket with peaches. Individuals who are exposed to FR schedules of reinforcement tend to respond at a high rate, *once they start responding.* It has been found, however, that with large FR schedules (for example, FR50), people will often cease responding for a period of time following reinforcement (apparently, taking a break before the long haul ahead). The decrease in response rate following a reinforcement on an FR schedule is called a "post-reinforcement pause." The pauses are usually of shorter duration than those which occur on FI schedules.

The fourth type of schedule is the "variable-ratio (VR) schedule." A VR schedule delivers reinforcement after an individual makes a certain number of responses, which varies from one reinforcement to the next. On a VR15 schedule, for example, reinforcement follows an *average* of one out of fifteen responses. Reinforcements may be separated from each other by 20, 1, 29, 10, 2, and 28 responses, but on the average one out of 15 responses will be reinforced. (Note that the average of 20, 1, 29, 10, 2, and 28 is 15.) Hence, the first reinforcement occurs after twenty responses. The second reinforcement occurs after one more response is made. The third response occurs after an additional twenty-nine responses are made, and so on. An example of a VR schedule is betting that a head will come up when a coin is flipped. In this case, a VR2 schedule is in effect, and the bettor is reinforced on the average of one out of every two coin flips. VR schedules eliminate the post-reinforcement pauses which occur on FR schedules, and they produce the highest and steadiest rates of behavior of the four intermittent reinforcement schedules discussed in the present section.

Teachers may wonder what relevance schedules of reinforcement have to classroom management. Admittedly, the use of reinforcement schedules would be difficult to implement in most classroom situations. Perhaps the points for a teacher to note are that it is usually possible to employ behavior modification procedures effectively by reinforcing only a portion of the correct behaviors, and that a child should be reinforced according to the number of appropriate behaviors he makes, rather than the passage of time. Also, intermittent reinforcement is less likely to result in satiation and, as will be discussed later, such schedules usually produce more durable behavior once the reinforcement is discontinued than is the case with continuous reinforcement schedules.

Conditioned and Token Reinforcement

The types of reinforcers mentioned earlier have varied from candy treats to teacher smiles. It is probably apparent to most readers that food reinforcers fall into a different category from social reinforcers, such as smiles and praise. The distinction between the two types of reinforcers is the source of their reinforcing capacity, with some reinforcers classified as unconditioned reinforcers and others as conditioned reinforcers. An "unconditioned reinforcer" is one whose ability to reinforce behavior is independent of an association with other reinforcers. Such reinforcers are also called "primary reinforcers." Examples of unconditioned reinforcers include food when an individual is hungry, liquid refreshment when one is thirsty, and sexual activities at all times. Unconditioned reinforcers are associated with satisfying a biological need.

A "conditioned reinforcer" is one whose ability to reinforce behavior results from an association with other reinforcers. Conditioned reinforcers are also called "secondary" or "acquired" reinforcers. In order to establish a neutral item or event as a conditioned reinforcer, it is necessary that the item or event be present before or during the time an already established reinforcer is presented. An example of the process of establishing an event as a conditioned reinforcer might involve a father who is feeding his baby. During the time he is feeding him, he will smile at the baby, pat his back, use the words "good boy," and show other forms of affection. Initially, the father's patting, for example, will have little effect on the infant's behavior. As a result of an association with food, however, patting is established as a conditioned reinforcer and the child will behave in such a manner as to acquire his father's pats. Sometimes this means that the child will make particular sounds and at other times it means that he will perform certain "tricks" for his father's pats. In other words, the pats on the back become conditioned reinforcers and the child will work for them in the same manner as he will work for other reinforcers.

There is a tendency to regard conditioned reinforcers as something less than "real" reinforcers. In fact, conditioned reinforcers are a potent and important source of reinforcement, and teachers should always attempt to establish conditioned reinforcers for their students. This can be done by praising, smiling at, and making physical contact with children at the same time they are being awarded treats and privileges. Once such social events are associated with established reinforcers, they become conditioned reinforcers; it then becomes possible for teachers to withdraw privileges and treats as reinforcers and to maintain student progress with social reinforcers alone.

In addition to social events such as praise, attention, and smiles, money can serve as a conditioned reinforcer. A young child learns that if she gives a storekeeper a certain number of pennies, she will receive her favorite candy. As a result of repeatedly pairing the pennies with the candy, the pennies eventually become conditioned reinforcers. After this procedure has been established, parents find that their child will more readily perform a certain task if she is paid for her efforts than if she is not.

Money has a considerable advantage over most other types of conditioned reinforcers in influencing behavior. Rather than being associated with only one type of primary reinforcer, money is associated with many types of reinforcers. In addition to different kinds of candy, money can be used to purchase toys, for admission to a favorite event, to buy soda pop, and so on. A conditioned reinforcer which is associated with a large number of positive reinforcers is termed a "generalized conditioned reinforcer" or a "generalized reinforcer."

A type of generalized reinforcer which is of great importance in classroom management and instruction is the "token reinforcer." The token reinforcer can be an object, such as a star or a poker chip. It can also be a symbol, such as a checkmark in a notebook or on the blackboard. Birnbrauer, Wolf, Kidder, and Tague (1965) point out that token reinforcers, in and of themselves, are unlikely to have reinforcing power. They attain reinforcing value, however, by being exchangeable for a variety of items which are reinforcing. Thus, a student may receive nine checks for behaving appropriately during the arithmetic period, and exchange the marks for three pieces of candy at the end of the school day. The items for which the tokens may be exchanged are called "back-up reinforcers."

There are several advantages in using a token reinforcement system over other types of reinforcement systems. Some reinforcement systems use a single item or privilege as a reinforcer, and their effectiveness is, therefore, dependent on the degree to which the students have been deprived of the intended reinforcer. If candy, for example, is used as a reinforcer, a reinforcement program may fail because the pupils have become satiated on the candy. Token reinforcement procedures, however, are not bound by this limitation because the tokens may be exchanged for a large variety of reinforcers—at least one of which should be reinforcing to each student. Tokens also provide the possibility of furnishing reinforcers of greater value than is the case when a single reinforcer is employed, since the tokens can be saved over a period of time and can be exchanged for an item or privilege of increased reinforcing value. A third advantage of token programs is that the presentation of a token after a desired behavior does not disrupt the classroom routine as does the awarding of a piece of candy or a toy.

McKenzie, Clark, Wolf, Kothera, and Benson (1968) pointed out a fourth advantage of token systems. They indicated that report card grades have been a customary token reinforcement arrangement in public school systems. The problem with the practice, however, is that the delay between the academic behavior and the resulting consequence is often between six and nine weeks. Thus, an association between the behavior and the consequence it produces is not likely to develop. Token reinforcement systems employed in behavior modification studies avoid this difficulty by presenting the token soon after an appropriate response occurs. Token systems also ensure a systematic relationship between the number of tokens which are earned and the products for which the tokens may be exchanged. This is in contrast to report card grades, in which such a relationship is often unsystematic or nonexistent.

There has been extensive use of token reinforcement procedures in classroom settings (see Axelrod, 1971; O'Leary and Drabman, 1971; and Kazdin and Bootzin, 1972, for review articles). Token programs have been successful in reducing the frequency of disruptive behavior and in improving academic performance. O'Leary and Becker (1967) provided an example of how a teacher could use a token reinforcement program to drastically reduce inappropriate behavior in a classroom of seventeen emotionally disturbed children. Following a ten-day baseline period in which inappropriate behaviors were occurring 76 percent of the time, a token reinforcement system was implemented. First, the following rules were written on the board:

In Seat
Face Front

Raise Hand
Working
Pay Attention

Next, the teacher rated each child daily with a score from 1 to 10 according to her estimate of how well the youngsters had obeyed the classroom rules. The ratings the students received were exchangeable for a variety of candies and toys. Thus, a child with a rating of 9 could buy more items, or items of greater value, than a child with a rating of 5. In this case the ratings constituted the token reinforcers and the candy and toys were back-up reinforcers.

Data obtained by an outside observer indicated that inappropriate behaviors decreased to 10 percent during the twenty-five-day token phase. In a later article (O'Leary, Becker, Evans, and Saudargas, 1969) the authors admitted that the rating procedure used to determine how many tokens each student would receive were based on subjective teacher judgments, but claimed that such a tactic is easier for a single teacher to implement than a tactic using more precise evaluations. My own experience indicates that the 10-point rating system is both effective and easy to implement, and I recommend it highly for a variety of classroom management problems.

Wolf, Giles, and Hall (1968) did a token reinforcement study which was directed toward improving the academic development of sixteen inner-city fifth- and six-grade students. All students were at least two years below grade level on the reading section of the Stanford Achievement Test (S.A.T.). In addition to attending regular school sessions, the students took part in a remedial program which was conducted for a 2$^1/_2$-hour period after school, on Saturdays, on school holidays, and during the summer months. It was during the remedial sessions that the token reinforcement procedures were in effect. The youngsters received reading, arithmetic, and English assignments obtained from commercially prepared materials. Each child had a folder containing pages which were divided into sixty or one hundred squares. After a student successfully completed an assignment, the teacher placed a slash mark in one of the squares. Initially, the slash marks were awarded after each problem was done correctly, but gradually the amount and difficulty of the work required for the marks were increased (an example of shaping). The marks were exchangeable for a variety of back-up reinforcers, such as snacks and novelties, which were awarded at the end of each period. Other back-up reinforcers, such as clothes, field trips, and secondhand bicycles, were available only if a student saved his tokens (that is, slash marks) over a longer period of time.

By the end of the year, the youngsters made a median gain of 1.5 years on the S.A.T. The authors pointed out that the study cost an average of $225 per student, but claimed that the amount of money should be contrasted with the economic and human loss which results from inadequate education. Anecdotal evidence indicating the degree to which the children enjoyed the remedial program was provided when the students were given a choice as to whether to attend classes during school holidays. Each time the choice was presented, a majority of the students voted to have class. On Thanksgiving and Christmas, however, the teachers refused to work.

Feedback

Reinforcers derive their ability to modify behavior from two sources. First, they serve as motivators for student performance. This means that a youngster is likely to study very hard for a spelling test if his father promises him a trip to the circus for a score of 80 percent or more. Similarly, students will work diligently on an assignment if they are permitted free time upon completion of the assignment. The second function of a reinforcer is to provide feedback to students, that is, information that they performed the right behavior. Therefore, a token, in the form of a checkmark next to a correct arithmetic computation lets a student know that his answer was accurate. Likewise, a smile and a pat on the back from the teacher inform the youngster that he has been working well.

Sometimes feedback alone is sufficient to produce an improvement in behavior. A critical aspect of programmed instruction materials, for example, is that the materials contain the correct answers to questions that are posed. Thus, a student quickly learns whether his own answers are correct or not. If they are correct, he proceeds further along the learning task. If they are not correct, he returns to the same problem, or to an easier section, and tries again.

Feedback procedures have been used in a variety of other ways to modify student and teacher behavior. At times teachers have made up charts on which student scores were posted each day. After a child completed an academic task the teacher or the child would enter the day's score. The scores of many children improve as they try to surpass their previous high score. Feedback is also helpful in modifying teacher behavior. A teacher might find, for example, that his rate of praising students is low and as a result of such information tries to increase his rate of praise. The information can be attained with the aid of outside personnel or by having the teacher keep a record of his own behavior.

As was the case with reinforcement, immediate feedback is more helpful than delayed feedback. An excellent demonstration of this principle was given in a study by Leach and Graves (1973). The study took place in a regular seventh-grade language arts classroom that met each day for fifty minutes. Two students, Betty and Jane, were having problems with correct sentence writing. The teacher defined a correct sentence as one which consisted of at least five words, which was punctuated and capitalized correctly, which had agreement between the subject and verb, and in which the subject and verb were identified. Each day the teacher asked Jane and Betty to write ten sentences. During Baseline$_1$ the teacher graded the students' papers and returned them to the girls the following day. Figure 1-3 shows that Betty averaged 54 percent and Jane received 61 percent during the Baseline$_1$ phase.

In the Immediate Correction$_1$ phase, the teacher continued to request that

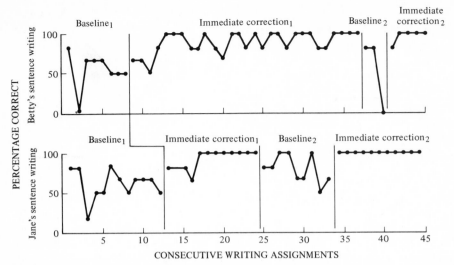

Figure 1-3 The percentage of correctly written sentences by two seventh-grade girls. The youngsters wrote ten sentences daily for a language arts assignment. *(From D. M. Leach and M. Graves, "The Effects of Immediate Correction on Improving Seventh Grade Language Arts Performance," in A. Egner (ed.),* Individualizing Junior and Senior High Instruction to Provide Special Education within Regular Classrooms. *Burlington, Vt.: University of Vermont, 1973, p. 17. By permission of the publishers.)*

the girls write ten sentences but immediately graded the papers and returned them to the girls. After three days the scores of each of the girls increased to high levels, with Betty reaching an average of 90 percent and Jane an average of 93 percent. On sixteen of twenty-nine days Betty had a perfect score, and on eight of eleven days Jane's scores were perfect. When baseline and immediate correction were reinstated during the third and fourth stages of the study, the remarkable effect of immediately correcting papers was verified. Desirably, the effectiveness of the immediate-correction procedure will encourage teachers to grade students' papers soon after they are completed. Teachers who find this task difficult to implement should consider using aides, students, and volunteer parents as graders. For further verification of the importance of immediate feedback, the reader should contemplate the chaos that would result in the game of "hot and cold" (p. 9) if delays in the words "hot" and "cold" occurred fifteen or more seconds after appropriate and inappropriate behaviors.

MEANS OF DECREASING THE RATE OF BEHAVIOR

Although educators are greatly concerned with means of teaching new behaviors, there are times when they find it necessary to decrease the rate of unacceptable student behaviors. Teachers who do not have behavior modification skills often must resort to sending disobedient children to the principal, demanding parent-teacher conferences, or referring students for psychological examination in the hope that an alternative placement will be recommended.

Teachers *with* behavior modification skill, on the other hand, are usually able to deal directly with disruptive behavior and thereby help both their students and themselves. In the remainder of this section I have described several procedures that teachers can apply in order to obtain classroom control.

Reinforcing an Incompatible Behavior

Perhaps the most obvious way to decrease the rate of one behavior is to *reinforce an incompatible behavior,* that is, one incompatible with the disruptive behavior. Hence, if a teacher is concerned that her students are too frequently out of their seats, she might reinforce them when they are in their seats. Or, if she is concerned that her students too frequently talk out without permission, she can reinforce them when they raise their hands. A third, and more ambitious, example would be to provide a more exciting and interesting school day for a student with a history of truancy. Desirably, the student would then find the school environment more reinforcing than alternative environments and would decrease his truancy. The tactic of reinforcing an incompatible behavior is a simple derivative of procedures for increasing the rate of behavior and need not be discussed further. I suggest, however, that teachers faced with inappropriate behavior should first seek a means of reinforcing a behavior incompatible with the problem behavior before attempting the punishment procedures to be discussed later.

Extinction

A second procedure which is used to reduce the rate of an undesirable behavior involves discontinuing the reinforcement which follows the behavior. In other words, the behavior of interest is ignored. When the frequency of the behavior decreases to a relatively low level, "extinction" is said to have taken place. Extinction procedures have often been used in classrooms when it was suspected that the attention a teacher showed to a student for misbehaving accounted for his inappropriate behavior. In these cases, the procedure involves ignoring the student following disruptive behaviors.

Hall, Fox, Willard, Goldsmith, Emerson, Owen, Davis, and Porcia (1971) used an extinction procedure with Mike, a fifteen-year-old boy in a classroom of fifteen junior high school educable mentally retarded pupils. The problem behavior was arguing and disputing with the teacher. The teacher recorded an inappropriate behavior whenever Mike argued with the teacher, failed to comply with a teacher's request within ten seconds, or shook his head during a discussion of assignments. The reader should note the precision with which the teacher defined disputing behaviors. As is presented in Figure 1-4, disputes averaged eight during the seven-hour school day for the ten days of Baseline$_1$. Beginning with Day 11, the teacher turned around and walked away from Mike following each incident in which he began to dispute. Mike continued to receive teacher attention and was praised when he behaved appropriately. The mean number of disputes continually decreased, reaching a mean of one for the nine days in which the extinction procedure was in effect ("Ignore and Praise$_1$").

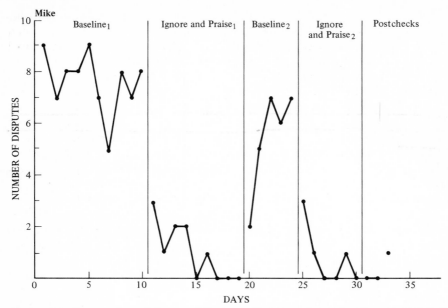

Figure 1-4 The number of disputes Mike had with his teacher daily. *(From R. V. Hall, R. Fox, D. Willard, L. Goldsmith, M. Emerson, M. Owen, F. Davis, and E. Porcia, "The Teacher as Observer and Experimenter in the Modification of Disputing and Talking-Out Behaviors,"* Journal of Applied Behavior Analysis, *4, 142, 1971. By permission of the publishers.)*

When baseline conditions were reinstated, misbehaviors quickly increased to an average of five per day. When ignoring procedures were reapplied, Mike's average dropped to a mean of less than one per day. Postchecks taken on three different days over a two-week period indicated a continued low level of disputing behaviors. During the postchecks period, the extinction procedure was still in effect, but measurements were not taken daily. Six weeks after the termination of the study, Mike's disputing behavior was no longer considered a problem.

Extinction operations have been particularly useful in eliminating temper tantrums in the classroom. Zimmerman and Zimmerman (1962) used such a technique with an eleven-year-old boy of normal intelligence who often had tantrums in the form of crying, kicking, and screaming during English class. The authors noted that the boy consistently received attention from those in his environment when he behaved inappropriately, and they surmised that eliminating this attention would reduce the rate of the tantrums. The teacher therefore ignored the youngster when he "acted out" but continued to attend to him when he behaved properly. It was found that the tantrums were completely eliminated in English class after several weeks of extinction. In other classes inappropriate behaviors continued to occur, probably because the tantrums still received attention in these situations.

The wide range of behaviors to which extinction techniques can be applied was indicated in a remarkable study by Wolf, Birnbrauer, Williams, and Lawler (1965). Laura, the student in the study, was a nine-year-old mentally retarded girl who vomited almost every day in class. Drug therapy proved ineffective in alleviating the problem. Whenever Laura vomited on her dress, the teacher dismissed her from class and sent her to the dormitory, where she was cleaned and comforted by the aides.

The authors hypothesized that the child's vomiting was due to the possibility that the dormitory contained more reinforcers for Laura than the classroom. Thus, it was considered feasible that vomiting was an operant (that is, voluntary) behavior which was reinforced by placement in the dormitory. Wolf et al. (1965) tested their suspicion by having the teacher ignore Laura whenever she vomited in class. During the extinction procedure, Laura had to remain in class regardless of the amount of vomit which accumulated on her dress. For the first twenty-nine days of extinction, vomiting occurred seventy-eight times. On one day, twenty-one episodes were recorded. Beginning with day 30, however, vomiting ceased entirely and stayed at the zero level for a period of more than fifty days.

The results of the study do not imply that all vomiting is under the control of consequent events. Certainly, antecedent agents, such as emetics, can elicit vomiting. The study does indicate, however, that some behaviors, previously considered involuntary, are maintained by the consequences which follow the behavior. Thus, a child may initially vomit because of an illness but continue to vomit because of the attention and privileges which follow the vomiting.

There are several factors which limit the effectiveness of extinction procedures in the classroom. Watson (1967) points out that if an individual consistently ignores a misbehaving child, and the individual is the only source of social reinforcement to the child, disruptive behaviors will generally decrease. The problem which may arise in a classroom is that although the teacher ignores the inappropriate behavior, the child's classmates may reinforce it with laughter and attention. If this case arises, it may be possible to eliminate peer attention by giving the entire class a reinforcer (for example, extra free-play time) for ignoring the child's misbehaviors.

A second problem which Watson (1967) points out is that extinction procedures will eliminate only those behaviors which are maintained by an additional source of reinforcement. If a student's temper tantrums are maintained by teacher attention, removal of attention will usually eliminate the temper tantrums. Some behaviors, however, may themselves be reinforcing. Maintenance of these behaviors would be independent of additional sources of reinforcement. For example, if a teacher ignores a pair of students who are frequently conversing with each other at inappropriate times, her extinction procedure will probably fail because the students' conversation is itself reinforcing. In such cases, reinforcing nontalking behavior may solve the teacher's problem.

A third difficulty with an extinction procedure is that when some behaviors are ignored, they will *initially* occur more frequently or intensely than they did during the baseline period. That is, a student whose temper tantrums are suddenly ignored may first increase the intensity of his tantrum before his tantrum ceases. Thus, if a teacher weakens during the period in which the problem appears to have worsened and attends to the pupil, she will actually be reinforcing a worse form of the behavior. Perhaps the information that this problem is frequent in extinction procedures will help the teacher to ride out the storm before the lull. It should be kept in mind, however, that an extinction procedure is not for the weak-willed teacher.

"Resistance to extinction" (for positive reinforcement) refers to the number of responses an individual makes once reinforcement no longer follows the behavior. A discovery which the reader may find surprising is that behaviors which have been learned on an intermittent reinforcement schedule result in a greater resistance to extinction than behaviors which have been learned on a continuous reinforcement schedule (Humphreys, 1939). Therefore, if a teacher wishes that a student continue to perform a certain behavior (for example, study behavior) after reinforcement has been discontinued, it would appear that an intermittent reinforcement schedule would be preferable to a continuous reinforcement schedule. On the other hand, learning is generally more rapid with continuous rather than intermittent reinforcement schedules.

These findings produce a slight dilemma for a teacher who is trying to decide how often to reinforce a certain behavior. The solution to the problem is to initially reinforce the desired behavior as often as possible. After the desired behavior is well established, however, the teacher should use an intermittent reinforcement in order to increase the durability of the behavior.

Punishment

A third procedure that a teacher can use to reduce inappropriate behavior is "punishment." This is a process in which the consequence of a behavior reduces the future rate of that behavior (Azrin and Holz, 1966). The events in our society which can serve as punishers range from a raised eyebrow to a jail sentence. No event can be classified as a punisher, however, unless the behavior of interest decreases in rate. Thus, if a teacher deprives a class of recess for talking out during study time, and the rate of talking out decreases, losing recess is a punisher. If the rate of talking out remains the same, however, depriving the class of recess cannot be considered a punisher.

A study reported by Hall, Axelrod, Foundopoulos, Shellman, Campbell, and Cranston (1971) demonstrated the use of punishment in a classroom for ten emotionally disturbed boys. The teacher observed that the students were "roaming around the room" at a rate that hindered academic development. To decrease the level of out-of-seat behaviors, the teacher listed each boy's name on a paper attached to a clipboard which the teacher carried with him. Each time a student left his seat without permission, the teacher placed a mark next to the child's name and required that the youngster remain after school for five minutes for each mark. A child with three marks, for example, had a fifteen-minute detention.

The procedure was in effect during the mathematics and reading periods. As depicted in Figure 1-5, the boys averaged twenty-three out-of-seat behaviors during the eight days of Baseline$_1$. During the ten days in which the punishment contingency was in effect, out-of-seat behaviors immediately decreased to low levels. On five of the days there were two or fewer out-of-seat behaviors, and the mean for the entire phase was two. When the punishment procedure was withdrawn during Baseline$_2$, out-of-seat incidents immediately increased to a higher level. (Following Baseline$_2$, a punishment procedure was reinstated, and again out-of-seat behaviors decreased in frequency. The authors did not include the results, however, since the data were obtained over the entire school day and therefore are not comparable with the previous figures, which were based only on the mathematics and reading periods.)

Hall, Axelrod, et al. (1971) reported another study in which punishment was used in a classroom. The problem child was Andrea, a seven-year-old retarded girl, who bit and pinched herself, her classmates, the teacher, and classroom visitors. It is understandable that Andrea was not socially popular. Figure 1-6 shows that during the six days of Baseline$_1$, the child averaged seventy-two bites and pinches per school day. The teacher used a punishment procedure that consisted of pointing at the child and shouting "No!" following each bite or pinch. When this contingency was in effect, Andrea's mean rate of bites and pinches immediately decreased and was rarely occurring at the end of the punishment phase. The average number of bites and pinches was only five. During a three-day Baseline$_2$ phase, the teacher made peace for the purposes of the experiment and discontinued the punishment procedure. Bites

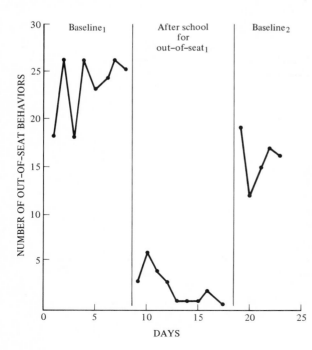

Figure 1-5 Out-of-seat behaviors of ten emotionally disturbed boys. *(From R. V. Hall, S. Axelrod, M. Foundopoulos, J. Shellman, R. A. Campbell, and S. Cranston, "The Effective Use of Punishment to Modify Behavior in the Classroom,"* Educational Technology, **11***, 1971, as reprinted in K. D. O'Leary and S. G. O'Leary (eds.),* Classroom Management: The Successful Use of Behavior Modification. *New York: Pergamon Press, 1972, p. 178. By permission of the publishers.)*

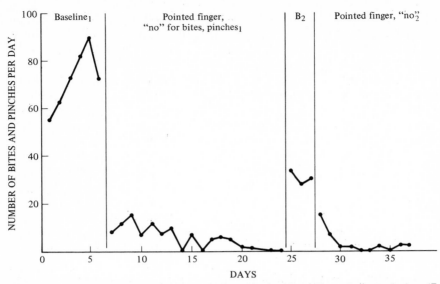

Figure 1-6 The number of times Andrea bit or pinched herself or others each day. *(From R. V. Hall, S. Axelrod, M. Foundopoulos, J. Shellman, R. A. Campbell, and S. Cranston, "The Effective Use of Punishment to Modify Behavior in the Classroom,"* Educational Technology, **11**, *1971, as reprinted in K. D. O'Leary and S. G. O'Leary (eds.),* Classroom Management: The Successful Use of Behavior Modification. *New York: Pergamon Press, 1972, p. 175. By permission of the publishers.)*

and pinches increased to thirty per day. When the punishment procedure was reinstated in the final phase, however, the problem behaviors quickly decreased to low levels.

The outcome of punishment procedures has created a considerable amount of controversy among behavior modifiers. It has been claimed that the effects of punishment procedures are temporary, and that they can result in the punished individual aggressing toward other people in the environment. Azrin and Holz (1966) found, however, that punishment produced durable changes in behavior, whereas a study by Risley (1968) gave no evidence that punishment resulted in aggressive behavior. It has also been alleged that an individual who is being punished may avoid the punishment by evading the environment in which the punishment takes place (Skinner, 1968). A teacher, for example, may give a child a long detention for talking out in class. The teacher hopes that the student will avoid future detentions by behaving appropriately in school. The student, however, may eliminate the possibility of receiving detentions by playing "hooky" from school.

Finally, although a punishment procedure may eliminate an inappropriate behavior, it will not necessarily teach an appropriate one. Thus, a punishment tactic may effectively stop a child from hitting his classmates, but this does not mean that he will learn appropriate social behavior in the process.

In spite of some disadvantages associated with the procedure, I believe that punishment techniques can be a useful tool for the teacher. One reason is that punishment tends to be effective in situations in which alternative techniques such as reinforcing an incompatible behavior and extinction do not work. Also, punishment procedures often produce a faster reduction in undesirable behaviors than other techniques.

When punishment procedures are called for, certain guidelines should be followed. First, the teacher should use the mildest form of punishment that is effective. Secondly, the criteria for punishment should be determined and clearly stated in advance. In this manner both the teacher and the students will have certain rules to guide their behavior, and the application of the procedure will be systematic rather than whimsical. Third, teachers should reinforce behavior incompatible with the undesirable behavior. Thus, if out-of-seat behavior has been a problem, in addition to punishing students for being out of their seats, the teacher might reinforce the children with praise or special privileges when they are in their seats. Finally, after punishment procedures have been effective, teachers should attempt to gradually substitute other procedures, such as positive reinforcement, for the punishment tactic.

Regardless of the position a teacher takes with respect to using punishment in the classroom, it should be understood that it is impossible to eliminate punishers from a youngster's environment. Every time a child stubs his toe on a bedpost, burns his hand on a hot pot, or bangs his head against another child's head, he has been punished. Hence, in many situations the problem is not how to eliminate punishers, but learning to live with them. Teachers should also not fear that if they occasionally punish a student the child will automatically dislike the teacher or the school. A tree will punish an adult who drives a car into it, but most adults still find trees reinforcing. The important element in developing good social relations with students is to have reinforcing actions far outweigh punishing ones.

The terms "punishment" and "negative reinforcement" should *not* be used interchangeably; such a practice is a common error. The difference between the two operations is that punishment serves to decrease the rate of the target behavior, whereas negative reinforcement produces an increase in the rate of the target behavior. Examples of each procedure are given below:

Punishment	Negative reinforcement
1. A child keeps off his neighbor's lawn after being bitten by the neighbor's dog. (*Trespassing decreased.*)	1. A child runs away from a dog which is chasing him. (Child's *rate of moving increased* in order to avoid the dog.)
2. A pigeon ceases pressing a bar after receiving an electric shock for each bar press. (*Bar presses decreased in rate.*)	2. Only by pressing a bar can a pigeon avoid electric shock. The pigeon presses the bar at a high rate. (*Bar pressing increased in frequency.*)
3. A child ceases pulling a classmate's hair after receiving a detention. (*Hair pulling decreased in rate.*)	3. A child sits quietly during a detention in order to have the detention terminated. (*Sitting quietly increased in rate and the child "escaped" the detention*).

Time Out

A punishment procedure that is sometimes used to reduce the rate of inappropriate classroom behaviors is termed "time out from positive reinforcement" or, more commonly, "time out." "Time out" is defined as removing access to reinforcement following an unacceptable behavior. In classroom situations, time out usually takes the form of isolating a disruptive child for a period of time following an inappropriate behavior. Hence, the child does not have the opportunity to engage in the reinforcing events which are occurring in the classroom. Madsen and Madsen (1968) demonstrated how a time-out procedure could be used to reduce the rate of disruptive talking by six junior high school girls. The time-out procedure consisted simply of requiring each girl who talked out to leave the classroom for a period of time. During the four weeks in which this procedure was employed, the rate of talking out decreased to one-eighth of its original level.

Two conditions must exist in order for a time-out technique to be effective. First, it is necessary that the area (for example, a classroom) in which the problem behavior is occurring be reinforcing to the student. If this is not the case, it is *un*likely that requiring a youngster to leave the classroom will be punishing to him. Secondly, the *time-out area must be one in which reinforcers are not present.* If the time-out area permits activities which are reinforcing to the student, he may actually prefer the time-out area to the area from which he has been excluded. Thus, when parents send children to their bedrooms for misbehaving, the procedure is often ineffective because the childs' rooms might contain toys, phonographs, and color television sets.

A time-out procedure used by Birnbrauer, Wolf, Kidder, and Tague (1965) was more precise in ensuring that the above conditions were met than was the case in the Madsen and Madsen (1968) study. In the Birnbrauer et al. study, the time-out area consisted of a bare 8×22 foot room devoid of reading and play materials. Behaviors for which a pupil might be sent to the time-out room included aggression toward other students, temper tantrums, and destroying class materials. Students performing these behaviors were warned, "Stop and return to work or go to the hall [p. 223]." If the child did not comply with the warning, he was sent to the time-out area; after ten minutes, he could reenter the classroom, provided he had been quiet for the preceding thirty seconds. If he did not enter the classroom within two minutes of being invited back to class, he spent another ten minutes in the time-out room. In other studies, time-out areas have not only been barren but have contained some means of restraining children so that they could not injure themselves or the property.

I realize that many readers will consider time-out to be a radical and inhumane method for dealing with disruptive behavior. It is my opinion, however, that the judgment as to whether or not a procedure is humane should be based more on its long-term effects than by the immediate discomfort which results. Few people would consider a surgeon or dentist, whose operation is painful, to be cruel if the procedures ultimately improve the health or extend the life of a patient. Similarly, placing a child in a time-out area should be considered a benevolent procedure if a considerable reduction in serious misbehaviors results.

A child who is aggressive toward other students and who frequently has temper tantrums may spend many years in school being shunned by his classmates and making minimal academic gains. In fact, many such students have been labeled "emotionally disturbed" and have been permanently removed from regular classes and placed in special classes or institutions. Procedures which involve relatively brief periods of time out and result in elimination of misbehaviors would seem to be more humane and efficient than long-term or permanent removal, which may be the only alternative. In addition, it has been found that, when applied properly, time-out procedures usually need be used only a limited number of times. Bijou, Birnbrauer, Kidder, and Tague (1966), for example, used a time-out area only eight times in two years with a class of seventeen pupils.

In recent years an increasing number of school systems have adopted time-out procedures with little or no success. The problem seems to be that in many situations the educational personnel cannot quite bring themselves to employ time-out procedures in the appropriate manner. Uncomfortable with the notion of completely isolating a child for a period of time, they rename the time-out area a "quiet room," a "meditation area," or a "cooling-off room." As such, the educators might talk to a student while she is in "time out," have the child's psychotherapist come to see her, or provide reading materials for her. All such tactics defeat the purpose of a time-out room, which is to punish behavior. When educators are unable to set up a time-out room as an isolation area, they should seek alternative techniques. By misusing time out, many educators have positively reinforced exactly those behaviors which they wished to eliminate.

Differential Reinforcement of Other Behavior

In addition to reinforcement of an incompatible behavior, extinction, punishment, and time out (which is a punishment procedure), a fifth technique for reducing the frequency of an inappropriate behavior is a "differential reinforcement of other behavior (DRO) schedule." A DRO schedule is one in which reinforcement is delivered only if a particular behavior does *not* occur for a specified period of time. Suppose a DRO five-minute (DRO5) schedule is used to reduce talking-out behavior. According to such an arrangement, reinforcement will be delivered only if talking-out does *not* occur for a five-minute period. Each time talking-out behavior does occur, a new five-minute cycle is begun and a reinforcer will be delivered only if the behavior of interest does not occur for the next five minutes. Following each reinforcement, a new five-minute cycle is begun.

There are few examples of the use of DRO schedules in classroom settings. In one case, however, Schmidt and Ulrich (1969) used a DRO10 schedule to reduce the excessive noise of twenty-nine fourth graders. For a period of fifty minutes each morning, the entire class received a two-minute addition to the gym period and a two-minute break for every ten minutes in which the noise level stayed below 42 decibels (dB). A sound-level meter measured the intensity of the noise. When the students met the criterion for reinforcement, a buzzer sounded which indicated that the students had earned the additional gym and break time. A new ten-minute cycle then began. Each time the students exceeded 42 dB, a whistle was sounded and another ten-minute cycle started. No reinforcement was delivered. Figure 1-7 represents the noise level during the four phases of the study. For the ten baseline sessions before the DRO schedule was used, the mean sound intensity was 52.5 dB. When DRO10 was in effect, the sound level immediately decreased to a stable level of 39 dB. During a reversal period in which the DRO10 schedule was not used, the mean quickly increased to a higher level; it decreased when the DRO procedure was reinstated. The Schmidt and Ulrich study may be classified as a token reinforcement procedure in which the buzzer was a token and the additional gym and break times were back-up reinforcers.

Although DRO schedules can be effective, they are somewhat difficult to implement for a teacher who does not have additional personnel available. In addition, a DRO technique contains the disadvantage that a student will be reinforced for performing *any* other behavior than the target behavior. It is, therefore, possible that a teacher who uses a DRO procedure to reduce

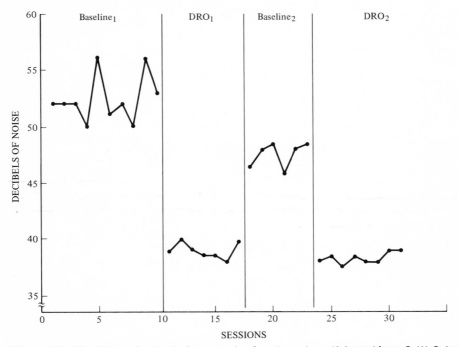

Figure 1-7 The daily noise level of twenty-nine fourth graders. *(Adapted from G. W. Schmidt and R. E. Ulrich, "Effects of Group Contingent Events upon Classroom Noise,"* Journal of Applied Behavior Analysis, **2**, *172, 1969. By permission of the publishers.)*

out-of-seat behaviors will find herself reinforcing a youngster when he is staring out the window or punching his neighbor in the back. For such reasons DRO schedules have had rather limited use in classroom settings, and most teachers will find the previously described procedures for reducing the level of undesirable behaviors more useful.

Further Means of Decreasing the Rate of Behavior

The procedures described above by no means constitute an exhaustive list of the methods by which teachers can reduce the rate of undesirable behaviors. In my opinion, however, the procedures which were discussed are the most thoroughly investigated and (in most cases) the most easily implemented procedures for teachers. For a discussion of additional techniques, the interested educator might consult articles by Foxx and Azrin (1973) on the topic of "overcorrection," an ingenious and amusing study by Ayllon (1963) on the use of satiation, and a book by Wolpe and Lazarus (1966) on desensitization. It should also be noted that although the topic of feedback was discussed as a means of increasing behavior, feedback can also be used as a means of decreasing undesirable behavior. Thus, showing a student a graph indicating the number of times he talked out might be a sufficient means for reducing the rate of instances of talking out. Similarly, giving a teacher a record of the number of times he screamed at his students might help him to reduce his rate of screaming.

Each of the procedures mentioned thus far has been described individually. There is no reason, however, why combinations of techniques cannot be employed. A teacher might, therefore, reinforce appropriate behavior at the same time that he or she extinguishes or punishes inappropriate behavior. In this manner faster changes in behavior are likely to occur and the students will learn not only what they should not do, but also what they should do.

ADDITIONAL BASIC PROCESSES AFFECTING BEHAVIOR

The principles and procedures discussed in the earlier parts of the chapter account, in large measure, for the behavior of human beings. There are, however, additional factors and processes affecting human behavior. The reader may wonder, for example, what influence the behavioral traits of adults and peers have on children. Or the reader might wish to know how children learn that it is appropriate to perform a behavior in one situation but not in others, or curious as to how behavior transfers from one situation to another. There is also the question of how complex behaviors are formed. The remaining portions of the chapter will be devoted to describing processes that lend answers to each of the above questions.

Imitation

One of the most common means through which children learn new behaviors is by observing and *imitating* the behaviors of other people. Casual observation of children indicates that many youngsters have the same idiosyncratic facial mannerisms and speech patterns as their parents. Adults are well aware of the influence that children have on each other and, therefore, they encourage their youngsters to associate with some children and to avoid others. The imitation process is so powerful that it is possible to learn a complex behavior, or a large portion of it, by simply observing other individuals perform the behavior. Thus, many people have a "good idea" how to drive a car the first time they sit behind the steering wheel.

Certain behaviors are difficult to learn through imitation alone. In such cases a combination of imitation and shaping is often helpful. Lovaas, Berberich, Perloff, and Shaeffer (1966) used this tactic to teach speech behavior to mute schizophrenic children. Briefly, the *model* (in this case, the speech therapist) would make a particular sound. If the child made an adequate imitation of the sound, the therapist would reinforce him. After the youngster consistently imitated one sound, the therapist would make other sounds and more complex sounds. Again the child would receive a reinforcer for an appropriate imitation. As the training sessions proceeded, the children were required to imitate entire words and sentences in order to receive the reinforcers. As a result of such procedures, the foundations of language behavior were established in many children whose cases were previously regarded as hopeless.

The imitation process can have a positive or negative influence on children. Presently, there is much controversy about the effect that television violence has on youngsters. Some psychologists with a psychoanalytic orientation claim that observing violence actually relieves children of the desire to be belligerent. Others claim that because the violent characters are typically punished for their actions, children are unlikely to imitate such behaviors. Still others suggest that by observing violence, children will learn such behaviors and emit them at opportune moments.

A study by Bandura (1965) supports the last position. The investigation involved three groups of children who observed a filmed model display a variety of aggressive behaviors and verbalizations. Group I observed the model being punished for aggression; in Group II the model was reinforced for aggressive behavior; and for Group III there was no consequence for aggression. After the films were completed, it was found that the youngsters who had observed the model being punished imitated fewer aggressive behaviors than the children in Groups II and III. Later, however, when the children were offered reinforcers if they imitated the aggressive behaviors of the model, each group of children displayed a similar number of aggressive behaviors. There is, therefore, much justification to the concern over television violence, since mere observation of a violent activity seems to add a behavior to a child's repertoire; the aggressive behavior may then be emitted under advantageous circumstances.

Imitation operations can lead to the learning of undesirable behaviors; on the other hand, they can also lead to the remediation of behavioral problems. In one case O'Connor (1969) found that when preschool children with a history of isolate behavior observed a film depicting social interaction, they later displayed substantial amounts of social activity. The film showed preschool youngsters interacting with each other at a high rate and receiving reinforcers for their social activities. When an apparently shy child in the film joined his peers in play, for example, the other children would offer him toys, talk to him, and smile at him. The social gains which accrued to the youngsters were maintained throughout the school year, according to teacher reports.

Teachers and education textbooks alike often claim that certain students have leadership qualities that influence the behavior of other students. The behavior of the leaders is then seen as a key to classroom control, since both their desirable and their undersirable behaviors are likely to be imitated by their classmates. A study by West and Axelrod (1975) supported this notion. The authors used a procedure in which three classrooms of adolescent, emotionally disturbed, and learning-disabled children could earn dimes by reducing the level of their disruptive behavior. In two classes the procedure markedly reduced disruptive behavior. In the third class chaos resulted. Led by George, a husky, intelligent thirteen-year-old boy, the class rejected the procedure as "baby stuff" and "dippy." The percentage of the class's inappropriate behavior rose substantially over baseline levels.

The senior author, Ms. Mina West, suspected that if George modeled appropriate behavior, his classmates would be likely to imitate his improved behavior. A conversation between George and Ms. West indicated that the youngster wished to have a position of greater responsibility. Ms. West then suggested that George become her consultant to help bridge the "generation gap." George readily agreeed to assuming a role as a student consultant, and his classroom behavior improved immediately. Taking their cue from George, the remainder of the students improved in their behavior markedly, even though there was no contingency on their behavior. The authors suggested that more research be done on the effects a prestigious student can have on his classmates' behavior.

Discrimination

There is probably no behavior that should be performed in all situations. It is proper, for example, for a youngster to sit quietly in the school library, but it is a cause for concern if the youngster sits quietly on the school playground. Smiling is desirable when greeting an acquaintance but is inappropriate at a funeral. Even a behavior such as breathing, which is almost always appropriate, should not occur under water. When a behavior consistently occurs in some situations but does not occur in others, the behavior is said to be "discriminated." Discrimination is brought about by reinforcing a behavior in certain situations and extinguishing or punishing it in other situations.

Whaley and Malott (1968) showed how a twelve-year-old, severely retarded girl, Leslie, could learn to discriminate *her* name from another name with a combination of positive reinforcement and time out. The authors constructed two cards, one with "Leslie" written on it and the other with the name

"Carmen." If the youngster picked the correct card, one of the authors said, "Good," and placed a piece of candy in Leslie's mouth. If she picked the wrong card, the author said "No," removed both cards, and placed the cards beneath the table for ten seconds before continuing the session. After sixty-five trials, Leslie consistently chose the correct card, and the authors concluded that she had learned the discrimination task. The fact that the girl's IQ was 20 indicates that rather than assuming that some youngsters are incapable of learning, educators should concentrate on developing techniques which are suitable for children at all levels.

The ability to make certain key discriminations is an important one, and those who are particularly adept at it are often called "sensitive." Thus, a teenage boy who is capable of making sensitive discriminations will ask a girl to dance if she smiles at him but will not do so if she consistently fails to make eye contact with him. A "clod" will ask the girl to dance regardless of the cues she emits. Similarly, effective teachers will learn when their students are likely to be receptive toward praise and when they are likely to reject it. They will respond to their students accordingly.

It should be understood that the discrimination process goes on whether educators want it to or not. Speech therapists, for example, should not be surprised when a child who is being reinforced for verbal behavior emits certain speech behaviors during a therapy session but does not exhibit the same verbalizations outside therapy. The problem is that the youngster has learned to discriminate. The child has learned that verbal behavior in the presence of the therapist will bring reinforcement but that the same behavior outside therapy will not lead to reinforcement. The solution to the therapist's problem, of course, is to provide reinforcement for speech behavior in a variety of situations. Similarly, a teacher should not expect children to be well behaved during *reading* class because she has devised a procedure that will motivate them to be well behaved during *mathematics.* If the teacher wants the children to be well behaved during reading, she should apply a behavior modification procedure during the reading period. In other words, teachers should realize that children are likely to discriminate those situations which are likely to lead to reinforcement from those that will not, and should plan their educational programs accordingly.

Stimulus Generalization

It sometimes happens that a behavior which is learned in one situation also occurs in other situations. For example, if a child learns that a temper tantrum at home will result in adult attention, it is likely that she will have temper tantrums in school at opportune moments. When a child learns a behavior in one situation but also emits the behavior in other situations, "stimulus generalization" is occurring. Of course, if it turns out that temper tantrums in school are ignored by the teacher, a discrimination will be formed and the youngster will cease her tantrums in school but continue to have them at home. Thus, generalization is the opposite of discrimination. Research has shown that the more similar the new situation is to the situation in which the original learning occurred, the more likely it is that stimulus generalization will occur.

Examples of stimulus generalization (more frequently termed "generalization") are common in daily life. The diner who responds to several waiters as if they were his own is generalizing. After a sufficient number of confused or hostile reactions, the patron will eventually learn to discriminate among the various waiters. A child who refers to all adult males as "Daddy" is making a generalized response based on the similarity of his own father to other men. Once again, environmental contingencies are such that a discrimination had better be achieved. When a pupil learns to read in school and later exhibits reading behaviors with comic books, generalization from a school experience has occurred. In the case of reading, however, the behavior will be reinforced in the new situation and is therefore likely to continue to occur.

Patterson (1965) did a study which indicated that a behavior learned in one situation will sometimes generalize to other situations. After observation of a hyperactive student for several hours, it was decided that the majority of Earl's misbehaviors could be broken down into pushing, hitting, and talking. A small box with a light bulb and an electric counter was then placed on Earl's desk. If he did not perform any inappropriate behaviors for a period of time (which increased as sessions progressed), the light flashed and the counter clicked. At the end of each day, all members of the class divided up an amount of candy or pennies which corresponded to the number of points on the counter.

During the time the procedure was used, Earl's classroom misbehaviors dropped to about one-fourth of their baseline rate. In addition, the teacher reported that destructive behavior decreased on the school playground and Earl's mother noted improved peer relationships at home, even though the reinforcement system was not employed on the playground or at home. Hence, there was generalization of the effect of the reinforcement system from the classroom where it was employed to other environments.

It is frequently desirable, from an educational standpoint, that behavior learned in a setting in which a certain procedure was applied also occur in settings in which this technique is not employed. If a teacher has effectively used contingent reinforcement to reduce the noise level during reading, she would hope that the improvement in behavior would generalize to other situations in which reinforcement is not employed. At times such generalization has been noted (for example, Patterson, 1965). As indicated in the section on discrimination, however, it is more likely that the improvement resulting from a given procedure will be restricted to the circumstances in which the procedure was applied *unless* specific measures are taken to extend the effects to other situations. As Baer, Wolf, and Risley (1968) pointed out, "Generalization should be programmed, rather than expected or lamented [p. 97]."

An example of a successful effort to achieve generalization from one classroom setting to another was provided by Walker and Buckley (1968). The youngster in the study was Philip, an intelligent (WISC IQ:116) nine-year-old boy who exhibited a variety of disruptive behaviors in the regular classroom. A series of observations in the regular classroom indicated that he attended to assignments only 42 percent of the time. While he was in the fourth grade, Philip was placed in a class for "behaviorally disturbed" children, where he experienced a token-reinforcement system designed to increase the rate at which he attended to assigned work. Though he did well in this setting, he still attended to tasks less often than desired. Therefore, an individualized program was devised for Philip and implemented on a daily basis within a special room adjoining the main classroom. Philip was informed that each time he engaged in study behavior for the entire duration of a specified time interval, he would receive a point, and that the points could be exchanged for a prize at the end of the period. The interval was initially thirty seconds but was gradually increased to twenty minutes.

Under the individual token system, Philip's average on-task rate was 93 percent. Subsequently, Philip was returned to his regular classroom. Rather than merely *hoping* that Philip's increased attending rate would generalize to the regular classroom, the authors took steps to establish generalization. Philip experienced a point system similar to the one he had been exposed to in the special class. The regular class teacher checked Philip's behavior at varying intervals and gave him a point if he was attending to his assignments. During the period that the token procedure was used in the regular classroom, his attending rate exceeded 80 percent on every occasion but one. It will be recalled that prior to the reinforcement procedure, Philip's regular-class attending rate was only 42 percent. It may therefore be concluded that Walker and Buckley succeeded in programming generalization from the special class to the regular class setting.

The reader should realize that generalization is not a mystical process but rather is best accomplished by structuring additional sectors of the environment to reinforce the behavior of interest. The failure of generalization to occur automatically is often disappointing, but one consolation is that behaviors learned in one setting are relatively easy to relearn in other settings.

Chaining

Thus far, when I have written about a behavior, such as walking, I have described it as if it were a singular act. Actually, walking is a complex act composed of many simpler behaviors. One breakdown of walking might consist of raising a foot off the ground, extending the foot for a distance, balancing oneself on the other foot, placing the ball of the foot on the ground, placing the heel of the foot on the ground, and raising the other foot. Although a physical therapist or medical doctor might be appalled at my analysis, the point is that almost every behavior is composed of smaller components. The series of behaviors comprising a larger act is called a "behavior chain," or, more simply, a "chain." Each link in the behavior chain serves as a cue for the next response in the chain. For example, raising a foot off the ground serves as a cue to extend one's foot for a distance. The element that maintains the links in the chain is the reinforcer at the end of the chain.

Performing a new behavior often involves combining already learned responses in a chain. Thus, a girl named "Robin" might be able to write every letter in the alphabet but not be able to write her name. The child must first learn to write an "R", that the "R" is a cue to write an "O", that "O" is a cue for a "B", and so on. Similarly, students may be able to enunciate every word in the "Gettysburg Address" but must learn to link each of the words together in a behavior chain.

It is possible that dissimilar behaviors will become linked together in a chain and cause problems for a teacher. Suppose a student has a temper tantrum for thirty minutes and then settles down for a few seconds. If the teacher immediately attends to the child, the youngster might learn that he can acquire his teacher's attention by misbehaving for a long period of time and then behaving appropriately for a brief interval. In such a situation I recommend that a teacher initially wait until the problem behavior has ceased for about a minute before attending to the child. On subsequent occasions the amount of time between the cessation of the problem behavior and teacher attention can be gradually lengthened; in this manner the child should associate reinforcement with appropriate behavior rather than with temper tantrums.

The examples of the chaining process cited above have all involved "forward chaining." This is a process in which a student initially learns the first link in the behavior chain, then the second one, the third one, and so forth, until she can perform the entire chain. Another way of learning a task is through "backward chaining." With such a procedure a student first learns the last link in the chain, then she learns the next-to-last link, until finally she learns the initial link. This might sound like an Abbott and Costello comedy routine, but many behaviors are naturally learned by backward chaining.

Consider the process by which a child learns the way home from his grandmother's house, which is five blocks away from his own. Early in life he learns to return home from a few feet away from his front door. A little later in life, he learns how to return home from the lawn in front of his house. At still later points in his life, he finds his way home from the sidewalk in front of his house, then from the neighbors' house, then from a block away, and so forth, until he learns to return home from his grandmother's house. With "forward" chaining, the learning process would begin by teaching the child the appropriate direction to take from his grandmother's house and guiding his path from there.

It is possible to teach a variety of school tasks through "backward" chaining. In order to teach Robin to spell her name with backward chaining, for example, a teacher might present the girl with the following work sheet:

ROBI–

If the youngster consistently filled in an *N*, she would be reinforced and would receive the following worksheet:

ROB––

Later, it would be,

RO---

then,

R----

and, finally,

When she consistently writes "ROBIN," she would have learned to spell her name with backward chaining. In another case, Sulzer and Mayer (1972) describe how they taught a six-year-old boy in a special education class to assemble a four-piece puzzle using backward chaining. First, all pieces but one were assembled and the youngster was required to replace only one piece. Each time he succeeded, he received a reinforcer. When the first step was mastered, two pieces were removed, then three, and finally all four pieces were removed and the child had to assemble the entire puzzle.

There is some controversy concerning whether a teacher should use forward chaining or backward chaining when both procedures are feasible. Although there is an absence of definitive experimentation on the topic, behavioral researchers tend to favor backward chaining. The question is still an open one, but one advantage in backward chaining is that the child who completes a step successfully experiences the reinforcer of observing a completed task. This is often not the case with forward chaining.

SUMMARY

There are two types of behaviors—"respondents" and "operants." Respondent behaviors are involuntary and consist of such responses as pupil dilation and sweating. "Operant" behaviors are voluntary and include behaviors such as hand-raising and reading. Behavior modifiers working in school settings have been mostly concerned with operant behaviors. The frequency of operant behaviors is influenced by events which follow the behavior. These events are known as "consequences." When consequences are arranged "contingent" upon a certain operant behavior, the behavior will either increase or decrease in rate. The process by which the behavior increases or decreases is known as "operant conditioning."

There are a number of ways to increase the rate of a behavior. One procedure is known as "positive reinforcement" and involves presenting a student with something he enjoys (for example, praise or privileges) contingent upon his performing a desirable behavior. Another tactic, known as "negative reinforcement," involves the removal of something he dislikes (for example, homework) if he performs an appropriate behavior. Both positive and negative reinforcement serve to increase the rate of behavior; but in the case of positive reinforcement the target behavior results in the presentation of something desirable, whereas in the case of negative reinforcement the behavior results in the removal of something objectionable.

When a student seldom, or never, performs a behavior, "shaping" procedures are often useful. The tactic involves reinforcing closer and closer approximations to the behavior until the desired behavior occurs. In other cases the target behavior does occur, but *not* in certain desirable situations. In such cases a "fading" procedure can be used. The process involves gradually changing the conditions under which the behavior occurs from the original situation to the new situation.

When each desirable behavior is followed by reinforcers, a "continuous reinforcement schedule" is in effect. It has been found, however, that it is possible to use an "intermittent" or "partial reinforcement schedule" to maintain existing behaviors or to teach new ones. Some intermittent reinforcement schedules are known as "interval schedules" and provide reinforcement only after a certain amount of time has elapsed since the previously reinforced behavior. Another type of reinforcement schedule is a "ratio schedule," in which reinforcement occurs after the student performs a certain number of appropriate behaviors. Ratio schedules tend to produce higher and steadier rates of response than interval schedules.

Reinforcers can be "unconditioned" or "conditioned." Unconditioned reinforcers, such as food and water, operate independently of an association with other reinforcers. Conversely, conditioned reinforcers, such as praise and money, owe their effectiveness to an association with other reinforcers. When conditioned reinforcers are associated with many other reinforcers, they are known as "generalized" reinforcers. A type of generalized reinforcer which has been useful in classroom situations is a "token" reinforcer. Tokens are items or symbols (for example, checkmarks) which can be exchanged for a variety of reinforcers, known as "back-up reinforcers."

Behaviorally oriented teachers have a variety of methods for decreasing inappropriate behaviors. One technique is to reinforce a behavior incompatible with the undesirable one. Thus, a child who is often truant can be reinforced for attending school. A second technique is to use an "extinction" procedure in which the reinforcement that has typically followed a behavior is discontinued. A teacher might, for example, not attend to a child when he is having a tantrum. Often the tantrum will decrease in rate. Another procedure is to "punish" the behavior. This can be done by keeping a student after school for five minutes each time he hits a classmate. A particular type of punishment procedure which has been largely effective is known as "time out." The operation involves not permitting a student access to reinforcement following an undesirable behavior. In most cases the child is isolated from his classmates for a period of time. An additional procedure for decreasing behavior is known as "differential reinforcement of other behavior," an arrangement in which a student receives reinforcement if he performs behaviors other than the undesirable one for a specified interval of time.

There are other basic processes which affect the occurrence of behavior. It has been noted, for example, that students will "imitate" the behaviors of other individuals in their environment. Hence, there is a need to provide appropriate "models" for children. In many cases, students learn to "discriminate" those conditions in which it is appropriate to perform a behavior from those situations in which the behavior is inappropriate. The process can be brought about by reinforcing student behavior in certain situations and extinguishing the same behavior in other situations. Discriminations do not always occur, however, and in some cases a behavior which has been learned in one situation will occur in other, similar situations. The process is known as "generalization" and is a transitory one, unless specific measures are taken to ensure the maintenance of the behavior in the new situations.

QUESTIONS AND ACTIVITIES

1 Distinguish between respondent and operant behaviors.
2 What is a noncontingent relationship? Give an example of a noncontingent relationship.
3 Make a list of ten events that might be positive reinforcers in your classroom. Do not use any examples given in the present chapter.
4 How is positive reinforcement similar to negative reinforcement? How do the processes differ?
5 Distinguish between differential reinforcement and shaping.
6 Consider a child whom you know who is lacking a certain skill. Indicate how you might use a shaping procedure to teach this skill. Be certain to indicate the child's present level of functioning, the terminal behavior, the intermediate steps, and how you will determine a reinforcer for him.
7 Give seven advantages of token reinforcement systems, at least three of which are not stated in the present chapter.
8 How might a teacher use the information presented on schedules of reinforcement to improve his teaching routine?
9 Take a classroom management problem and propose a procedure that might be an effective punishment technique. Do not use any example included in the present chapter.
10 Distinguish between punishment and extinction.
11 Indicate how a teacher might use a combination of imitation and reinforcement to achieve better classroom control of misbehaving children.
12 Give a situation in which you would like to see students exhibit discrimination behaviors and another situation in which you would like to see them exhibit stimulus generalization.
13 How might a teacher use a fading procedure to teach a child to print the letter "L"?
14 Indicate how a child would be taught long division, using forward chaining and using backward chaining.

REFERENCES

Axelrod, S.: "Token Reinforcement Programs in Special Classes," *Exceptional Children*, **37**, 371–379, 1971.

Ayllon, T.: "Intensive Treatment of Psychotic Behaviour by Stimulus Satiation and Food Reinforcement," *Behaviour Research and Therapy*, **1**, 53–61, 1963.

Azrin, N. H., and W. C. Holz: "Punishment," in W. K. Honig (ed.), *Operant Behavior: Areas of Research and Application* (New York: Appleton-Century-Crofts, 1966), pp. 213–270.

Baer, D. M., M. M. Wolf, and T. R. Risley: "Some Current Dimensions of Applied Behavior Analysis," *Journal of Applied Behavior Analysis*, **1**, 91–97, 1968.

Bandura, A.: "Influence of Models' Reinforcment Contingencies on the Acquisition of Imitative Responses," *Journal of Personality and Social Psychology*, **1**, 589–595, 1965.

Bijou, S. W., J. S. Birnbrauer, J. D. Kidder, and C. E. Tague: "Programmed Instruction as an Approach to Teaching Writing and Arithmetic to Retarded Children," *Psychological Record*, **16**, 505–522, 1966.

Birnbrauer, J. S., M. M. Wolf, J. D. Kidder, and C. E. Tague: "Classroom Behavior of Retarded Pupils with Token Reinforcement," *Journal of Experimental Child Psychology*, **2**, 219–235, 1965.

Foxx, R. M., and N. H. Azrin: "The Elimination of Autistic Self-stimulatory Behavior by Overcorrection," *Journal of Applied Behavior Analysis*, **6**, 1–14, 1973.

Hall, R. V., S. Axelrod, M. Foundopoulos, J. Shellman, R. A. Campbell, and S. Cranston: "The Effective Use of Punishment to Modify Behavior in the Classroom," *Educational Technology*, **11**, 24–26, 1971.

———, R. Fox, D. Willard, L. Goldsmith, M. Emerson, M. Owen, F. Davis, and E. Porcia: "The Teacher as Observer and Experimenter in the Modification of Disputing and Talking Out Behaviors," *Journal of Applied Behavior Analysis*, **4**, 141–149, 1971.

———, D. Lund, and D. Jackson: "Effects of Teacher Attention on Study Behavior," *Journal of Applied Behavior Analysis*, **1**, 1–12, 1968.

Haupt, E. J., V. J. Van Kirk, and T. Terraciano: "An Inexpensive Fading Procedure to Decrease Errors and Increase Retention of Number Facts," in E. Ramp and G. Semb (eds.), *Behavior Analysis: Areas of Research and Application* (Englewood Cliffs, N.J.: Prentice-Hall, 1975), pp. 225–232.

Humphreys, L. G.: "The Effect of Random Alternation of Reinforcement on the Acquisition and Extinction of Conditioned Eyelid Reactions," *Journal of Experimental Psychology*, **25**, 141–158, 1939.

Kazdin, A. E., and R. R. Bootzin: "The Token Economy: An Evaluative Review," *Journal of Applied Behavior Analysis*, **5**, 343–372, 1972.

Leach, D. M., and M. Graves: "The Effects of Immediate Correction on Improving Seventh Grade Language Arts Performance," in A. Egner (ed.), *Individualizing Junior and Senior High Instruction to Provide Special Education within Regular Classrooms* (Burlington, Vt.: University of Vermont, 1973), pp. 15–21.

Lovaas, O. I., J. P. Berberich, B. F. Perloff, and B. Schaeffer: "Acquisition of Imitative Speech in Schizophrenic Children," *Science*, **151**, 705–707, 1966.

Madsen, C. H., and C. R. Madsen: *Teaching/Discipline* (Boston: Allyn & Bacon, 1968).

Martin, G. L., G. England, E. Kaprowy, K. Kilgour, and V. Pilek: "Operant Conditioning of Kindergarten-Class Behavior in Autistic Children," *Behaviour Research and Therapy*, **6**, 281–294, 1968.

McKenzie, H. S., M. Clark, M. M. Wolf, R. Kothera, and C. Benson: "Behavior Modification of Children with Learning Disabilities Using Grades as Tokens and Allowances as Back-up Reinforcers," *Exceptional Children*, **34**, 745–752, 1968.

O'Connor, R. D.: "Modification of Social Withdrawal through Symbolic Modeling," *Journal of Applied Behavior Analysis*, **2**, 15–22, 1969.

O'Leary, K. D., and W. C. Becker: "Behavior Modification of an Adjustment Class," *Exceptional Children*, **33**, 637–642, 1967.

———, W. C. Becker, M. B. Evans, and R. A. Saudargas: "A Token Reinforcement Program in a Public School: A Replication and Systematic Analysis," *Journal of Applied Behavior Analysis*, **2**, 3–13, 1969.

———, and R. Drabman: "Token Reinforcement Programs in the Classroom: A Review," *Psychological Bulletin*, **5**, 379–398, 1971.

Patterson, G. R.: "An Application of Conditioning Techniques to the Control of a Hyperactive Child," in L. P. Ullmann and L. Krasner (eds.), *Case Studies in Behavior Modification* (New York: Holt, Rinehart, and Winston, 1965), pp. 370–375.

Risley, T. R.: "The Effects and Side Effects of Punishing the Autistic Behaviors of a Deviant Child," *Journal of Applied Behavior Analysis*, **1**, 21–34, 1968.

Schmidt, G. W., and R. E. Ulrich: "Effects of Group Contingent Events upon Classroom Noise," *Journal of Applied Behavior Analysis*, **2**, 171–179, 1969.

Skinner, B. F.: *The Behavior of Organisms* (New York: Appleton-Century-Crofts, 1938).

———: *The Technology of Teaching* (New York: Appleton-Century-Crofts, 1968).

Sulzer, B., and G. R. Mayer: *Behavior Modification Procedures for School Personnel* (Hinsdale, Ill.: Dryden Press, 1972).

Tribble, A., and R. V. Hall: "Effects of Peer Approval on Completion of Arithmetic Assignments," in F. W. Clark, D. R. Evans, and L. A. Hamerlycnk (eds.), *Implementing Behavioral Programs for Schools and Clinics: Third Banff International Conference* (Champaign, Ill.: Research Press, 1972), pp. 139–140.

Walker, H., and N. K. Buckley: "The Use of Positive Reinforcement in Conditioning Attending Behavior," *Journal of Applied Behavior Analysis*, **1**, 245–250, 1968.

Watson, L. S.: "Application of Operant Conditioning Techniques to Institutionalized Severely and Profoundly Retarded Children," *Mental Retardation Abstracts*, **4**, 1–18, 1967.

West, M. M., and S. Axelrod: "A 3D Program for LD Children," *Academic Therapy*, **10**, 309–319, 1975.

Whaley, D. L., and R. W. Malott: *Elementary Principles of Behavior* (Kalamazoo, Mich.: Behaviordelia, 1968).

Wolf, M. M., J. S. Birnbrauer, T. Williams, and J. Lawler: "A Note on Apparent Extinction of Vomiting Behavior of a Retarded Child," in L. P. Ullmann and L. Krasner (eds.), *Case Studies in Behavior Modification* (New York: Holt, Rinehart, and Winston, 1965), pp. 364–366.

———, D. K. Giles, and R. V. Hall: "Experiments in a Remedial Classroom," *Behaviour Research and Therapy*, **6**, 51–64, 1968.

————, T. R. Risley, and H. L. Mees: "Application of Operant Conditioning Procedures to the Behaviour Problems of an Autistic Child," *Behaviour Research and Therapy*, 1, 305–312, 1964.

Wolpe, J., and A. A. Lazarus: *Behavior Therapy Techniques: A Guide to the Treatment of the Neuroses* (New York: Pergamon Press, 1966).

Zimmerman, E. H., and J. Zimmerman: "The Alteration of Behavior in a Special Classroom Situation," *Journal of the Experimental Analysis of Behavior*, 5, 59–60, 1962.

Chapter 2

Derivative Procedures for Modifying Student Behavior

The processes and principles described in the initial chapter are of basic importance to an understanding of the practice of behavior modification and to an ability to apply the methods in classroom situations. A reader of the relevant literature will notice that the operations are consistently recurring in behavior modification studies. The procedures described in the present chapter have been derived from the fundamental principles and have been found to be useful in classroom situations.

The topics to be discussed in the first section of this chapter involve various means for presenting reinforcement. Thus, there will be a description of the effects of increasing and decreasing the amount of reinforcement that is presented, procedures for gradually removing reinforcement, and programming group consequences. The second section consists of a variety of procedures by which children can learn to modify their own behavior, including the popular topic of contingency contracting. In the third section, means by which students can influence the behavior of each other and of their teacher are presented. The final section discusses the effects of various classroom arrangements on student behavior.

ALTERNATIVE PROCEDURES FOR PRESENTING CONSEQUENCES

Varying the Amount of Reinforcement

So far, the ability of reinforcers to increase the rate of a behavior has been discussed in some detail. However, the manner in which the *amount* of reinforcement can affect a behavioral change has not been mentioned. Other factors being equal, it is well known that adults prefer a job which pays a good salary to one that offers a poor salary. It is possible, therefore, that the behavior of schoolchildren is also influenced by the quantity of reward that is available for desirable behavior. Thus, some behavior modification procedures might fail, not because of the *kind* of reinforcer that is offered, or because of other procedural problems, but because not enough reinforcement is provided. This point was dramatically demonstrated in an investigation by Wolf, Giles, and Hall (1968). One of the boys in the study, Al, had a history of completing only a small portion of his reading assignments each day. A reading assignment consisted of about 200 words and a set of 12 or 13 questions. Initially, Al could earn sixty points for completing a reading unit and could later exchange his points for a variety of back-up reinforcers. Nevertheless, as shown in Figure 2-1, during a nineteen-day period Al never once completed an assignment. In the second stage of the study, the teacher offered Al 120 points for each unit he completed, and he promptly completed two stories on the first day. For the twenty days in which the increased incentive was available, Al completed two units on five occasions and one unit on six days, and averaged almost one story per day for the entire phase. When he could again earn only sixty points per story in the final phase, Al failed to complete a unit on any day. The lesson to be learned from Al is that he was willing to work, but the price had to be right.

A second study in the same article involved eleven students and showed

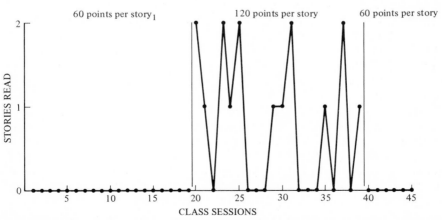

Figure 2-1 The number of units Al completed during each class session. *(Adapted from M. M. Wolf, D. K. Giles, and R. V. Hall, "Experiments in a Remedial Classroom,"* Behaviour Research and Therapy, **6**, *p. 56, 1968. By permission of the publishers.)*

how a redistribution of points could be used to motivate children to work on subject areas they had previously neglected. For an hour each day, the students could choose to do assignments from reading, arithmetic, or English workbooks. Each of the assignments was worth a specified number of points. Under these conditions the students tended to work with only one or two types of materials. The teacher then shifted the number of points a student could earn on each assignment, in an attempt to induce the students to work more frequently with the materials they had previously ignored. Thus, if a student worked only on English assignments, the points available for English might be cut in half whereas points for arithmetic and reading might be tripled. In all cases the effect of changing the point distribution was the same. The students consistently worked with those materials which offered the possibility of earning the most points. The results of the study present a possible solution to a problem which many teachers face. Rather than fussing with students who are reluctant to perform certain assignments, it might be possible to arrange a point system which would make it sufficiently attractive for children to perform those academic tasks which they have previously neglected.

That increasing amounts of reinforcement were effective in the above study does not mean that teachers should automatically offer children large sums of reinforcement. Rather, they should estimate the amount of reinforcement that is likely to motivate a student and determine the effectiveness of that quantity. Children who experience large amounts of tangible or social reinforcement over a short period of time are likely to become satiated on the reinforcer and diminish their efforts. It is better to initially offer a certain amount of reinforcement and increase the quantity only when the original amount proves ineffective.

Thinning Schedules of Reinforcement

The prior section showed that by increasing the amount of reinforcement that is available for a certain task, it is sometimes possible to stimulate reticent students into action. There are other cases in which students are already engaging in a task for the available reinforcers, but the teachers wish to eliminate programmed reinforcers without producing a decrease in student performance. Reasons for this might be that a teacher is using tangible reinforcers and is finding the system expensive, or that the behavior modification procedure the teacher is using is difficult to implement. For such teachers it was probably disappointing that when the consequences were eliminated in the majority of the previously presented studies, the students' behavior tended to revert to their original baseline levels. The reader should note, however, that in these studies the reinforcement or punishment contingencies were halted *abruptly.* It may be that by removing the consequences in a gradual manner, much of the improvement could have been maintained.

In an article by O'Leary and Becker (1967), the authors suggested that "by requiring more appropriate behavior to receive a prize and increasing the delay of reinforcement it was hoped that transfer of control from the token reinforcers to the more traditional methods of teacher praise and attention would occur [p. 639]." A procedure in which reinforcement gradually becomes available less often is known as "thinning the schedule of reinforcement."

The termination of the school year prevented O'Leary and Becker (1967) from trying out their suggested procedure. A similar approach, however, was employed in a study by Egner, Pitkin, and McKenzie (1970). Initially, the teacher awarded reinforcers at a relatively high rate but gradually discontinued all programmed reinforcement. The youngsters in the study were twenty pupils in their second year of an ungraded elementary school, and the object of the study was to increase the proportion of the time in which the students were in their seats. During all phases of the study, an oven timer was set to ring six times a day. Following each of the bell rings, all students were rated as being "in seat" or "out of seat." During Baseline$_1$ the students were in their seats between 53 and 83 percent of the time, with a mean of 63 percent (see Figure 2-2). In the Token$_1$ phase the teacher gave a token to each pupil who was in his seat from the time the bell rang until she reached his desk. The token was a

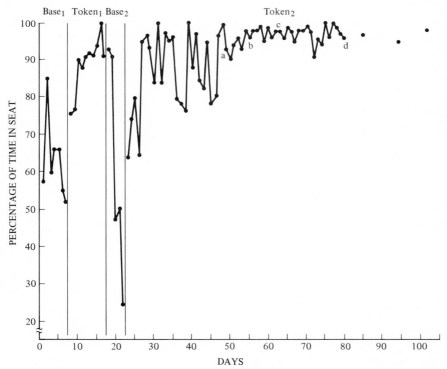

Figure 2-2 The percentage of time twenty second-grade students spent in their seats. *(Adapted from A. Egner, P. Pitkin, and H. McKenzie, "In Seat Token Project," in H. McKenzie (ed.), 1968–1969 Report of the Consulting Teacher Program: Vol. II. Burlington, Vt.: Consulting Teacher Program, College of Education, University of Vermont, 1970, p. 222. By permission of the publishers.)*

square piece of oaktag containing the word "Good." At the time the teacher delivered the token, she also complimented the student. The tokens were not exchangeable for any back-up reinforcers and therefore may be regarded as tangible pieces of social reinforcement. The teacher ignored students who were out of their seats when the bell rang. During the Token$_1$ stage, in-seat behavior increased steadily and reached a mean of 88 percent. In Baseline$_2$, tokens were removed *abruptly* and the teacher did not praise students who were in their seats when the bell rang. In-seat behavior decreased sharply.

The fourth stage (Token$_2$) consisted of a reinstatement of the tokens and teacher praise. For the twenty-six days of this phase, the average rate of in-seat behavior was 87 percent. This stage was a necessary prerequisite to the schedule-thinning procedure. At point "a" in Figure 2-2 the teacher began to dispense tokens for in-seat behavior on every other occasion that the bell rang. Thus, although the bell still rang six times a day and measurements continued to follow all rings, reinforcement was delivered on only three occasions a day. In spite of the less frequent reinforcement, the average rate of in-seat behavior increased to 92 percent. At point "b," reinforcement was available during only two of the six bell rings, with the mean rate of in-seat behavior reaching 95 percent. At point "c" there was only one occasion out of the six rings when the tokens and praise were delivered, but the average proportion of in-seat behavior increased slightly. Finally, at "d" the token reinforcement procedure was completely discontinued, but the rate of in-seat behavior remained at a high level. The thinning procedure used by Egner et al. (1970), therefore, holds considerable promise as a means of gradually removing a programmed reinforcement system from a classroom.

In accordance with the practice of thinning a schedule of reinforcement, it is sometimes possible to switch from one type of reinforcer to another, after student behavior improves sufficiently. Consider the dilemma of a special education resource room teacher who notes that a student of his is more motivated by candy and other tangible reinforcers than he is by privileges and teacher approval. The teacher could use candy as a reinforcer for academic improvement, but he would be diminishing the chances of returning the child to the mainstream of education because regular classroom teachers often find candy an unacceptable reinforcer. Given this situation, the teacher might initially use candy in the resource room to reinforce academic improvement. As the child becomes more competent in performing the behavior, the resource room teacher can often maintain the improvement by using less powerful (for this child) reinforcers, such as classroom privileges and teacher approval. Now that the behavior is being maintained by more easily implemented reinforcers, the regular classroom teacher should find it feasible to continue the reinforcement procedures of the resource room teacher and, thereby, to maintain student improvement.

Reinforcer Sampling

It probably seems to most readers that once an event has demonstrated an ability to reinforce behavior, it will be able to reinforce the same behavior in different situations and will be able to reinforce different kinds of behaviors. A thorough explication of the subject by Ayllon and Azrin (1968) indicated, however, that some caution should be exercised before reaching such a conclusion. Ayllon and Azrin refer to a considerable amount of evidence that indicates that when a reinforcer is initially presented in a novel situation, the individual will often refuse the proposed reinforcer. The phenomenon exists even though the individual may have readily consumed or engaged in the reinforcing event in different situations in the past. Ayllon and Azrin (1968) first presented the results of studies with subhumans to support their contention. They noted, for example, that pigeons which are reinforced with a certain type of food for performing a task will eat the food in the home cage but will often reject the same food in a novel cage. In addition to rejecting the food, the pigeon may flap its wings repeatedly, appear startled, and back away from the food. Frequently, however, the bird will later approach and consume the food.

Ayllon and Azrin (1968) reported similar findings with humans. The authors cited information from a study by Sommer and Ayllon (1956) in which several college women initially refused to accept money as a reward for taking part in an experiment. Remarks such as, "Oh, keep it, I don't really need it," and "Give it to someone else" were common in the early sessions. Speech therapists who are attempting to reinforce appropriate verbal behavior often notice that a child will reject a piece of candy placed in his mouth. After an adaptation period, however, most children will readily accept the candy.

The importance of these findings is that if a student is going to reject some event as a reinforcer, a system requiring him to perform an academic task to acquire the intended reinforcer is likely to fail. If children refuse the intended reinforcer, they will probably not work for it. A solution to the problem is to allow the students to sample the object or event before it is used as a reinforcer. This is known as "reinforcer sampling." If toys are to be used as a reinforcer, for example, the teacher can permit the students to play with the objects for a short period before a reinforcement procedure is used. Similarly, the students should be allowed to sample small amounts of candy if candy is to be employed as a reinforcer.

If it is important to use a reinforcer sampling procedure when children are familiar with the intended reinforcers, it is all the more important to use such a tactic when children are *not* familiar with the intended reinforcers. Thus, a teacher should not attempt to reinforce children with a new classroom game before she allows the students to become acquainted with the game. As Ayllon and Azrin state, "The sampling of the event does not guarantee that the event will, in fact, be reinforcing to the individual; rather, the sampling allows any reinforcing properties to be exhibited if the event has any potential reinforcing properties. If the individual does not seek the event after it has been sampled, it will not be because of a lack of familiarity with it [p. 92]."

Only a few classroom studies have employed a reinforcer sampling tactic. Miller and Schneider (1970), for example, used a token reinforcement system to develop handwriting skills in a preschool classroom. During the first day in which tokens were employed, the children were permitted to sample each of the play activities which were to be used as back-up reinforcers. On subsequent days, of course, it was necessary for the children to earn the opportunity to engage in the reinforcing events. Likewise, Hall, Panyan, Rabon, and Broden (1968) employed a classroom game as a reinforcer for study behavior. Before the game was used as a reinforcer, however, the children had the opportunity to play the game. In such a manner the children had a chance to become familiar with the game and to come into contact with the reinforcing properties of the activity.

Ayllon and Azrin (1968) describe some of the ways in which reinforcer sampling is used in our daily lives. Car salesmen, for example, will permit prospective customers to try out a new car over the weekend. The assumption is that the individual who experiences the reinforcing properties of the new automobile will be more likely to purchase it. It was also pointed out that such procedures are used by book and record companies.

My personal recommendation is that reinforcer sampling procedures be used by speech, psychological, and other types of therapists as well as by teachers. Rather than abruptly using a behavior modification technique in which a child must immediately begin to earn the reinforcers, it would be better to set aside a period of time in which the students can engage in the reinforcing activities noncontingently. Overdoing the plan can cause more problems than it solves.

Group Contingencies

Many of the studies mentioned thus far have been concerned with the problem behaviors of one or two children in a classroom. Some teachers, however, may have situations in which there is a general level of disruptiveness, or poor academic development, and therefore prefer techniques which are applicable to an entire classroom. Using a system in which individual records and different reinforcers must be employed for each student is often a cumbersome and impractical scheme. A possible solution to the problem is to use a "group contingency." This is a procedure in which the consequence (that is, reinforcement or punishment) that each student receives depends not only on his own behavior, but also on the behavior of other members of his group.

An example of a group contingency is found in the sport of professional baseball. After the World Series has been completed, all members of the winning team receive the same pay, even though their individual performances may have varied greatly. The team has been scored as a unit. Similarly, all members of the losing team receive the same, smaller share, in spite of the fact that the performance of some members of the losing team may have exceeded that of some of the players on the winning team (or so the losers might claim). Another example of a group contingency occurs when an individual purchases automobile insurance. The premium he pays is determined not only by his own driving record, but by the driving performance of other people in his neighborhood, as well as of people of the same sex and age range. A third example of a group contingency is the electoral system. A citizen casts a vote for a particular candidate but receives her choice only if a sufficient number of members of the electorate vote in a similar manner. If she is outvoted, she must endure the majority choice until the next election.

Gallagher, Sulzbacher, and Shores (1967) showed how a group contingency procedure could be used in a classroom for five emotionally disturbed boys. Although the children were performing a variety of disruptive behaviors, the authors concentrated only on reducing out-of-seat behaviors. They hypothesized that if the youngsters remained in their seats, the rate of other inappropriate behaviors would also decrease. During baseline, the students left their seats, without permission, an average of seventy times a day. The teacher then informed the students that they could have a maximum of a twenty-four-minute Coke break at the end of the school day if they did not leave their seats without permission. She posted the numbers "24, 22, 20, . . . , 4, 2, 0" on the chalkboard. These figures represented the number of minutes for the Coke break. Each time a student left his or her seat without permission, two minutes were marked off the amount of time for the Coke break, for the *entire* class. Thus, if there was one out-of-seat incident, all students received a twenty-two-minute break. If there were two incidents, the children had a twenty-minute break. If there were twelve or more out-of-seat behaviors, the class did not receive a Coke break (since all twenty-four minutes would have been marked off). Each child's name was assigned a different color chalk. Whenever a student left his or her seat without permission, the teacher marked off two minutes with the designated chalk color. In this way the students could identify who was responsible for costing them a portion of their break time. For the fifteen days in which the group contingency procedure was employed, the mean number of out-of-seat behaviors decreased to 1.0 per day, and an overall decrease in other disruptive behaviors was also reported.

A procedure such as the one above, in which a certain number of minutes (or points, or pennies, and so on) is removed following an inappropriate behavior, is known as "response cost." The reader should note that even though the students might ultimately receive a consequence that they enjoy, response cost is classified as a punishment procedure. This is the case in the Gallagher et al. study, for example, because the students lost minutes of free play contingent on leaving their seats; since the behavior on which there was a contingency (that is, out-of-seat behaviors) decreased in rate, the procedure qualifies as punishment.

With slight adaptations, the author has found the Gallagher et al. procedure exceedingly effective. The tactic might involve vertically listing the numbers "15, 14, 13, . . . , 1, 0" on the board. The numbers might refer to minutes of free-play time available for the entire class. Each time a student violates a classroom rule, the teacher crosses the highest intact number off the board (see Figure 2-3). It would be difficult to use different colors of chalk with large-size classes. The teacher, therefore, uses chalk of only one color, but places the name of the deviating student next to the crossed-off number. With such a procedure, the author has often found that a teacher, *without assistance,*

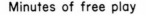

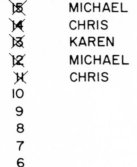

1̶6̶	MICHAEL
1̶4̶	CHRIS
1̶3̶	KAREN
1̶2̶	MICHAEL
1̶1̶	CHRIS
10	
9	
8	
7	
6	
5	
4	
3	
2	
1	
0	

Figure 2-3 Hypothetical chart of a response-cost group contingency arrangement.

can quickly eliminate one or more inappropriate behaviors in a regular-size classroom. In addition, since free-play time can be used as the reinforcer, the technique does not place a burden on the teacher's pocketbook. If one or two students consistently violate the rules and preclude the possibility of the other children receiving the privileges, the problem can sometimes be solved by placing the problem child(ren) on a separate, individual system.

Some behaviorists have speculated that group contingency operations are effective partly because of the role of peer pressure. It is possible, for example, that when a particular child misbehaves several times, his classmates will coerce him into obeying the classroom rules. If peer pressure is indeed a factor in group contingencies, such procedures should produce a greater decrement in disruptive behaviors than a similar system programming individual consequences. An investigation by Axelrod (1973) in two classes did not verify this position. The study compared an individual contingency with a group contingency in reducing out-of-seat and disruptive behaviors. In both classes the individual and group contingency systems were equally effective in controlling misbehaviors. Overall, however, the group contingency operation seemed easier to implement. Not only was the record-keeping process simpler, but there was less trouble in administering the privileges, since all students received the same consequence.

The question of the fairness of group contingency procedures is frequently raised. To many teachers it seems unfair to penalize an entire class for the misbehaviors of one child. To answer this criticism, I again ask the reader to view the long-term effects of such a procedure. A student who is generally cooperative will suffer in academic and social development if his classmates are continually disruptive. If a teacher uses a technique which will reduce the level of inappropriate behaviors, it is reasonable to expect that all students will eventually benefit from the procedure. This does not mean that I am recommending group contingencies over individual contingencies. If a teacher has devised an individual contingency system that is effective, she should use it. In cases where it is unrealistic to attempt many individual contingencies, however, a group contingency tactic should be considered.

Classroom Games

A "classroom game" is a particular type of group contingency that teachers have commonly used. Anyone who has observed children playing dodgeball or "multiplication baseball" is aware of the enthusiasm that such games generate. The children will urge their classmates on to greater heights and will vehemently congratulate them when they succeed. The question that arises is whether teachers can take advantage of the reinforcing value of winning a game so as to motivate the children to perform appropriate school behaviors.

Barrish, Saunders, and Wolf (1969) did a study that indicated an affirmative answer to the above question. The teacher of the class was dealing with twenty-four fourth graders—many of whom were chronic discipline problems. When baseline observations indicated that out-of-seat and talking-out behaviors were occurring more than 80 percent of the time, the authors devised a "good behavior" game. The teacher divided the students into two teams, according to the rows in which they sat. She informed the youngsters that they were going to play a game in which there were some rules relating to out-of-seat and talking-out behavior. Each time a student violated one of the rules, the teacher placed a mark against his team on the chalkboard. The team that had the fewer marks at the end of the period was declared the winner. If both teams had five or fewer marks, they both won the game. Besides winning the game, the members of the winning team received victory tags, free-play time at the end of the day, and a star next to their names on the winner's chart.

Since the students were scored as a team, and since each team member received the same consequence, the procedure is classified as a group contingency. The procedure had an immediate and substantial effect on the behavior, with instances of talking out and out-of-seat behaviors decreasing to less than one-fourth of the baseline level. In addition, it was found that both teams won the game 82 percent of the times it was played.

A difficulty which arose during the study was that two students sometimes performed disruptive behaviors at a high rate. Both students were on the same team and were capable of negating the efforts of their teammates. When the problem occurred, the teacher managed the situation by placing each deviant child on a team by himself. Under these conditions their misbehaviors were managed on an individual basis and kept the other members of the team in contention for the winners' privileges.

Perhaps the main contributions of the Barrish et al. study were that the authors used an easily applied procedure (that is, a game) which was similar to those in which schoolchildren engage, and that the reinforcers were privileges which are available in any classroom. Although the expenditure of money which is required when costly tangible reinforcers are employed is undoubtedly worthwhile, the problem frequently arises that funds are difficult to procure or are unavailable. In such cases, it is necessary that a teacher use his ingenuity to devise a system using the many reinforcers which are already available in the classroom.

The Barrish et al. study used the winning of the game, as well as a variety of privileges, as consequences for the students' behavior. The reader may wonder whether winning the game without the privileges would be sufficient to motivate improved student performance. Axelrod and Paluska (1975) found that winning alone was not always enough. In the Baseline₁ phase, the teacher, Ms. Jolena Paluska, gave the students six spelling words and tested the students on the words the next day. Figure 2-4 indicates that the average for this phase was 3.5 words correct, or 58 percent accuracy. In the Game₁ stage,

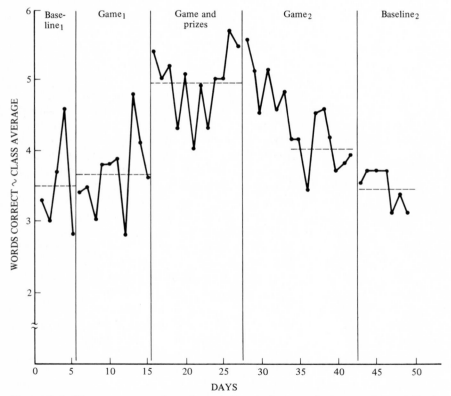

Figure 2-4 The average number of words the students spelled correctly on daily six-word spelling tests. *(From S. Axelrod and J. Paluska, "A Component Analysis of a Classroom Game on Spelling Performance," in E. Ramp and G. Semb (eds.),* Behavior Analysis: Areas of Research and Application. *Englewood Cliffs, N.J.: Prentice-Hall, 1975, p. 280. By permission of the publishers.)*

Ms. Paluska divided the children into the "Blue" team and the "Red" team. The teams were matched according to their Baseline$_1$ scores. After giving the students their daily test, the teacher added the scores of the two teams and announced the team with the higher overall score. She then read aloud the names of the winners and permitted the winners to stand by their desks and cheer for themselves. Although the students were enthusiastic about the game, their average spelling accuracy increased only 3 percent—to 3.65 words correct. In the "Game plus Prizes" phase, the children on the winning team continued to receive social reinforcement, but each student was also awarded a prize, such as a candy bar, a pencil, or a toy car, after his team won. The class's spelling accuracy increased to 5.0 words a day, or 83 percent correct. Hence the awarding of prizes for the winners furnished the motivation for improved spelling performance that the game alone failed to provide. When the game alone and baseline conditions were later reinstated, the children's spelling accuracy decreased. The study again emphasizes the importance of teachers measuring student performance, since the enthusiasm the youngsters exhibited during Game$_1$ and Game$_2$ would probably mislead many teachers into believing that the game alone was increasing student achievement.

SELF-CONTROL OF BEHAVIOR

Some educators admit to the effectiveness of behavior modification procedures but object to the fact that the teacher rather than the child himself modifies the youngster's behavior. Thus, although a teacher might devise and conduct a reinforcement system that enhances the academic development of the student, some educators would prefer that the child learn to modify his own behavior. One argument behind this notion is that students who are able to control their own behavior will not have to depend on the skills of their teachers in order to develop scholastically.

A considerable amount of research has been done on self-control procedures in clinical settings but relatively little in classrooms. Nevertheless, some studies have shown that when students learn to record their own behavior, they are able to increase their attending behavior and reduce their disruptiveness. Other studies have shown that when students determine the amount of reinforcement they should receive for a particular task, their performance of the task often improves markedly. Finally, contracting procedures employed in some school systems have shown that students can effectively participate in the entire process of setting goals and determining reinforcement levels.

Self-Recording

Many people have found that by recording some aspect of their behavior, they are able to modify that behavior. In one case a law student used a wrist counter to keep a daily record of the number of cigarettes he smoked. After baseline observations indicated that he smoked more than forty cigarettes a day, he set progressively lower goals of cigarette consumption for himself, until he ultimately ceased smoking. In another case a graduate student was concerned about his consumption of alcoholic beverages. Before baseline he figured out the ethanol content of each of his favorite drinks. Thereafter, he recorded the amount of ethanol in each drink that he had. During baseline he found that he was consuming the equivalent of eight bottles of beer a day. He then set successively lower goals for himself in much the same manner as the law student did with his smoking behavior. Two years later he reported that his alcoholic consumption was at half of its original level. In still another case an associate found that he could increase the rate at which he complimented other people by keeping a daily record of the number of positive statements he made.

Although self-recording procedures have seldom been used in classroom situations, Broden, Hall, and Mitts (1971) showed that such techniques can sometimes be useful. Two students took part in the investigation. One of the youngsters was Liza, an eighth-grade girl who had received a D– in history class. Liza met with her counselor on a weekly basis, during which time she expressed a desire to become a better student. The counselor then approached Liza's history teacher and asked him to use a social reinforcement system with the youngster. The history teacher, however, declined the request because he felt that the behavior modification tactic would interfere with the lecture format of his course. The authors then decided to determine the effect of having Liza record her own behavior.

An outside observer kept a record of Liza's study behavior; "study behavior" consisted of attending to classroom assignments and following teacher directions. The data which the observer collected were used to assess the effectiveness of the behavior modification technique. The observer did not apply any contingency to Lisa's behavior, nor did she inform Lisa of the results. Baseline data collected over seven days indicated that Liza's study rate was only 30 percent, despite two conferences with the counselor in which she promised to "really try." On day 8 the counselor met with Liza and discussed the definition of "study behavior" with her. She also gave Liza a slip of paper and directed her to take such a slip to history class each day. Her instructions were to rate her behavior as "study" or "nonstudy," "when she thought of it," during history class. She was to place a "+" in one of the boxes if she had been studying for the previous few minutes, and a "–" if she had not been. With the self-recording procedure, Liza's study rate increased to an average of 78 percent. In addition, her history grade increased from a D– to a C.

A second case reported by Broden et al. involved Stu, an eighth-grade boy who continually talked out in mathematics class, disturbing both his teacher and his classmates. In the self-recording phase, the teacher asked Stu to place a mark on a piece of paper (see Figure 2-5) each time he talked out without permission. No contingencies were placed on his talking-out behavior, nor did the teacher remind him to mark his paper each time he talked out. The data of a classroom observer indicated that the self-recording procedure reduced Stu's talking out to about one-fourth of its Baseline$_1$ level.

At least three points concerning the studies are worth mentioning. First, it

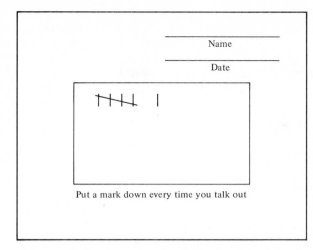

Name

Date

Put a mark down every time you talk out

Figure 2-5 Sample self-recording sheet used by Stu. *(From M. Broden, R. V. Hall, and B. Mitts, "The Effect of Self-Recording on the Classroom Behavior of Two Eighth-Grade Students," Journal of Applied Behavior Analysis, **4**, p. 196, 1971. By permission of the publishers.)*

was demonstrated in Liza's situation that someone (in this case, the counselor) could institute procedures to modify behavior, even though she could not be present to observe the student and apply consequences to her behavior. Secondly, it was indicated that a method which systematically increases an individual's awareness of a certain behavior might also help the individual to change that behavior. Finally, the self-recording procedure can be seen as a feedback technique in which individuals provide themselves with information concerning their own behavior.

Teachers should consider using self-recording procedures to improve various aspects of their teaching repertoire. They might, for example, keep a record of the number of times they praise and reprimand students. By setting a progressive series of goals, they can try to reach the point at which they make, say, ten praise comments for every reprimand. They might also keep a record of the amount of time it takes to grade student papers and attempt to decrease their return time or keep it at a low level. A self-recording procedure is probably less effective than a programmed contingency, but it has the outstanding advantage of eliminating the need for second-party participation.

Self-determined Reinforcement

In almost all cases in which positive reinforcement procedures have been employed in classrooms, the teachers determined the amount of reinforcement the students would receive for performing in a certain manner. Some educators might wonder whether children can participate in the process of deciding how much reinforcement a particular task is worth and whether such participation enhances the youngsters' performance on the task. Also, if children can responsibly take part in the process of setting goals and determining reinforcement levels, they would have taken a step toward regulating their own behavior—an outcome which most educators would look upon favorably.

Lovitt and Curtiss (1969) showed that it was a feasible arrangement to have a student determine how much reinforcement he should receive for completing academic assignments. They also demonstrated that the student's academic output improved in the process. The youngster in the study was a twelve-year-old boy in a class for children with behavioral disorders. The boy was working on a token system in which the points he earned for scholastic performance were exchangeable for minutes of free-play time. The teacher kept a record of the rate at which the child completed work in eight different academic areas.

In the first stage of the study, the teacher determined the amount of work the youngster would have to accomplish in order to receive a specified amount of free time. The contract which she devised included ten mathematics problems for one minute of free time, one page of reading without errors for two minutes of free time, and writing twenty letters for one minute of free time. Figure 2-6 indicates that, for the thirteen days that this procedure was employed, the median rate of academic performance was 1.6 responses per minute. In the second stage of the study, the student himself specified the payment which he would receive for completing tasks in each of the eight academic areas. The contracts he derived included ten mathematics problems for two minutes of free time, reading one page for three minutes of free time, and writing ten letters for two minutes of free time. The youngster was consistently more generous to himself than the teacher was. For the thirteen days in which this procedure was used, his median rate increased to 2.3 responses per minute. Later, when teacher-specified contracts were again used, his median performance decreased to the earlier level.

An obvious criticism that could be raised against the Lovitt and Curtiss

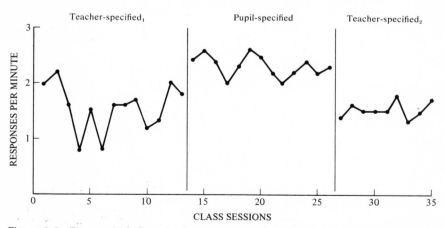

Figure 2-6   The number of academic responses a twelve-year-old boy made in eight different areas. *(Adapted from T. C. Lovitt and K. Curtiss, "Academic Response Rate as a Function of Teacher- and Self-imposed Contingencies,"* Journal of Applied Behavior Analysis, **2**, p. 52, *1969. By permission of the publishers.)*

(1969) study is that the improvement which occurred in the second phase of the study might have been due to the increased level of reinforcement the student received, rather than the fact that the student devised the contracts. Indeed, the previously described study (pp. 45–46) by Wolf et al. (1968) indicated that increasing the amount of reinforcement which is available for a certain behavior can increase the rate of that behavior. A second study which Lovitt and Curtiss (1969) presented clarified the issue. In the first phase of the study, the student worked under the contracts which the teacher initially used in the first experiment. In the second stage of the study, the teacher informed the child that the youngster would be working with the contracts which he himself had previously determined. Thus, the student worked for a more generous amount of reinforcement, but now the contracts were *imposed* on him by the teacher. In the final stage of the investigation, the teacher again employed the original, less generous contracts. Unlike the Wolf et al. (1968) study, it was found that the larger amount of reinforcement did not produce results superior to the smaller amounts of reinforcement. Thus, the critical factor in the original Lovitt and Curtiss (1969) study was whether the teacher or the student determined the contracts rather than the quantity of reinforcement which was available.

Glynn (1970) performed another experiment concerned with student-determined reinforcement. The subjects for the study were girls in ninth-grade classes in a Canadian school. Each day, the students received reading sheets describing various aspects of history and geography. After they read the material, the girls answered twenty multiple-choice questions concerning the content of the reading sheets. Based on the number of questions answered correctly, the students received tokens in the form of slips of paper which were exchangeable for a variety of prizes. One class of girls was exposed to a condition in which the author determined how many tokens the students should receive for their performance; in another condition with the same class, the judgment was made by the students. For another class of students, the amount of reinforcement the girls received was determined by chance. One of the findings of the study was that self-determined reinforcement was at least as effective as experimenter-determined reinforcement in improving academic behavior. A surprising discovery was that when the girls themselves determined how many tokens they deserved for their test performance, they tended to be less benevolent to themselves than the experimenter was. This finding conflicts with that of the Lovitt and Curtiss (1969) study and appears to reveal an area requiring further investigation.

Many teachers might find the notion of having students determine reinforcement amounts desirable. Nevertheless, teachers should *not* assume that all youngsters will behave in a reasonable manner when given such a task. In some cases students will demand excessive amounts of reinforcement for performing relatively easy tasks. In these situations, teachers might find it necessary to guide students through the process by initially granting students a small amount of responsibility and gradually increasing the student's participation. If these measures fail, it may be necessary for the teacher alone to make the decisions.

Contingency Contracting

Perhaps the most ambitious endeavor for teaching children to manage their own behavior is found in the practice of "contingency contracting." A "contingency contract" is an agreement between a teacher and a student stating that upon the student's reaching a certain goal, the teacher will reward the student with an event, activity, or object that he likes. A contingency contract differs from other contingencies in that the terms are devised by both the teacher and the student and the particulars are usually spelled out in writing.

The main advocate of contingency contracting is Lloyd Homme. In his book on the topic, Homme (1969) points out that in many cases teachers have imposed negative contingencies on children. These are arrangements in which a student must behave in a certain manner in order to avoid a punisher. Thus, an example of a negative contingency would be a teacher's stating, "If you behave well today, I won't send a note home to your mother," or, "If you finish your work on time, you won't be kept in at recess." Also, the legal systems in most countries are examples of negative contingencies.

Rather than using negative contingencies, Homme proposes instead that teachers use positive contingencies. Such operations take the form, "When you show you have learned a little more, you can engage in an even more enjoyable task"; or, "If you refrain from a certain inappropriate behavior, you will receive a special privilege." An example of a positive contingency is permitting a child to play a game with a classmate if he answers 90 percent of his mathematics problems correctly. Another example is to allow a youngster to be a messenger if he fails to hit his classmates during the entire morning.

The process of arriving at a contract involves negotiation between the teacher and the student. The parties discuss both the amount of the task to be accomplished and the amount of reinforcement to be provided. Initially, it is expected that the teacher will have the main responsibility for determining the terms of the contract. As the learning process continues, the distribution of the responsibility should gradually shift to the student, until he has the main responsibility for arriving at the specifics of the agreement. After a contract is devised, the terms should be written down, with a copy of the terms going to each party. In this manner there can be no question about the obligations of the teacher and the student, and changes in the contract should come about only following a new agreement between the parties.

Homme (1969) states some guidelines for writing an appropriate contract. Many of the suggestions are applicable to any behavior modification program:

1 The payoff should be immediate. This is especially important in the early stages of learning when the student is first becoming familiar with contracting.

2 The contract should provide frequent, small rewards for slight improvements in behavior, rather than one large reward for a great change in behavior. Thus, it is better to give a student one piece of candy after completing two arithmetic problems than to reward him with an entire box of candy for doing twenty-five problems. This also is most important during the early stages of learning.

3 Both sides of the agreement should be of relatively equal weight. Hence, a student should not receive a trip to the zoo after working for a minute, nor should he be required to spell fifty words correctly for two minutes of free time.

4 The terms of the contract should be clear. A student should know, for example, that he is required to do *five* arithmetic problems for a certain reward rather than to do *some* problems for the reward.

5 Because of the different learning levels and learning rates of children, it is better to devise individual rather than group contracts.

6 The tasks should be short enough so that they can be completed in the allotted amount of time.

Lates and Egner (1973) showed how a contingency contract could be used with a junior high school student. The youngster of concern was Jethro, an eighth-grade boy who had been sent to the principal's office for discipline problems on numerous occasions. At a meeting with the guidance counselor, assistant principal, and his parents, Jethro agreed to the following contract: On each day in which Jethro completed all of his assignments in each class, he would receive one privilege at home. The privileges were compatible with Jethro's interests and included visits to friends' homes, fishing trips, permission to stay up late at night, and time at the youth center. Once the contract was introduced, Jethro never again was sent to the principal's office. Both his parents and teachers were impressed with the results. Comments on Jethro's report card included:

"His behavior has improved tremendously."
"Most improved student in whole class."
"Attitude and effort have also improved."

Another example of contingency contracting was provided by Tymchuk (1974). The student in the program was a twelve-year-old boy who was having difficulties with reading. An examination of the boy's background revealed that the parents seldom showed interest in their son's scholastic activities. It was also concluded that the youth's chief desire was for praise from his father and to spend time with him in athletic activities or talking about "men things." The parents and boy agreed that the father would spend more time with the boy as his reading performance improved. According to the contract, the youngster read portions of stories to his parents and received a checkmark for each paragraph he read correctly in thirty minutes. Each time he received a check, he could exchange it for a penny. He could also exchange fifteen checks for fifteen minutes of television time, twenty checks for an opportunity to work on building a boat with his father, and fifty checks for a basketball game with

Father. Both the terms of the contract and the daily results were pinned to the kitchen wall. The data revealed a steady increase in the number of paragraphs the boy read correctly and a steady decrease in the number of errors he made.

ALTERNATIVE BEHAVIOR MODIFICATION AGENTS

Most of the studies described so far have involved teachers applying contingencies to the behavior of their students. There are times, however, when children might be more effective agents of change—particularly adolescent youngsters. Thus, some of the studies in the present section will discuss procedures by which children have modified the behavior of their classmates. In one case the effect was programmed; in another case it occurred even though it was not planned. Still another study describes the means by which students can act as effective tutors for their classmates.

A second topic to be discussed is the influence that student behavior has on the behavior of teachers. It turns out that in the process of instructing their students, teachers are subject to the same principles of reinforcement, extinction, and punishment as their students. Thus, attentive student behavior will reinforce certain teacher behaviors, whereas blank faces and yawning will decrease the rate of other behaviors. The reader will note that the application of such principles can influence a variety of behaviors that ranges from minor idiosyncracies to the full cluster of instructional techniques.

Peer Reinforcement

Teachers are undoubtedly aware of the effect that peer approval and disapproval can have on a child. A student who is cheered by his classmates for helping his team to win a game may strut around the classroom in a manner resembling the proverbial peacock. Another pupil who is ridiculed for his inability to speak properly might cry or pout. In some behavior modification studies it has been noted that when children have the chance to earn rewards for the entire group, their classmates will reinforce their success. Thus, in the previously described (p. 35) study by Patterson (1965), Earl had the opportunity to earn points which were exchangeable for candy or pennies, to be shared by the entire class. Under these conditions the author noted that Earl's classmates would usually applaud him after his final score was announced, and that they frequently complimented him during classroom breaks. The social reinforcement afforded by the students may have augmented the success of the token reinforcement program.

The occurrence of peer reinforcement in the Patterson (1965) study was noted anecdotally. A more systematic investigation of the process was provided by Axelrod, Hall, and Maxwell (1972). Jimmy, the student of concern, had a history of classroom discipline problems. On several occasions his teacher and the school principal reprimanded him for behaving inappropriately in class and for fighting with his schoolmates outside of class. The authors conducted a five-session Baseline$_1$ phase to determine the percentage of time

Jimmy engaged in study behavior. As indicated in Figure 2-7, during this period Jimmy was studying an average of 55 percent of the time.

From sessions 6 through 10 the authors attempted to induce the classroom teacher to give Jimmy attention when she observed that he was behaving properly. As the lower portion of Figure 2-7 indicates, the authors' efforts were fruitless. At no time did the teacher administer social reinforcement to Jimmy. Sessions 6 to 10 were therefore considered to be an extension of Baseline₁. As the disgruntled experimenters prepared to abandon their efforts, good fortune struck. During session 10 Jimmy completed an assignment and asked the teacher to grade it. After the teacher ignored him, he brought the paper to Anthony Maxwell, the class's most outstanding student, and the third author of the article. Anthony graded the paper as 100 percent correct and Jimmy returned to his seat. A few moments later, Jimmy again approached Anthony

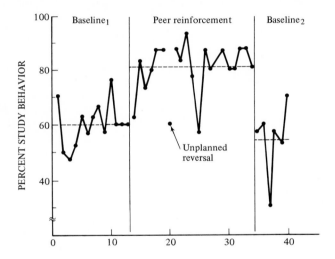

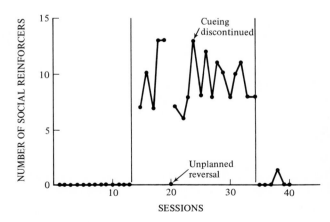

Figure 2-7 The top graph depicts the percentage of time Jimmy was engaged in student behavior, whereas the bottom graph shows the number of social reinforcers he received. "Unplanned reversal" refers to a day in which Anthony was absent. *(From S. Axelrod, R. V. Hall, and A. Maxwell, "Use of Peer Attention to Increase Study Behavior," Behavior Therapy, 3, p. 350, 1972. By permission of the publishers.)*

and asked him to write "Very good" on the paper. Anthony, of course, complied with the request. The authors then decided that they were working with the wrong person. They gave up on the teacher and decided, instead, to work with Anthony as the agent of social reinforcement. During sessions 11 to 13 Anthony was seated next to Jimmy, but was given no instructions on administering social reinforcement. The sessions were, therefore, considered a further extension of Baseline$_1$. During the entire Baseline$_1$ phase, Jimmy's study rate averaged 60 percent, with a range of 46 to 78 percent.

Following Baseline$_1$ the senior author asked Anthony if he would like to teach Jimmy to become a "better student." Anthony readily agreed to do so and then received information on how to deliver social reinforcers. Beginning with session 14, Anthony would wait until Jimmy was behaving properly. He would then tap him on the shoulder and make a comment such as "Jimmy, you're doing a good job." or "Keep up the good work." Initially, one of the authors would signal Anthony when it was an opportune moment to reinforce Jimmy. By session 23, however, Anthony had learned the job so well that cueing became unnecessary and Anthony acted on his own. Jimmy apparently found Anthony's praise reinforcing, as his study rate quickly increased, until it stabilized at a rate above 80 percent. The verification of the reinforcing effectiveness of peers is interesting, but perhaps the most important point of the study is that when teachers find it difficult to carry out a behavior modification technique, an alternative strategy might be to have a student implement the procedure.

An area which is receiving increasing attention is the use of students to tutor other youngsters in academic subjects. An excellent source for such studies is a portion of a book entitled *Behavior Analysis and Education—1972* (Semb, Green, Hawkins, Michael, Phillips, Sherman, Sloane, and Thomas, 1972). One of the studies (Willis, Crowder, and Morris, 1972) employed eighth graders as reading tutors for children in grades two through eight. The tutors spent their free periods each day working with pairs of students on programmed reading materials. They lavished praise on the students and gave them tokens each time the students read a sentence without error. Although the tokens were not exchangeable for back-up reinforcers, they provided concrete evidence for the children that they had read the material correctly. The performance of the tutors was rated with respect to twenty items, such as "Praises often when correct," "Shows enthusiasm," and "Corrects errors." The authors praised the tutors when they performed well and gave teams of tutors the opportunity to win a trophy when their collective ratings exceeded those of the other team of tutors. Evidence of the effectiveness of the student tutors was given by the fact that children in the tutored group gained 1.3 years in reading achievement level during the school year, as compared with 0.58 year for a similar group in the regular remedial program. The authors pointed out that in addition to being more effective, the tutoring procedure cost less than half the amount of money that was spent on the regular remedial program.

Student tutoring is also one of the only feasible means by which students can receive a large amount of teaching on a one-to-one basis.

Modifying the Modifier's Behavior

It is likely that every teacher is a behavior modifier. As Lovitt (1970) points out, the alternative to being a modifier is to be a "behavior maintainer" [p. 85]. Since teachers use techniques to develop reading behaviors in nonreading students and attempt to convert lazy students into industrious ones, they qualify as modifiers rather than maintainers. Given that a teacher's behavior can modify a student's behavior, one might raise the question of whether the converse is also true. That is, does a student's behavior have an effect on the teacher's behavior? A courageous experiment by Southern and Zey (1969) indicated that the answer to the above question is "yes."

Southern and Zey were students in a college education course who noticed that the instructor often used the word "alright." Since they were also students in a behavior modification course, they knew how to do something about it. Sessions consisted of fifteen-minute blocks of time during class, and there were usually five sessions per class during Baseline$_1$. The range of the number of "alrights" was from one to twelve, with a mean of 5.5 per fifteen-minute session. In the second condition of the study, the students coughed aloud each time the instructor said, "Alright." It was indicated that the coughs were loud enough so that the entire class could hear them but did not appear to disturb the other students or the instructor's lecture. During the twelve sessions in which this procedure was applied, the average number of "alrights" decreased to slightly less than half of the baseline rate. In the third stage Southern and Zey (1969) returned to baseline conditions and soon enough everything was again "alright."

Perhaps the Southern and Zey study is appropriate at a time when college students are attempting to achieve greater rights. Modifying a professor's behavior can be considered a step in the desired direction. A study reported by Whaley and Malott (1968), however, may have been the ultimate in student revolutions, since in this case the professor whose behavior was being modified was, himself, an instructor of a behavior modification course. The problem that the professor had was that he consistently lectured from the right side of the classroom. Students on the left side had difficulty hearing him, whereas the pupils on the right became exhausted from his persistent presence. During one fifty-minute class period, it was found that he spent forty-six minutes on the right side of the class with most of the remaining time being spent in the middle of the room at the podium. Occasionally he ventured to the left side, in order to write on that side of the board.

Anyone who has spoken before audiences would agree that the attention that listeners exhibit is very reinforcing to the speaker. The students of the class decided to take advantage of this fact. Their plan was to give the professor complete attention when he stood on the far left of the class, and to ignore him at other times. When the class began, the professor immediately walked to the right side and began to lecture. All students' eyes were faced downward, away from the professor, for about ten minutes. At the end of that time, he had filled the right side of the blackboard and was forced to move to the far left of the room. When he turned and faced the class, thirty-five pairs of eyes gazed at him in rapt attention. The students appeared to be orgastically awaiting each word he enunciated. He remained on the left for five minutes. When he moved to the other side, the attention of the audience suddenly dissipated. The professor then began to pace from one side of the room to the other as he delivered his lecture. With about twenty minutes remaining in the period, he stopped on the far left of the room and stayed there for the remainder of the period. Student records indicated that the professor spent about twenty-eight minutes on the far left of the room.

At the next class the students confessed their modification procedure to their professor. He indicated that he had been unaware of their scheme. The professor claimed that he had noticed the poor attention in the beginning of the period, but he had attributed this to the effects of the evening meal which preceded his class. He had also credited the increased attention which later occurred to the exciting nature of his lecture.

In a more serious vein, Gray, Graubard, and Rosenberg (1974) showed that junior high school children were capable of modifying important behaviors of their teachers. The students were members of a class for youngsters who were considered incorrigible by previous teachers. One child, Jess, had a history which included hitting other students with beer bottles and chairs. At one point Jess was suspended for forty days for assaulting a principal with a stick. The seven students each day attended a class in which a special education teacher instructed them in behavior modification techniques. The students were to apply their newly learned techniques in their other classrooms.

During Baseline$_1$ the students kept a record of the number of times the teachers responded to them positively and negatively. The mean number of positive comments was 7.5 and the mean number of negative comments was 18.5 per period. In the Intervention stage of the study, the students reinforced their teachers if they behaved appropriately. If a teacher responded positively to a student, the youth might reward the teacher with a smile, by sitting up straight, or making a comment such as, "I like to work in a room where the teacher is nice to the kids." If the teacher made a negative comment, the student might state, "It's hard for me to do good work when you're cross with me." If the teacher explained a concept adequately, the youngster would exclaim, "Ah hah! Now I understand! I could never get that before."

Under such procedures, positive teacher comments increased each week for five weeks and ultimately averaged twenty-three per period. Negative comments decreased each week until there were no such comments during the final week. Thus, the behavior of teachers is as modifiable as that of students, and teacher supervisors should keep behavioral principles in mind when training new and in-service teachers. This can take the form of providing social reinforcement for improvement in teaching behavior and frequent and immediate feedback for various aspects of their performance.

CLASSROOM ARRANGEMENTS

Teachers sometimes make important decisions on the arrangement of their classroom and the physical placement of students without being fully aware of the effects of their actions. Thus, one teacher will place a disruptive child near her desk so that she can "keep an eye on him," whereas another teacher will place a similar student in a rear corner of the classroom "to prevent him from disturbing his classmates." In other situations a teacher will rearrange the desks of all students according to some formation which she believes will improve the performance of her students. In each of the above cases, the teachers may have made a correct or incorrect decision. The purpose of the present section is to explore the effects of various physical arrangements on student performance and to stress the importance of having teachers make the relevant judgments on the basis of carefully collected data rather than according to arbitrary speculations.

Seating Arrangements

It is not unusual for a teacher to conjecture that a certain student's behavior is influenced by other pupils in the vicinity. In cases in which there is a great deal of inappropriate interaction between two neighboring children, the teacher might separate the students in the hope that the new seating arrangement will produce an improvement in behavior. A portion of a study by Burdett, Egner, and McKenzie (1970) showed that such manipulations will sometimes have a beneficial effect on student performance.

The youngster in the investigation was a six-year-old, first-grade boy who will be referred to as Wayne. In the Boy_1 condition, Wayne sat at the base of a U-shaped desk arrangement. On one side of Wayne sat a boy, whereas a girl was on the other side. As indicated in Figure 2-8, for the eleven days in which this seating arrangement was in effect, Wayne attended to teacher assignments between 30 and 100 percent of the time, with a mean of 68 percent. During this period Wayne's teacher observed the tendency for Wayne and his male neighbor to distract each other from classroom tasks. Thus, in the second phase of the study, the boy who sat next to Wayne was moved to another seat and was replaced with a girl. As a result, there was a girl on either side of Wayne. It can be seen that on the first day the procedure was used, Wayne's attending rate increased to 100 percent and remained at that level for the remainder of the $Girl_1$ phase. When each of the conditions was reinstated during the third and fourth phases of the study, the superiority of having a girl on either side of Wayne was verified.

A reaction which the reader might have to the Burdett et al. study could be that the effectiveness of such a procedure is common knowledge. I disagree with this position. The manipulation of the seating arrangements "worked" in

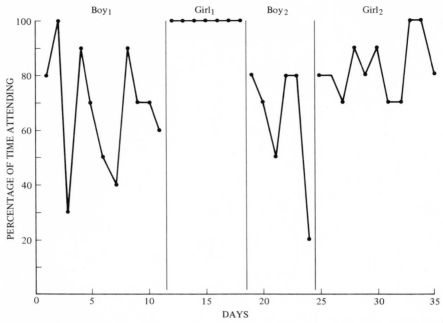

Figure 2-8 Percentage of time Wayne attended to teacher assignments with differing seatmates. *(Adapted from C. Burdett, A. Egner, and H. McKenzie, "P 14," in H. McKenzie (ed.), 1968–1969 Report of the Consulting Teacher Program: Vol. II. Burlington, Vt.: Consulting Teacher Program, College of Education, The University of Vermont, 1970, p. 87. By permission of the publishers.)*

the case presented by Burdett et al. It will not work in other cases. The contribution which the authors made was that rather than assuming that the procedure would work or making a subjective evaluation of its effectiveness, the investigators *measured* the efficacy of their operations. With their objective data they could confidently conclude that their procedure was indeed effective. If the results of the new seating arrangement had not been favorable, the investigators would also have had this information, and they could then have attempted a new tactic to remedy the behavioral problem. A teacher who does not measure the effectiveness of such a technique might arrive at an erroneous decision and fail to proceed in the manner most conducive to classroom progress. The reader may argue that measurement is helpful but is difficult to accomplish with a busy schedule. Evidently this was not a troublesome task in the present study. The teacher rated Wayne every three minutes during a thirty-minute study period. The requirement of only ten measurements a day did not produce any apparent disruption of the teacher's normal routine. In the next chapter I will describe additional examples of observation techniques which require little time or effort from the teacher.

The previous study verified the commonly held notion that children are

Table 2-1 Percentage of Time Attending

		Condition	
Student	Baseline₁	Praise Edwin, ignore Greg	Ignore Edwin, praise Greg
Edwin	31%	81%	62%
Greg	33	58	82

Source: Adapted from M. Broden, C. Bruce, M. A. Mitchell, V. Carter, and R. V. Hall, "Effects of Teacher Attention on Attending Behavior of Two Boys at Adjacent Desks," *Journal of Applied Behavior Analysis, 3,* 199–203, 1970.

influenced by the behavior of students who sit next to them. This idea was taken one step further by Broden, Bruce, Mitchell, Carter, and Hall (1970), who showed that reinforcing one student's behavior can influence the behavior of the student who sits next to him. The study involved two second-grade boys, Edwin and Greg, who were seatmates. Both children were considered by the teacher and principal to be discipline problems. Their permanent record cards revealed a history of disruptive behavior since they entered school. As shown in Table 2-1, during Baseline₁ Edwin's mean rate of study behavior was 31 percent and Greg's was 33 percent. During the next phase, the previously described (p. 7) technique used by Hall, Lund, and Jackson (1968) was applied to Edwin. The teacher praised and attended to Edwin at times when she noticed that he was behaving appropriately. Edwin's rate of study eventually increased to a mean of 81 percent. This compares with the original level of 31 percent. More interestingly, Greg's rate of study behavior increased to 58 percent, as compared with the baseline rate of 33 percent, even though the procedure was not applied to him. In a later condition, the technique was applied to Greg but not to Edwin. During the last seven sessions in which this procedure was applied, Greg's rate of study behavior increased to 82 percent whereas Edwin was at the 62 percent level (see Table 2-1). Thus it appeared that the greatest effect of the reinforcement procedure was experienced by the child to whom it was applied, but that there was a considerable influence on the child in the adjacent seat. Broden et al. (1970) speculated that a "possible explanation for the increased study in the second pupil might be that when study behavior for one of the pair was increased, he was less likely to look at, laugh at, talk to, or otherwise provide social reinforcement for the behavior of his neighbor" [p. 203].

The two prior studies were concerned with the effect students who sat next to each other had on one another. An additional factor influencing student behavior is the manner in which the desks are arranged throughout the classroom. Traditionally, teachers have arranged the desks in a row formation as follows:

```
A    B    C    D    E

F    G    H    I    J

•    •    •    •    •

•    •    •    •    •

•    •    •    •    •
```

More recently, however, an increasing number of teachers have been arranging students in a "cluster" or table formation as follows:

```
A  B        E  F        •  •        •  •

C  D        G  H        •  •        •  •
```

Child A sits next to child B and directly faces child C. Child D faces B and sits next to C. A similar relationship exists for E, F, G, and H and the other clusters of children.

A study by Axelrod, Hall, and Tams (1972) compared the performance of seventeen second-grade students in each of the seating arrangements. Initially children sat in table formation. Figure 2-9 shows that during the nine-day Tables$_1$ period, the average daily rate of study behavior was 62 percent. During the Rows$_1$ phase, the children sat in a row formation and their study level immediately increased and reached a level of 82 percent. When the children again sat in a table arrangement, their study rate decreased to 63 percent but rose to 83 percent when row formation was reinstated. There are several reasons why the table formation may have been associated with more disruptive behavior. First, in such an arrangement children are facing each other and, therefore, find it easy to start a conversation. This tendency is further enhanced by the fact that the children are sitting close to each other in the table arrangement. Another reason is that it is easier for children who are engaged in conversation to escape the detection and reproof of their teachers when they sit in table formation than when they sit in rows. Finally, in the table arrangement a discussion between two students can easily attract the attention and contributions of the other children in the same cluster.

Reinforcement Areas

Ready access to reinforcers is an important factor in the teaching process. In giving training in fluent speech to a child who stutters, for example, a therapist who has his reinforcers near him will generally be more effective than a therapist who must fumble around to locate the reinforcers. Likewise, it has been found that sectioning off a portion of the classroom as a reinforcement area is an effective and convenient means of providing rewards for desirable behavior.

Hopkins, Schutte, and Garton (1971) provided an excellent example of the usefulness of a reinforcement area with twenty-four first and second graders

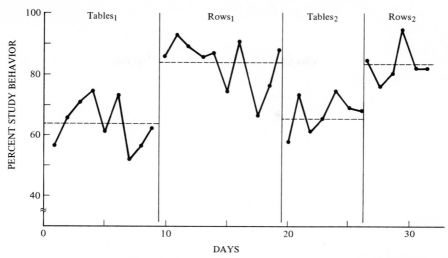

Figure 2-9   The percentage of time second-grade children engaged in study behavior during different seating arrangements. *(From S. Axelrod, R. V. Hall, and A. Tams, "A Comparison of Common Seating Arrangements in the Classroom." Paper presented at the Kansas Symposium on Behavior Analysis in Education, Lawrence, Kans., May 1972. By permission of the authors.)*

who were having difficulty completing printing and cursive writing assignments. Each day the teacher wrote on the chalkboard a printing assignment of about 200 letters for the first graders and a cursive writing assignment of approximately 250 letters for the second graders. She then passed out sheets of paper and asked the students to copy the lesson. During Baseline₁ the students gave their completed papers to the teacher and were instructed to return to their seats and to sit quietly. The children then had to wait for the last student to hand in his paper and have it graded before proceeding to the next subject. Under these conditions the group of first graders printed an average of six letters per minute, whereas the second graders wrote approximately 7.25 letters per minute.

In the second phase of the study, the teacher gave the students in both groups fifty minutes to complete their assignments. If a child finished his assignment before the fifty-minute period was over, he was allowed to go immediately to a play area in the back of the classroom for the remainder of the session. The play area was separated from the remainder of the classroom by an L-shaped partition and consisted of a television set and a variety of games and toys. The children were allowed to bring toys and games from home to supplement those provided by the teacher (thus ensuring that at least some items would be reinforcing to each of the children). When this procedure was in effect, the printing rate of the first graders went up 25 percent and the writing rate of the second graders increased 56 percent.

A later phase of the study consisted of allowing the students only forty-five minutes to complete the assignment and continuing to permit them to go to the play area. With less time to do their work, the first graders further increased their printing rate and the second graders their writing rate; both rates continued to increase when the assignment time was decreased to forty minutes and later to thirty-five.

I consider the procedure employed by Hopkins et al. an outstanding one. The main asset of their technique is the manner in which they provided reinforcement for the students as soon as they completed their assignments. Immediately after a student had finished his work, he could walk to the back of the classroom and engage in the reinforcing activities. In addition, the administering of the reinforcing activities required little effort on the part of the teacher, who was, therefore, able to continue with other classroom duties. Many other reinforcement systems do not contain these advantages. In a social reinforcement system, for example, teachers are not always able to praise students immediately after they behave appropriately. Other teachers find it difficult to administer praise to all children, particularly when the classrooms are large. Likewise, token reinforcement tactics are sometimes hampered by practical problems such as record-keeping chores, preventing stealing of tokens and back-up reinforcers, and replenishing popular reinforcers.

There are at least two difficulties that can arise with the present procedure. First, it is possible that the children will be noisy during the time they are playing, thus interfering with the work of their slower classmates. In the Hopkins et al. study, the teacher avoided the problem by making a rule that if a child became particularly noisy, he would have to leave the play area and return to his desk. The authors reported only three incidents of this nature. Secondly, it is possible that the students will carelessly rush through an assignment in order to gain quick access to the play area. In order to avoid this difficulty, the authors kept track of the number of errors the students made during each condition. Surprisingly, they found that, in general, the faster the students completed an assignment, the *fewer* errors they made. During the final phase of the study with the first graders, however, an exception to this rule was noted: some of the first graders were making more errors as their speed increased. This situation was remedied by requiring the students to recopy a portion of their assignment if their error rate exceeded an individually determined criterion.

Homme (1969) gives detailed recommendations on the organization of a reinforcement area. First, he describes the layout of a classroom containing a reinforcement area. As illustrated in Figure 2-10, the teacher's and students' desks are on one side of the room and there is an L-shaped partition separating the reinforcement area from the rest of the room. He then lists events that can take place in the reinforcement area for various age groups. They are as follows:

[Three to five years old]
    a Being read to
    b Looking at books

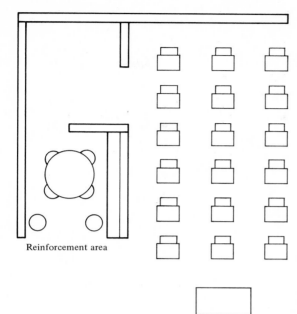

Reinforcement area

Figure 2-10 The suggested layout of classroom containing a reinforcement area. *(From L. Homme, How to Use Contingency Contracting in the Classroom, Champaign, Ill.: Research Press, 1969, p. 84. By permission of the publishers.)*

    c Playing with crayons
    d Painting
    e Working puzzles
    f Cutting and pasting
    g Playing with clay

[Six to eight years old]
    a Reading stories
    b Playing with cards
    c Drawing
    d Painting
    e Playing with Tinker Toys
    f Playing dominos
    g Working puzzles

[Nine to eleven years old]
    a Reading comics
    b Reading science fiction, mystery stories, etc.
    c Working puzzles
    d Playing chess
    e Playing checkers
    f Drawing
    g Painting

[Twelve to fourteen years old]
    a Playing chess
    b Playing cards

    c Writing letters
    d Reading magazines, books, comics
    e Playing dominos
    f Talking
    g Playing tic tac toe

[Fifteen to sixteen years old]
    a Talking
    b Playing tic tac toe
    c Playing chess
    d Reading books, magazines, comics
    e Working jigsaw puzzles
    f Playing checkers
    g Writing letters

Homme also makes the following suggestions with respect to reinforcement areas:

1 After determining the reinforcing events, the teacher should make up a reinforcement "menu." The menu consists of the activities the students may engage in while they are in the reinforcement area. It can also indicate the amount of time the students are permitted to participate in the activities. The menu should be posted adjacent to the reinforcement area so that it will be accessible to the students.

2 The children should spend no less than three minutes nor more than ten in the reinforcement area. With less than three minutes, the students cannot become sufficiently involved in an activity to make it interesting, and with more than ten, they may become satiated on the privileges.

3 In order to control the amount of time a student is in the reinforcement area, timing devices such as oven and memo timers can be used. Teachers can also use sign-in and sign-out sheets on which the students are required to state the time of entry and exit. The teacher can make periodic checks to make sure the students are not exceeding their time limits.

Undoubtedly, there are a variety of problems that might confront teachers in setting up a reinforcement area. It is usually worth the trouble that is involved, however, since the associated contingency is often effective with children at a variety of age and learning levels.

SUMMARY

There are numerous procedures for modifying student behavior that can be derived from basic behavioral principles. Hence, there are alternative ways by which teachers can present consequences, techniques by which students can learn to control their own behavior, procedures with which students can modify their classmates' and teachers' behaviors, and classroom arrangements that facilitate the learning process.

It has sometimes been found that when students fail to complete assignments for a certain amount of reinforcement, if the amount of reinforcement is increased, the students will complete their work at an acceptable rate. On the other hand, when students *are* working for a specific amount of reinforcement, it is sometimes possible to "thin the schedule of reinforcement" without a decrement of the behavior. The thinning process can consist of requiring an increased number of appropriate behaviors or progressively lengthening the delay between appropriate behaviors and the awarding of reinforcers. When a teacher uses a new reinforcer, or when she introduces an existing reinforcer into a novel situation, some students will initially reject the reinforcer. A means of avoiding this problem is to use a "reinforcer sampling" procedure in which students partake of the reinforcing event before being required to work for it. After the youngsters become familiar with the reinforcer, the teacher can present the reinforcer contingent on student behavior. In most behavior modification systems, consequences are programmed according to each student's behavior. There are times, however, when a "group contingency" is helpful. This is an arrangement in which students receive consequences on the basis of the entire group's performance. As such, the recording process and the awarding of consequences are often facilitated. Many classroom games are examples of group contingencies.

There is a variety of ways in which students can learn to modify their own behavior. Sometimes, when students keep a record of a behavior, an improvement results. Teachers therefore might encourage students to keep track of the number of times they call out without permission or to note the number of times they answer questions correctly. Another manner in which students can contribute to the modification of their own behavior is by determining the amount of reinforcement they should receive for completing academic tasks. Published studies have shown that many children will act responsibly when given such a task; in some cases the youngsters will work harder when they determine their own reinforcement levels than they will when the teacher imposes reinforcement levels. The most complete effort for the self-management of behavior is in "contingency contracting." This endeavor involves having students contribute to the process of setting goals and determining reinforcement levels. After students have reached an agreement with the teacher on each component of the contract, the particulars of the contract are publicly posted. The terms of the contract can be renegotiated as students show progress.

Most examples of behavior modification procedures presented earlier involved teachers modifying student behavior; it is also possible for *students* to modify the behavior of their classmates and their teachers. Students can modify the behavior of other children by complimenting them when they behave appropriately and tutoring them in academic areas. The use of student tutors is a rare source of inexpensive one-to-one instruction. Students can also improve the behavior of their teachers through their attentiveness to their lectures and by praising their instructional efforts.

Teachers should give consideration to the means by which they arrange

<u>their classrooms</u>. By carefully collecting data, teachers can determine whether one seating arrangement is more conducive to learning than other arrangements. Studies presented in this chapter found the traditional row arrangement to be superior to the table or cluster arrangement. It is also important to determine which students should sit near each other and to ascertain the appropriate location (that is, front, back, or middle) for disruptive children. Teachers will often find that by setting aside a particular portion of the classroom as a reinforcement area, they will have acquired a convenient and effective means of modifying student behavior. The reinforcement area can include a variety of games and activities appealing to the age group it serves.

QUESTIONS AND ACTIVITIES

1 Conduct a study in which you initially reinforce each appropriate behavior and then thin the schedule of reinforcement.
2 State three reasons why it would be worthwhile to thin a reinforcement schedule.
3 Give three advantages and three disadvantages to group contingency procedures.
4 Suppose Kevin did not wear his eyeglasses because his classmates accused him of looking like a professor. Devise a procedure that would motivate Kevin's classmates to stop ridiculing him and that would increase the likelihood of Kevin's wearing his eyeglasses.
5 Describe a situation in which a teacher might wish to use self-recording and self-determined reinforcement.
6 Devise a procedure that will motivate a student tutor to increase the academic achievement of his tutee.
7 Suppose you are a student in a college classroom. How might you get your professor to scratch his head less frequently? Do not use the procedure described on p. 65.
8 Suggest a classroom game that might improve the reading performance of sixth-grade students.
9 What is the purpose of a reinforcer sampling procedure? How might a teacher use reinforcer sampling in conjunction with a token reinforcement program?
10 Devise a contingency contract to improve a student's ability to do the multiplication tables. Indicate how it might be possible to transfer control of the system from the teacher to the student.

REFERENCES

Axelrod, S.: "Comparison of Individual and Group Contingencies in Two Special Classes," *Behavior Therapy*, **4**, 83–90, 1973.

———, R. V. Hall, and A. Maxwell: "Use of Peer Attention to Increase Study Behavior," *Behavior Therapy*, **3**, 349–351, 1972.

———, R. V. Hall, and A. Tams: "A Comparison of Common Seating Arrangements in the Classroom." Paper presented at the Kansas Symposium on Behavior Analysis in Education, Lawrence, Kans., May 1972.

———, and J. Paluska: "A Component Analysis of the Effects of a Classroom Game on Spelling Performance," in E. Ramp and G. Semb (eds.), *Behavior Analysis: Areas of Research and Application* (Englewood Cliffs, N.J.: Prentice-Hall, 1975), pp. 277–282.

Ayllon, T., and N. H. Azrin: *The Token Economy: A Motivational System for Therapy and Rehabilitation* (New York: Appleton-Century-Crofts, 1968).

Barrish, H. H., M. Saunders, and M. M. Wolf: "Good Behavior Games: Effects of Individual Contingencies for Group Consequences on Disruptive Behavior in a Classroom," *Journal of Applied Behavior Analysis*, **2**, 119–124, 1969.

Broden, M., C. Bruce, M. A. Mitchell, V. Carter, and R. V. Hall: "Effects of Teacher Attention on Attending Behavior of Two Boys at Adjacent Desks," *Journal of Applied Behavior Analysis*, **3**, 199–203, 1970.

———, R. V. Hall, and B. Mitts: "The Effect of Self-Recording on the Classroom Behavior of Two Eighth-Grade Students," *Journal of Applied Behavior Analysis*, **4**, 191–199, 1971.

Burdett, C., A. Egner, and H. McKenzie: "P 14," in H. McKenzie (ed.), *1968–1969 Report of the Consulting Teacher Program*, Vol. II (Burlington, Vt.: Consulting Teacher Program, College of Education, The University of Vermont, 1970), pp. 85–90.

Egner, A., P. Pitkin, and H. McKenzie: "In-Seat Token Project," in H. McKenzie (ed.), *1968–1969 Report of the Consulting Teacher Program*, vol. II (Burlington, Vt.: Consulting Teacher Program, College of Education, The University of Vermont, 1970), pp. 218–227.

Gallagher, P. A., S. I. Sulzbacher, and R. E. Shores: "A Group Contingency for Classroom Management of Emotionally Disturbed Children." Paper presented at the Kansas Council for Exceptional Children, Wichita, March 1967.

Glynn, E. L.: "Classroom Applications of Self-Determined Reinforcement," *Journal of Applied Behavior Analysis*, **3**, 123–132, 1970.

Gray, F., P. S. Graubard, and H. Rosenberg: "Little Brother is Changing You," *Psychology Today*, **8**, 42–46, 1974.

Hall, R. V., D. Lund, and D. Jackson: "Effects of Teacher Attention on Study Behavior," *Journal of Applied Behavior Analysis*, **1**, 1–12, 1968.

———, M. Panyan, D. Rabon, and M. Broden: "Instructing Beginning Teachers in Reinforcement Procedures Which Improve Classroom Control," *Journal of Applied Behavior Analysis*, **1**, 315–322, 1968.

Homme, L.: *How to Use Contingency Contracting in the Classroom* (Champaign, Ill.: Research Press, 1969).

Hopkins, B. L., R. C. Schutte, and K. L. Garton: "The Effects of Access to a Playroom on the Rate and Quality of Printing and Writing of First- and Second-Grade Students," *Journal of Applied Behavior Analysis*, **4**, 77–87, 1971.

Lates, R., and A. Egner: "Teaching Self-Discipline through Contingency Contracting," in A. Egner (ed.), *Individualizing Junior and Senior High Instruction to Provide Special Education within Regular Classrooms* (Burlington, Vt.: University of Vermont, 1973), pp. 45–52.

Lovitt, T.: "Behavior Modification: The Current Scene," *Exceptional Children*, **37**, 85–91, 1970.

——— and K. Curtiss: "Academic Response Rate as a Function of Teacher- and Self-Imposed Contingencies," *Journal of Applied Behavior Analysis*, **2**, 49–53, 1969.

Miller, L. K., and R. Schneider: "The Use of a Token System in Project Head Start," *Journal of Applied Behavior Analysis*, **3**, 213–220, 1970.

O'Leary, K. D., and W. C. Becker: "Behavior Modification of an Adjustment Class," *Exceptional Children*, **33**, 637–642, 1967.

Patterson, G. R.: "An Application of Conditioning Techniques to the Control of a Hyperactive Child," in L. P. Ullmann and L. Krasner (eds.), *Case Studies in Behavior Modification* (New York: Holt, Rinehart, and Winston, 1965), pp. 370–375.

Semb, G., D. R. Green, R. P. Hawkins, J. Michael, E. L. Phillips, J. A. Sherman, H. Sloane, and D. R. Thomas (eds.): *Behavior Analysis and Education—1972* (Lawrence, Kans.: Support and Development Center for Follow Through, Department of Human Development, University of Kansas, 1972).

Sommer, R., and T. Ayllon: "Perception and Monetary Reinforcement: The Effects of Rewards in the Tactual Modality," *Journal of Psychology*, **42**, 137–141, 1956.

Southern, B., and A. Zey: "Use of Contingent Coughing to Reduce a Professor's Disfluency." Unpublished manuscript, University of Kansas, 1969.

Tymchuk, A. J.: *Behavior Modification with Children* (Springfield, Ill.: C. C. Thomas, 1974).

Whaley, D. L., and R. W. Malott: *Elementary Principles of Behavior* (Kalamazoo, Mich.: Behaviordelia, 1968).

Willis, J., J. Crowder, and B. Morris: "A Behavioral Approach to Remedial Reading Using Students as Behavioral Engineers," in G. Semb, D. R. Green, R. P. Hawkins, J. Michael, E. L. Philips, J. A. Sherman, H. Sloane, and D. R. Thomas (eds.), *Behavior Analysis and Education—1972* (Lawrence, Kans.: Support and Development Center for Follow Through, Department of Human Development, University of Kansas, 1972), pp. 211–221.

Wolf, M. M., D. K. Giles, and R. V. Hall: "Experiments in a Remedial Classroom," *Behaviour Research and Therapy*, **6**, 51–64, 1968.

Chapter 3

Measurement and Research Design

Although the chapter on measurement follows those which discuss the various principles and techniques of behavior modification, its importance is second to none. Without carefully measuring behavior, a teacher does not have an information base on which to make important decisions. As a result, his application of the techniques is often done in a haphazard manner. With accurate data, a teacher has before him evidence as to whether or not his procedures are working, and he can make critical judgments accordingly. "Flying by the seat of your pants" is no more applicable to education than it is to medicine.

My plea for teachers to measure behavior should not scare them away. Measurement in behavior modification is usually simple. It does not involve complicated statistical analyses, nor does it involve giving intelligence, achievement, or personality tests. Many times, it involves nothing more than counting behavior. In other cases, a teacher will have only to note five times in a morning whether a child is performing a certain behavior. At still other times, a teacher will merely have to look at a wall clock to find out how long it took the youngsters to complete a task or how tardy a particular student is.

The first half this chapter I will discuss the importance of defining behavior and the means by which behavior can be measured. There will also be a discussion of the advantages of obtaining data on a daily basis and the means by which a teacher can check the accuracy of her data. The latter portion of the chapter describes the research designs characteristic of behavior modification studies.

MEASUREMENT OF BEHAVIOR

Defining Behavior

The first step in measuring behavior is to define the behavior in units that are specific and observable. Many of the expressions that educators use are so vague that it is difficult to be certain what the terms mean. Describing a student as "mischievous" or "bad," for example, is bound to cause confusion unless a more precise definition is provided. An exercise which I have used is to have a classroom of teachers write the definition of a term such as "disturbing others." One teacher might define the expression as incidents in which a student prevents a classmate from completing an assignment. A second teacher might define the term as a tendency to annoy classmates or the teacher. A third definition could include aggressive and noisy behaviors. The point being made is that, although the above definitions have much in common, they are not the same. Different people have different notions as to what "disturbing others" means.

In order to make such a term more meaningful, a teacher must break the expression down into smaller, observable units. A teacher might define "disturbing others" as incidents of hitting another student and grabbing another student's possessions. If the teacher wishes to include talking out in class, this also is permissible. The decision as to what the term denotes, however, must be made in advance, not as the behavior modification program proceeds and conditions change; and the definition must involve behaviors which are observable. One adequate definition of "disturbing others" was provided by Kuypers, Becker, and O'Leary (1968): "Grabbing another's objects or work, knocking neighbor's books off desk, destroying another's property, throwing objects at another without hitting, pushing with desk" [p. 102].

Measurement Procedures

Once the behavior of interest has been defined, it is necessary to measure its occurrence quantitatively. There are several different types of measurement techniques available. The decision as to which technique should be used will depend, first of all, on the nature of the behavior being studied, and secondly, on whether the observations are done by an outside observer or by the classroom teacher.

The measurement procedures fall into two general categories: measurement of lasting products, and observational recording. Observational recording, in turn, is of four types: event or frequency recording, duration recording, interval recording, and time-sampling recording.

Measurement of Lasting Products The measurement of lasting products will be presented first because it is the measurement technique closest to a teacher's experience. With such a technique a teacher measures the tangible output of a student's work. The resulting product is one that can be measured immediately after the student completes his work or at a later point in time. Examples of the measurement of lasting products include the grading of spelling words, arithmetic examples, English compositions, and the answers to reading comprehension questions. The product might be graded as 80 percent correct or 25 percent complete. Since the product is a lasting one, a teacher can grade the work at her own convenience, but it is usually best to mark the work as soon as possible after the student has completed it and inform the student of the results. The measurement of lasting products is not a new measurement procedure, of course. Teachers have been using it for many years. It is an important one, however, because it often gives an accurate representation of a child's academic progress.

Observational Recording Some behaviors are transitory. They occur at one point in time but not at another point. In addition, they do not leave a product which can be measured at a future time. Examples of such behaviors are talking out, hand raising, smiling, and striking another student. In order to obtain an accurate measure of such a behavior, it is necessary to record it at the time or soon after it occurs. The measurement of transitory behaviors which do not leave a lasting product is called "observational recording." Described below are four types of observational recording:

Frequency Recording Perhaps the best-known type of observational measurement is "frequency or event recording." With such a procedure, the observer keeps a tally of the number of times a particular behavior occurs over a certain period of time (for example, per hour, morning, and so on). For many years teachers have been obtaining frequency counts of student absences by placing marks in their notebooks. For other behaviors, frequency records can be obtained by using a pencil and paper. The paper can rest on the teacher's desk or can be carried with her as she moves around the classroom. In the study by Hall, Axelrod, Foundopoulos, Shellman, Campbell, and Cranston (1971), a teacher carried with him a clipboard with a piece of paper on which he recorded the frequency with which each of the students left his seat. The paper contained the name of each student; whenever a student left his seat without permission, the teacher placed a mark next to his name. (In a paragraph below it will be pointed out that the frequency recording is really not the best measurement procedure for out-of-seat behavior.) In some cases teachers will find the chalkboard suitable for frequency recording. A device which teachers have indicated is convenient for frequency recording is the wrist counter[1] which golfers use to keep a record of the number of strokes they take on a

[1]The wrist counter may be obtained from Behavior Research Company, Box 3351, Kansas City, Kans. 66103.

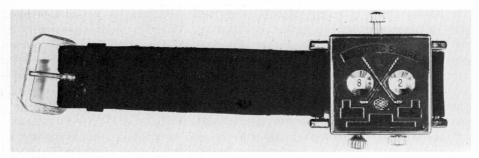

Figure 3-1   Golf wrist counter, useful for classroom frequency tallies.

certain day (see Figure 3-1). The counter is attached to the wrist in a manner similar to a wristwatch. Each time the target behavior occurs, the teacher presses the counter and advances the total by one. She thus avoids carrying paper or walking to the chalkboard to make a tally.

Some teachers have used frequency recording to obtain a measure of student progress on various academic tasks. In an instructional endeavor known as "precision teaching," the teacher will pinpoint an academic behavior such as reading from a standard textbook. Next, she will count the number of words the student reads correctly and the number he reads incorrectly during a period of time. The teacher will then record the frequencies of words read right and wrong on graph paper. By inspecting the frequency graph, the teacher can determine whether or not the procedure is effective with the youngster. (For a more complete description of "precision teaching," see Lindsley, 1969, or Gaasholt, 1970.)

Frequency recording is a good measurement procedure for short-duration behaviors such as hitting, talking out, and reading errors. Frequency recording would *not* be an appropriate measurement procedure for a behavior such as out-of-seat behavior, since a student may leave his seat without permission and stay out of his seat for an entire morning. A record showing that the child was out of his seat only one time during the morning session would give a poor idea of what the child was actually doing.

Duration Recording   A second kind of measurement procedure, known as "duration recording," would be more appropriate than frequency recording for behaviors such as out-of-seat behavior, pencil sharpening, and daydreaming. Duration recording gives a measure of how long a student engages in a certain behavior. For some behaviors a duration record is easy to obtain. If a teacher wished to know how tardy a student was, for example, she would merely have to subtract the time at which the youngster was due from the time he arrived in class. Thus, if Benji was due at 9:00 A.M. and appeared in class at 9:22 A.M., the duration of his lateness is twenty-two minutes. Similarly, if a teacher was interested in the amount of time it took a student to complete an assignment, she would subtract the time at which he began the assignment from the time at which he completed the task.

There are other behaviors for which it is more difficult to obtain a duration record. In these cases it is usually necessary to use a stopwatch. Consider the teacher who wishes to determine the amount of time Jonathan is out of his seat during the reading period. The teacher would start her stopwatch when Jonathan leaves his seat. When the youngster returns to his seat, she would stop her watch and record the amount of time that has elapsed. When Jonathan again leaves his seat, she would repeat the process. At the end of the reading period, the teacher would add up the times to determine the duration of Jonathan's out-of-seat behavior. Instead of using a conventional stopwatch, the teacher could save herself some time and effort by using a repeater stopwatch. With this type of watch the user can stop the watch and start it again where she left off without setting the watch back to the zero point. Thus, the teacher could save herself the trouble of recording various durations and adding them up at the end of the period.

A problem with duration recording is that, in measuring certain behaviors, a teacher must continuously attend to the child of concern. This would not be a major problem for an outside observer but it has obvious limitations for a teacher who is confronted with a variety of other tasks. As a result, duration recording tends not to be used by teachers who are conducting behavior modification studies. The time-sampling measurement procedure, to be discussed later, circumvents most of the difficulties associated with duration recording.

Interval Recording   A third measurement technique, known as "interval recording," is also useful for behaviors such as out-of-seat behavior and daydreaming. Interval recording gives some indication of both the frequency and the duration of a behavior. A data sheet for an interval record of out-of-seat behavior might appear as follows:

	Seconds					
	0 10	20	30	40	50	60
Minutes 1	+	+	+	−	−	+
2	−	−	+	+	+	−
•						
•						
•						
60	+	+	−	−	−	−

The data sheet is divided into ten-second intervals for a sixty-minute period (other data sheets could use different intervals). During each consecutive interval the teacher (or another observer) records whether or not the target behavior occurs. Suppose one is concerned with out-of-seat behavior, and "+" represents in-seat behavior while "−" means out-of-seat behavior. The observer watches the child for the ten-second interval. If the child remains seated for the *entire* ten-second interval, the interval is scored "+". *If at any time during the ten-second interval the student leaves his seat without permission, the entire interval is scored* "−". On the above data sheet the record for the first minute would be interpreted as follows: The child was in his seat for the first thirty seconds. At some time between thirty and forty seconds the child was out of his seat, as was the case between forty and fifty seconds. During the last ten-second interval the student was always in his seat. A long string of +'s would indicate that a student was staying in his seat for lengthy periods of time. Frequent alternation of +'s and −'s would mean that the student often left and reoccupied his seat.

Hooper (1970) provided an example of how a teacher could use interval recording for measuring talking-out behavior. The data sheet was divided into one-minute intervals from 9:00 A.M. to 9:20 A.M. daily and appeared (in adapted form) as follows:

9:01	02	03	04	05	06	07	08	09	10	11	12	13	14	15	16	17	18	19	20
		−				−									−				

Each time the teacher heard the student talk out, she looked at a desk clock and recorded a − in the appropriate box. Thus, if the talking-out behavior occurred after 9:03 but before 9:04, she placed a − in the third box. The data above indicate that the child talked out between 9:03 and 9:04, between 9:07 and 9:08, and between 9:16 and 9:17. The rest of the time, he was quiet. The reader should note that if there had been more than one talking-out instance during an interval, there would still be only one minus for the interval.

In the Hooper study, the teacher had only to attend to the problem behavior auditorally, and she was, therefore, able to engage in her usual teaching activities. When the target behavior is one that must be attended to visually, the undivided scrutiny of the teacher is required, and the task usually becomes too burdensome for her. As a result, teachers who must conduct observations without assistance will usually find interval recording almost as impractical as duration recording.

Time-Sampling Recording   A measurement technique that is more convenient than duration and interval recording and which provides an accurate record of student performance is called "time-sampling recording." With such a procedure the teacher notes only what a youngster is doing at the *end of the time interval.* Suppose a teacher is interested in determining the on-task rate of a certain student. She might choose to record the behavior at two-minute intervals for a twenty-minute period, using the following data sheet:

Minute	2	4	6	8	10	12	14	16	18	20
Behavior	+	−	−	+	+	−	−	+	+	+

At exactly the two-minute mark, the four-minute mark, the six-minute mark, and so on, the teacher would rate the student's behavior. If the youngster was "on task," he would receive a +. If he was not on task, he would receive a −. For recording purposes it does not matter what the child was doing immediately before or after a measurement was due. All that matters is what the student was doing at the two-minute marks. The present record shows that the student was on task at the two-, eight-, ten-, sixteen-, eighteen-, and twenty-minute marks, and that he was off task at the four-, six-, twelve-, and fourteen-minute marks. Thus, it would be estimated that the student was on task 60 percent of the time during the twenty-minute measurement period.

As is probably obvious to the reader, an advantage in time-sampling measurement is that the teacher need attend to the student's behavior only when a measurement is due. At other times she can engage in her usual teaching duties. Nevertheless, some teachers will still find it annoying to constantly check their timepieces to determine whether a measurement is due, and still other teachers will forget to make the checks. A solution to this problem was offered by O'Gorman, Schneider, and McKenzie (1970) in a study involving the finger-sucking behavior of an eleven-year-old boy. The teacher made use of an oven timer set to go off at certain intervals. Since the oven timer would ring when a measurement was due, the teacher did not have to continually check a timepiece. If the youngster did not have his fingers in his mouth when the timer went off, the teacher put a + on the data sheet. If his fingers were in his mouth when the timer rang, he received a −. In addition to rating the youngster's behavior, the teacher gave the student a reward if his fingers were out of his mouth when the timer went off (providing an example of how the administering of consequences can be combined with the measurement procedure).

The reader might wonder whether a student who is exposed to a procedure such as that employed by O'Gorman et al. might learn to remove his fingers from his mouth just before the bell is scheduled to ring and then resume finger sucking after the bell goes off. The answer to the question is "yes" as long as the rings occur at standard intervals. In order to avoid this difficulty, the teacher should vary the amount of time between bell rings. Hence, the first ring might occur at five minutes, the next one two minutes later, the third one twenty-five minutes later, the fourth one three minutes later, and so on. When the amount of time between rings varies, the student must keep his fingers out of his mouth at all times in order to be certain that he will receive the reinforcer.

When using an oven timer for time-sampling measurement, the teacher is relieved of the burden of constantly having to check the student or a timepiece. An even more convenient device than an oven timer is a memo timer.[2] The memo timer, which is essentially a portable oven timer, is a small (1.5 inches in diameter), inexpensive timing device which people sometimes use to remind themselves that their time on a car parking meter is about to expire. (See Figure 3-2.) The memo timer can be set for intervals varying from a few minutes up to an hour. When the time expires, a buzzing sound occurs which is usually audible to the entire class. The memo timer is more convenient than an oven

[2]The memo timer (also known as a "belt buzzer") may be obtained from Behavior Research Company, Box 3351, Kansas City, Kans. 66103.

Figure 3-2   Memo timer. Diameter is 1.5 inches (3.8 centimeters).

timer because it is less bulky and because it can be attached to a blouse, a shirt, or a belt loop and can even be removed from the chain to which it is affixed and glued to a watch band. If teachers find the noise of the oven timer obtrusive, they can sometimes mute the sound by placing clay along the perimeter. (For a more complete description of the memo timer, see Foxx and Martin, 1971.)

The reader may wonder how many times a teacher using time sampling must rate behavior during a given session in order to obtain an accurate measure of student performance for that session. Kubany and Sloggett (1973) compared the results that were obtained when student behavior was rated eighty times per session with those obtained when the behavior was rated five times per session, and found remarkably similar results. Thus, rating the behavior only five times a session appears sufficient for valid measurement and is probably adequate for most classroom studies.

In the preceding paragraphs measurement techniques have been presented, which teachers can employ, and have employed, as part of their normal teaching routine. The author realizes, however, that some teachers will still find the measurement of student behavior an unwieldy task. In such cases it might be worthwhile to train whatever other personnel are available to perform the measurement chores. These might include teacher aides, volunteer parents, students in the classroom, students from the higher grades, the guidance counselor, and education and psychology students from nearby colleges.

Continuous Measurement

In traditional educational research, measurement of student performance occurs infrequently. In a study involving a comparison of techniques for teaching reading, for example, students may take a standardized reading test at the beginning of the school year and retake the same test, or a similar one, at the end of the term. Judgments of the effectiveness of the techniques in question will be drawn by comparing the pretest and posttest scores of students exposed to each of the techniques. Eaton and Lovitt (1972) point out that difficulties with the practice of infrequent measurement include the possibilities that a student might guess well on the day of the test, or conversely, that he might be upset or ill on the testing day. Such problems might not be critical for the evaluation of groups of students but are of great importance when judging the progress of individual youngsters.

Behavior modifiers prefer to measure the behavior of interest continuously. It is likely that a teacher who is using a behavior modification technique to teach reading, for example, will obtain a *daily* measure of the number of words a child reads correctly. When daily measurement is used, the problem of a child guessing correctly or his having a "bad" day is greatly reduced, since it is unlikely that a child can guess correctly every day, or that each day will be a "bad" one. An additional advantage of continuous measurement is that it provides a teacher with frequent feedback on the effectiveness of her techniques. If her procedures are effective, she will receive the information early in the school term and can continue to use beneficial procedures. Conversely, if her techniques are ineffective, a teacher who measures continuously will also receive such information early in the year and can attempt alternative procedures. Teachers who depend on pre- and posttests to evaluate the effectiveness of their procedures are hampered by a lack of relevant information and might make the wrong decision as to whether they should continue or abandon the use of a certain technique. Inspection of the vast majority of graphs in this book will reveal the measurement of behavior on a daily or weekly basis.

Reliability

Whenever the behavior of interest cannot be recorded with automated equipment, the judgment as to the occurrence of the behavior is made by a human being. With only one person making the observations, there is a risk that the measurements will be biased in some manner. It is possible, for example, that the observer will inadvertently score a certain type of behavior as inappropriate during a baseline session but as appropriate during the reinforcement stage. One way to reduce this risk is to have a second person record the same behavior independently of the first observer. The second observer is called the "reliability observer," whereas the individual who is present at all sessions is called the "primary observer." The teacher can serve as either the primary or the reliability observer, or the entire measurement process can be conducted by outside personnel.

The method of calculating the degree of agreement between the observers, or the "reliability," depends on the measurement technique which is employed. If event recording is used, reliability is determined by dividing the record of the observer with the smaller number by the record of the observer with the larger number, according to the following formula:

$$\frac{\text{Smaller recorded frequency}}{\text{Larger recorded frequency}} \times 100 = \text{percent agreement}$$

Thus, if one observer records eighty instances of talking out in a day and a second observer records one hundred, the reliability would be $^{80}/_{100} \times 100 = 80$ percent. A similar formula would be used to determine the reliability of duration recordings. If, for example, one observer's records indicated that a student was out of his or her seat for fifty minutes whereas the figure for the second observer is forty-five minutes, the reliability would be $^{45}/_{50} \times 100 = 90$ percent.

For interval and time-sampling measurements, a different formula for reliability must be employed. Suppose the records of two observers on a child's rate of study behavior over a ten-minute period are as follows:

Observer 1:	+	−	−	−	+	+	−	−	+	+
Minute	1	2	3	4	5	6	7	8	9	10

Observer 2:	+	−	−	+	−	+	−	−	+	+
Minute	1	2	3	4	5	6	7	8	9	10

It can be seen that there was agreement between the two observers on all but minutes 4 and 5. Reliability can be calculated with the following formula:

$$\frac{\text{Number of agreements}}{\text{Total number of measurements}} \times 100 = \text{percent agreement}$$

In this case there were eight agreements out of ten measurements. Therefore, the reliability would be $^{8}/_{10} \times 100 = 80$ percent.

The formula for the reliability of lasting-products measurement also depends on the type of behavior being studied. For an exercise such as listing words which rhyme with "book," reliability would be determined by employing the same formula as was used for event and duration recording. Thus, if one grader found twenty correct words whereas the second grader indicated that there were nineteen correct words, reliability would be $^{19}/_{20} \times 100$, or 95 percent. For a spelling or arithmetic assignment, the graders would score each answer independently. Their grading would then be compared score by score to determine the percentage of times they were in agreement. Suppose a child were asked to spell the words "some," "duck," "find," "seven," and "break." Listed below is the way the student spelled the words and the manner in which each of the graders scored them. ("+" means correct and "−" means incorrect.)

	Grader 1	Grader 2
1. some	+	+
2. duck	+	+
3. finb	+	−
4. sevn	−	−
5. break	+	+

The graders agreed on all words except the third one. Thus, reliability would be $4/5 \times 100$ or 80 percent. The formula is the same as that used for interval and time-sampling measurements.

In order to be certain that reliable measurements are achieved when observational recording is employed, it is sometimes necessary to have practice sessions before experimental conditions are started. The observers should first discuss the definition of the behavior(s) of interest. If there are any disagreements or confusion as to how certain types of behavior should be rated, the observers should talk over the disparities until differences are removed. During the initial practice session(s), the observers might sit side by side (unless, of course, one of the observers is the teacher) in such a way that they can easily check each other's scoring and discuss any differences in ratings. During a later practice session, the observers should be separated from each other to determine whether independent measurements result in sufficiently high reliability for the study to be started.

When experimental sessions begin, it is imperative that the observers rate behavior independently. One way to increase the probability that the scoring will be done in an independent manner is to separate the observers from each other's view. This can be accomplished by placing some barrier, such as a portable blackboard, between the observers. Whenever possible, it is also better not to inform the observers which experimental condition is in effect. This should be done so that the expectations of the observers will not influence their ratings.

In a thorough description of recording procedures, Broden (1968) points out that although it is desirable that reliability measurements be taken every session, it is not economically or practically feasible to do so. There should, however, be at least one reliability check for each experimental condition. If reliability is high, there is probably no need to have more than three reliability checks during each of the experimental phases.

There are no absolute standards as to an acceptable level of reliability. Most researchers consider reliability of less than 80 percent too low for scientific purposes. If reliability is often below 80 percent, my suggestion is that the observers discuss their differences, conduct additional practice sessions, and reexamine their definitions of the target behaviors.

RESEARCH DESIGN

In describing the various studies which appear in the earlier sections of this book, the reader may have noticed that the author usually omitted terms such as "experimental group," "control group," and "statistical significance level." This is neither a coincidence nor an error. The expressions are characteristic of traditional educational research but not of behavioral research. In the present section of this chapter, the components of the research designs used in traditional educational studies will be briefly reviewed and the objections that behavior modifiers have to such research strategies will be pointed out. The research methodology preferred by behavior modifiers and the advantages of the tactics for teachers who wish to do research in their classrooms will be described in some detail later.

Traditional Educational Research Designs

Group Design   The research design most frequently used in educational studies is known as the "group design." An educational researcher will typically use the design in order to determine which of two or more procedures is best able to produce a certain desirable outcome. A hypothetical experiment might involve an attempt to determine whether children learn sight vocabulary words best when there is no consequence following their answers, when their correct answers are reinforced, or when incorrect answers are punished. The group design might involve randomly assigning the students to three different groups: a control group which receives no consequences (group C), and two experimental groups—group R, which receives reinforcement, and group P, which receives the punishment procedure. The investigators would try to obtain groups which were as large as was feasible. The groups would then be exposed to the respective procedures, and their sight vocabulary scores would be compared with an appropriate statistical test. If it were found, for example, that the scores of group R students were significantly better than those achieved by groups C and P, the reinforcement procedure would be considered the best of the three techniques.

Although there is some merit to the approach, behavioral researchers have generally rejected the use of the group design. One problem is that the group design does not give information as to which technique is best for each individual student. Although a particular procedure might be the best one for most students, there may be some students for whom one of the alternative techniques would be superior. Children in group R, for example, receive the reinforcement condition but not the punishment condition. Thus, if a particular child in group R would respond better to punishment than he would to reinforcement, this fact would not be known. A second element limiting the usefulness of the group design in educational research is the difficulty of obtaining groups of children demonstrating the same problems (Risley, 1970). Finally, even when it is possible to locate a large sample of children with similar characteristics, the realities of school systems often prevent the random assignment of children to different experimental conditions, as is highly desirable in group research designs.

Correlational Research A second kind of research popular in education involves finding correlations between certain environmental conditions and important behavior of students. A correlation between two variables is a measure of the degree to which they vary together. A "positive correlation" is one in which as one variable increases, the other variable also increases. A "negative correlation" is one in which as one variable increases, the other decreases. It is therefore likely that there is a positive correlation between the number of hours a student studies and scholastic success, since it would be expected that as the hours of studying increased, scholastic success would also increase. Likewise, one would expect to find a negative correlation between student absences and academic achievement, since as absences increased, one would expect academic success to decrease. Although correlational studies indicate many interesting relationships, behavior modifiers generally consider such investigations to be of limited value. This is so because, although two variables may be highly correlated with each other, one variable does not necessarily *cause* the other to occur.

As an example of this notion, suppose there were found a high positive correlation between the quality of students' shoes and the students' achievement levels in school. This would *not* mean that if society were to supply high-quality shoes to all low-achieving pupils they would suddenly do well in school. It is more likely that the pupils would continue to be low achievers, but with good shoes. Unquestionably, researchers doing correlational studies have not even implied that, if one variable is highly correlated with a second variable, it is causing the second variable to occur. The important point, however, is that educators are interested in the conditions that will *cause* student performance to improve, and correlational research is suggestive but not definitive.

Behavioral Research Designs

Behavior modifiers use research designs that eliminate the problem of obtaining large groups of children and that clearly demonstrate which factors cause an improvement in the performance of individual students. Also, as was the case with the measurement procedures, the behavior research designs are easy for teachers to carry out. Thus, teachers can participate in the development of their field by conducting research in their own classrooms and, desirably, publishing the results in various journals. This is in marked contrast to the realities surrounding group research design, which few teachers will ever be able to engage in.

The remainder of the present section will describe the two research designs most often employed in behavior modification studies. The more commonly used design is the "reversal" design, which was described briefly in the first chapter. An alternative design, which is coming into increased usage, is

known as the "multiple-baseline" design. The particulars of each of three types
of multiple-baseline designs will be presented.

Reversal Design   In order to point out how a teacher makes use of the
reversal design, I will make reference to a study by Alley and Cox (1971). The
classroom for the Alley and Cox study was the home of a newlywed couple, the
teacher was a recent bride, and the student was the new groom. The behavior
of concern was the husband's tendency to leave items of clothing in the living
room.

The first stage of almost every behavior modification study is called the
"$Baseline_1$" stage. (See $Baseline_1$, Figure 3-3.) $Baseline_1$ is a measure of the
behavior or interest under normal classroom conditions. During this phase the
teacher should be acting in her usual manner and should give no special
attention to the problem of concern. The reason for taking baseline measurements is to provide a basis for comparing the behavior under normal conditions
with behavior under conditions in which a special procedure is being applied.
Without a baseline phase there would be no way of determining whether or not
improvement later took place. During the seven-day $Baseline_1$ phase of the
Alley and Cox study, it was observed that the husband left between one and
three articles of clothing in the living room each day.

After the teacher conducts $Baseline_1$ measurements, "Experimental
$Phase_1$," is begun. During this period the teacher applies the procedure which is
intended to improve student performance and evaluates the effect. Data are
collected in the same manner as was done during $Baseline_1$: The technique
which is used can be reinforcement, extinction, punishment, changing seating
arrangements, or any other tactic which a teacher might feel would be

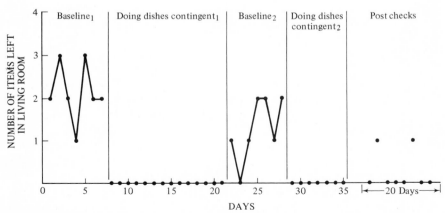

Figure 3-3 The number of articles of clothing left in the living room by a newlywed man.
*(From S. J. Alley and L. Cox, "Doing Dishes as a Contingency for Reducing a Husband's Rate
of Leaving Clothes in the Living Room," in R. V. Hall (ed.),* Managing Behavior, Part III,
Lawrence, Kans., 1971, p. 42. By permission of the publishers.)

effective. It is important that the teacher apply only one *new* condition at a time during this period. Thus, if a teacher wishes to determine the effect of reinforcement on arithmetic performance, she should reinforce a student's correct arithmetic answers but should *not* punish the incorrect ones. If a teacher *later* wants to know the effect of the combination of reinforcement and punishment, she should determine this only after she has found the effect of reinforcement or punishment alone. The reason for this is that if a teacher applies reinforcement or punishment simultaneously and student performance improves, she will not know whether the improvement was due to the reinforcement, the punishment, or the combination of the two procedures. Experimental Phase$_1$ in the Alley and Cox study (labeled "Doing Dishes Contingent$_1$," in Figure 3-3) consisted of an agreement that whoever left the greater number of articles of clothing in the living room for a given week would do the dishes the following week. In case of a tie, the wife would do the dishes the next week. For the fourteen days in which the dishes contingency was in effect, the husband never left any items of clothing in the living room, indicating that students of all ages can learn quickly when they have good teachers.

When student performance improves during Experimental Phase$_1$, teachers often wonder whether it actually was the procedure which they employed during this period which accounted for the change or whether other factors may have been responsible. A teacher might consider it possible that the change took place because she now knows her students better, because the weather changed, because the students had matured, or because certain youngsters had moved from her classroom. All such explanations could account for the change in behavior. To eliminate the possibility that these uncontrolled factors accounted for the improvement in behavior, a third experimental condition, known as "reversal" or "Baseline$_2$" phase, is necessary. (See Baseline$_2$, Figure 3-3.) During this stage the teacher ceases using the procedure employed during Experimental Phase$_1$. If students received reinforcement for correct arithmetic answers during Experimental Phase$_1$, for example, they will no longer receive such reinforcement during Baseline$_2$. If the behavior changes to a level similar to that which occurred during Baseline$_1$, the teacher can have confidence that the procedures she used during Experimental Phase$_1$ caused the improvement in behavior. If the rate of the behavior does not change, it is possible that uncontrolled factors were responsible for the improvement which occurred during Experimental Phase$_1$, or that the behavior modification procedure is no longer necessary.

Returning to our newlywed couple, Figure 3-3 indicates that when the husband was no longer required to do the dishes after leaving items of clothing in the living room, he quickly returned to his old ways. During the seven-day Baseline$_2$ phase, he left an article of clothing out every day but one. This provided convincing evidence that the contingency of doing dishes really did account for the improvement which occurred during the Doing Dishes Contingent$_1$ stage of the study.

For educational purposes it is usually undesirable to terminate a study while students are in the Baseline$_2$ phase. Thus, a fourth condition involves returning the children to the procedure used during Experimental Phase$_1$. This stage is known as "Experimental Phase$_2$" and is labeled "Doing Dishes Contingent$_2$" in Figure 3-3. It can be seen that when the "doing dishes" agreement was again employed, the husband's performance was consistently perfect. When behavior again improves during Experimental Phase$_2$, there is additional evidence that the procedure which the teacher used really was the cause for the change in performance.

The final stage of a behavior modification study is an extension of Experimental Phase$_2$. This phase, known as the "Postchecks" period, involves a continuation of the procedures of Experimental Phase$_2$. Measurements, however, are taken less frequently. If measurements were taken daily during Experimental Phase$_2$, they may be taken an average of only once a week during the Postchecks phase. This stage is important for determining whether the procedures have a long-lasting effect on the behavior of concern. Eight postchecks over a twenty-day period in the Alley and Cox (1971) study indicated that a total of only two items of clothing were left in the living room. (The reader should note that, although it is ideal that behavior modification studies employ all of the above phases, in practice many experiments do not include one or more of the stages. For scientific purposes, however, there should at least be Baseline$_1$, Experimental Phase, and Baseline$_2$ conditions.)

In the Alley and Cox (1971) study, the experimenters were interested only in comparing the "doing dishes" contingency with baseline conditions. Sometimes a teacher wishes to compare more than two conditions. In the hypothetical study involving sight vocabulary (p. 40), the investigators were concerned with comparing three conditions—no consequence, reinforcement, and punishment. Unlike the group design, the experimental design using reversal procedures might involve exposing an entire class of students to Baseline$_1$ (no consequence) conditions, followed by Reinforcement$_1$, Punishment, Reinforcement$_2$, and Baseline$_2$. Notice that all students experience all conditions. With such a design one could compare each student's performance under each of the conditions. Thus, it might be found that fifteen students did best with reinforcement, three did best with punishment, and two did best with no consequence on their answers. With this information a teacher could individualize a child's program in accordance with the conditions under which he or she worked best. This would not be possible with the group design, since each student would receive only one condition—no consequence, reinforcement, or punishment. The group design tells educators something about groups of students but little about individuals. The reversal design can give information on both groups and individuals.

Multiple-Baseline Design   Although the reversal design has been a useful research design for numerous behavior modification studies, there are at least two situations in which its use is not recommended. First, there are times when it might be dangerous to use a reversal design. Consider a situation in which a teacher attained a Baseline$_1$ record of the number of times a child poked classmates in the eyes. Next, suppose a behavior modification procedure was employed and the youngster's eye-poking ceased. Although it might be scientifically interesting to determine the effect of halting the procedure and returning to Baseline$_1$ conditions, it would be perilous and unethical to do so, since the child could harm her neighbors during the reversal period.

Another situation in which a reversal design should not be used is one in which the behavior of interest is unlikely to return to its Baseline$_1$ level following the cessation of a behavior modification procedure. Axelrod and Piper (1975) found, for example, that after a behavior modification procedure improved the reading performance of several students, removal of the procedure did not lead to a deterioration of the behavior. The authors proposed that the natural environment[3] provides so much reinforcement for reading that even when the original procedure is discontinued, reading behavior may persist.

When it is dangerous to use the reversal design, or when it appears likely that the behavior of interest is irreversible, teachers should consider the use of a multiple-baseline design (Baer, Wolf, and Risley, 1968; Risley and Baer, 1973). A description of each of the three types of multiple-base designs follows:

Different-Behaviors Multiple-Baseline Design The first type of multiple-baseline design involves taking baseline measurements of several different behaviors for a period of time (for example, sight vocabulary, spelling, and arithmetic). The behaviors could be those of an individual student or those of a group of students. Once the baseline level is well established for all behaviors, a behavior modification procedure is applied to only one of the behaviors. If the behavior changes in the desired direction, the procedure is continued with the first behavior but is also applied to the second behavior. If the second behavior improves when the procedure is applied to it, the procedure is then applied to the first, second, and third behaviors, and so on. If each of the behaviors improves when the procedure is applied to it, the teacher has provided strong evidence that the procedure he is using is causing the desired change in the behaviors.

Leonardi, Duggan, Hoffheins, and Axelrod (1972) employed this type of multiple-baseline design with a classroom of second graders. During a ten-day period a teacher trainee kept a record of the number of out-of-seat, disturbing-others, and talking-out behaviors the four most disruptive students engaged in during a one-hour period each day. Figure 3-4 indicates that the youngsters averaged twelve out-of-seat, sixteen disturbing-others, and twelve talking-out behaviors per hour during the ten-day period. From day 11 to day 16, a group contingency procedure similar to that used by Gallagher, Sulzbacher, and Shores (1967) was applied to out-of-seat behaviors but not to disturbing-others and talking-out behaviors. The procedure was in effect for all students, but the measurements were still restricted to the four most disruptive students. The

---

[3]The term "natural environment" refers to the variety of settings a student encounters in his daily routine.

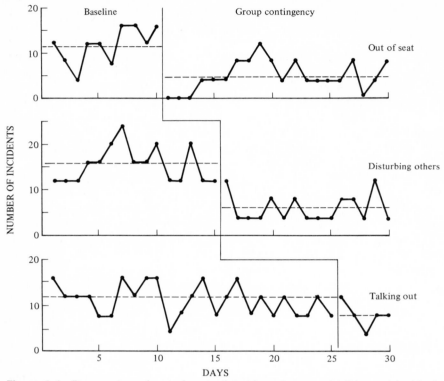

Figure 3-4 The number of out-of-seat, disturbing-others, and talking-out incidents in a second-grade classroom. *(From A. Leonardi, T. Duggan, J. Hoffheins, and S. Axelrod, "Use of Group Contingencies to Reduce Three Types of Classroom Behaviors." Paper presented at the meeting of the Council for Exceptional Children, Washington, D.C., March 1972. By permission of the authors.)*

teacher listed the numbers "24, 23, 22, . . . , 0" on the board. The figures represented the number of minutes of free play which the class could receive at the end of the morning. Each time a student left his seat without permission, the teacher crossed the highest intact number off the blackboard. Whenever a number was crossed off, the entire class lost a minute of free play. Figure 3-4 indicates that out-of-seat behaviors decreased from a mean of twelve during baseline to a mean of two during the "Group Contingency" phase for the four students. Disturbing-others and talking-out behavior, to which the contingency was not applied during days 11 to 16, changed little from the level of the first ten days.

Even though out-of-seat behaviors decreased when the group contingency was used, the possibility that uncontrolled factors were responsible for the improvement could not be ruled out. During days 16 to 25 more evidence of the effectiveness of the group contingency procedure was provided. During this period the students lost a minute of free play for out-of-seat behaviors *and* for disturbing others but *not* for talking-out behaviors. It can be seen that out-of-seat behaviors stayed below the baseline level, disturbing-others behaviors decreased to six a day, but talking-out behavior stayed at about the same level during this period. Thus, the group contingency was effective with the behaviors to which it was applied, but not to other behaviors. From days 26 to 30 the students lost free-play time for out-of-seat, disturbing-others, *and* talking-out behaviors. Figure 3-4 indicates that out-of-seat and disturbing-others behavior remained at low levels and that instances of talking out decreased somewhat from a baseline mean of twelve to a mean of eight. The fact that each behavior improved only when the procedure was applied to it provides a strong argument for believing that the group contingency procedure caused the change in behavior.

 Different-Settings Multiple-Baseline Design The first multiple-baseline design involved measuring several *different behaviors* of an individual or group and then initiating a procedure with each of the behaviors at different points in time. The second type of multiple-baseline design involves measuring the *same behavior* of an individual or group but in *different situations.* After baseline measurements are taken in all of the situations, the experimental procedure is applied to the behavior of concern in only one of the situations. If the behavior improves in the first situation, it is also applied in the second situation. If improvement is again noted, the procedure is applied in the third situation, and so on. If improvement consistently occurs when the behavior modification tactic is applied in each of the different situations, the teacher has furnished satisfactory evidence that the technique improved the behavior of the child or group of children. The different situations to which this design could be applied might involve the same behavior during different periods of time each day (for example, classroom and home), or with different playmates, and so forth.

 Hall, Cristler, Cranston, and Tucker (1970) made use of the second type of multiple-baseline design. The problem behavior was the tardiness of twenty-five fifth-grade students following the noon, morning, and afternoon recesses. A baseline of the number of students who were tardy after each of the recesses was established for thirteen days. (See Figure 3-5.) On day 14 the teacher informed the students that each child who was in his or her seat within four minutes of the end of the *noon* recess would have his name listed under a chart entitled "Today's Patriots." Figure 3-5 indicates that beginning with day 14 the procedure led to an immediate decrease in tardiness following the noon recess, but that tardiness following the morning and afternoon recesses stayed about the same. On day 22 the teacher told the children that it was necessary to be on time following both the *noon* and *morning* recesses in order to be a "patriot." Figure 3-5 shows that under these conditions tardiness was eliminated following the noon and morning recesses but was unchanged in the afternoon. On day 28 the teacher announced that in order to have his or her name placed on the patriots chart a student had to be punctual following *all three of the daily recesses.* Under these conditions there were no incidents of tardiness following any of the recesses. The type of multiple-baseline design used by Hall, Cristler,

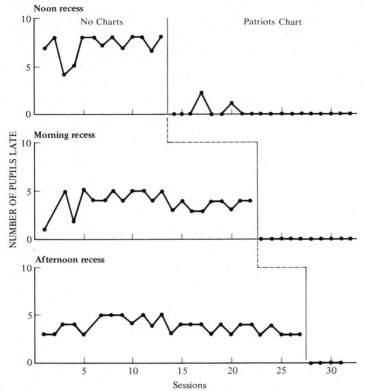

Figure 3-5 The number of tardy students following the noon, morning, and afternoon recesses. *(Adapted from R. V. Hall, C. Cristler, S. S. Cranston, and B. Tucker, "Teachers and Parents as Researchers Using Multiple-Baseline Designs,"* Journal of Applied Behavior Analysis, **3**, *p. 249, 1970. By permission of the publishers.)*

et al. (1970) clearly indicated that the "Today's Patriots" procedure was an effective one, since improvement occurred in a given situation (that is, following noon, morning, afternoon recess) only when the tactic was applied in that situation.

    Different-Students Multiple-Baseline Design The third type of multiple-baseline design involves applying a procedure to the same behavior of *different students.* First, a baseline on a particular behavior is established with each student. Next, a procedure is applied to one student but not to the others. If the behavior of the first student improves, the procedure is applied to both the first and the second student. If the behavior of the second student improves, the procedure is applied to the next student, and so forth, until all students have been exposed to the procedure. If the behavior of each individual improves when the procedure is applied to him, it has been demonstrated that the procedure caused the improvement in behavior. This type of multiple-baseline design can also be applied to different *groups,* by first applying the procedure to one group, then to a second group, then to a third group, and so on.

Another study reported in the Hall, Cristler, et al. (1970) article gave an example of the third type of multiple-baseline design. The subjects for the investigation were three high school students, Dave, Roy, and Debbie, who were consistently receiving D's and F's on French quizzes. Figure 3-6 indicates that during the first ten days of baseline the median grade for all three students was F. After the tenth quiz, the teacher informed Dave that she would "help" him with after-school tutoring following each instance in which he received a D or F on a quiz. Apparently, this was the type of help which Dave preferred to do without. His quiz grades improved immediately. At no time during the remainder of the study did he receive a grade of less than C, and, in fact, his median grade increased to A.

Meanwhile, between days 11 and 14 baseline conditions were in effect for Roy and Debbie. Figure 3-6 indicates that their performance did not improve during this period. Following day 15 Roy was told that he would be given after-school tutoring whenever he received a D or F on a French quiz. From session 16 to the end of the study, he received no grade below a C, with his median grade increasing to B. From the sixteenth to the twentieth sessions,

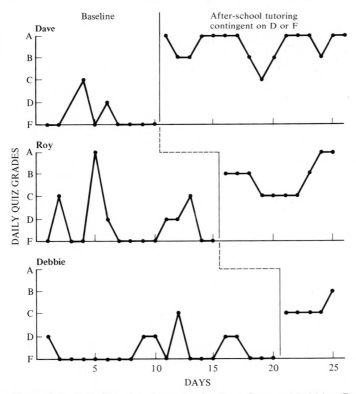

Figure 3-6 Daily French quiz grades for Dave, Roy, and Debbie. *(From R. V. Hall, C. Cristler, S. S. Cranston, and B. Tucker, "Teachers and Parents as Researchers Using Multiple-Baseline Designs,"* Journal of Applied Behavior Analysis, **3**, *p. 251, 1970. By permission of the publishers.)*

baseline conditions were in effect for Debbie, and her performance remained unchanged. When after-school tutoring for D's and F's was applied to her performance, following session 20, Debbie improved to the point that she never received a D or F and her median quiz score increased to C, as compared with a baseline level of F. The consequence of after-school tutoring can therefore be considered the factor causing the improvement in grades, since each student's scores increased at the point at which the contingency was applied to her.

GRAPHING DATA

Following each session in which data have been collected, it is wise for a teacher to graph the results. With a visual representation of the data, the teacher can determine whether or not the procedure he has been using has improved his students' behavior. If student performance has improved, the teacher will be reinforced for his efforts and is more likely to continue to use the procedure. If performance has not improved, the teacher will have this knowledge available to him and can devise an alternative strategy. It has been found that graphing data can also reinforce a student's behavior. On several occasions the author has observed students reacting enthusiastically as their graph showed an improving trend, or bragging to their classmates that their performance during a given session has reached to 100 percent level.

A conventional graph consists of a vertical and a horizontal axis. The vertical axis consists of a series of points (each of which is known as an "ordinate") giving a measure of the behavior of interest. The vertical axis might be labeled "Frequency of Temper Tantrums," "Number of Words Spelled Correctly," "Percentage of Time Studying," "Duration of Out-of-Seat Behavior," and so on. In the hypothetical data of Figure 3-7 the vertical axis has been labeled "Number of Hand Raises." The horizontal axis consists of a series of points (each known as an "abscissa") representing the element of time. Thus, the horizontal axis might be labeled "Days," "Hours," "Sessions," and so on. In Figure 3-7 the horizontal axis has been labeled "Days." In order to determine the level of a behavior on a given day, one must find where the appropriate point falls on the vertical and horizontal axes (that is, determine the ordinate and the abscissa). In Figure 3-7, for example, there was one hand raise on day 5 and there were nine on day 14.

In reading a graph it is sometimes helpful if the *mean* (that is, *average*) level of the behavior during an experimental condition is indicated. The mean can be noted with a horizontal dashed line. In Figure 3-7 the mean number of hand raises during Baseline$_1$ was 2.0. During the Praise for Raising Hand$_1$ stage, the mean was 8.6. The average for a given phase is attained by taking the sum of the data points and dividing by the number of data points. During Baseline$_1$ in Figure 3-7, the sum is $3 + 2 + 3 + 1 + 1 = 10$. The number of data points is five. Therefore, the mean is $^{10}/_5 = 2$.

Rather than showing the mean score, some people prefer to indicate the "median" score. The "median" is the middle point from a series of scores

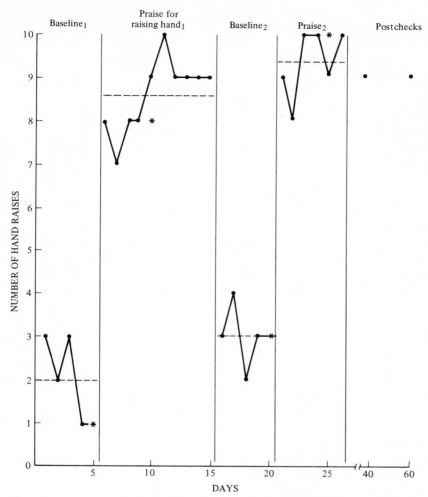

Figure 3-7 Hypothetical data of the number of times a student raised his hand each day.

which have been arranged in order of magnitude. To find the median of the Baseline$_1$ scores in Figure 3-7, the points 3, 2, 3, 1, 1 are arranged in the order 1, 1, 2, 3, 3. The middle point of the five scores is 2. Therefore, the median is 2. If there is an even number of scores, calculating the median is somewhat different. Suppose the data are 5, 2, 5, 4, 2, 3. When arranged in order of magnitude, the series becomes 2, 2, 3, 4, 5, 5. In this case there would be two middle scores: 3 and 4. The median is then found by adding 3 + 4 and dividing by 2. Therefore, the median would be 3.5. The median can also be represented on a graph with a horizontal dashed line.

The results of reliability checks are sometimes indicated on the graph. This can be done by using an asterisk to represent the data point of the reliability observer. Thus, in Figure 3-7 both observers recorded one hand raise on day 5, whereas on day 10 the primary observer recorded nine hand raises and the reliability observer recorded eight.

Hall (1971) made some suggestions for graphing data:

1   Experimental conditions should be separated by dark, vertical lines.
2   Experimental conditions should be labeled as descriptively as possible. The label "Praise for Raising Hand" is, therefore, preferable to the title "Reinforcement" or "Praise."
3   Data points between different experimental conditions should not be connected.
4   Data points between postchecks should not be connected.

Although the conventional graph is suitable for most purposes, there are investigators who sometimes use a "cumulative graph." With a cumulative graph the vertical axis indicates the *total number of behaviors which have occurred since the beginning of the study.* This differs from the conventional graph, in which the vertical axis indicates only the number of behaviors which occurred during each session. The horizontal axis will still represent the dimension of time (such as "Days"). An example of each type of graph should make the distinction clear. Suppose Randy's record of instances of talking out during a ten-day baseline period was: 6, 2, 0, 5, 3, 0, 4, 1, 3, and 5. The conventional graph of the data is represented in the top portion of Figure 3-8. The lower portion of Figure 3-8 is the cumulative curve of the same data. On day 1 Randy had six instances of talking out. On day 2 there were two more occasions of talking out, for a total of eight since the beginning of the study. On day 3 there was no talking out. Therefore, the total number of instances of talking out remained at eight. On day 4 there were five more instances of talking out, for a total of thirteen. After ten sessions a total of twenty-nine occasions of talking out was recorded. The same information can be derived from either graph, but the conventional graph gives a more convenient representation of daily performance whereas the cumulative graph gives a more convenient picture of the total number of behaviors since the beginning of the study. It is my opinion that the cumulative graph is of limited use for most classroom studies, and that the conventional graph is usually to be preferred.

The question as to how long an experimental condition (particularly the Baseline$_1$ phase) should be conducted is often raised. Aside from recommending that the Baseline$_1$ stage be carried out for a minimum of five sessions, my only suggestion is that the decision as to the length of each condition be based on an inspection of a graph of the data. If the data are fairly stable, a relatively short Baseline$_1$ phase is probably sufficient. Broden (1968) pointed out that "Five sessions indicating a behavior occurred 30%, 40%, 25%, 35%, and 30% of the time respectively might be all that is needed to substantially indicate a stable rate. More time might be needed if the percentages read 10%, 90%, 50%, 30%, and 60% simply because of the wide variability of the scores [p. 3]."

Another consideration which should be made with respect to the length of

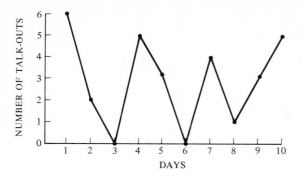

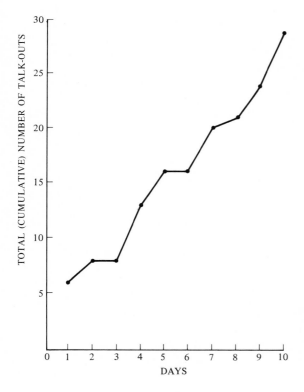

Figure 3-8 The top portion of the figure is a hypothetical conventional graph of the number of times Randy talked out each day. The bottom portion of the figure is a cumulative graph of the same data.

the Baseline$_1$ phase is the trend of the data. Suppose the data representing the rate with which a student hits his classmates during a five-day Baseline$_1$ phase are those presented in Figure 3-9. Since it is desirable that the frequency of the hitting behavior decrease, and the rate is already decreasing, it would be unwise to discontinue Baseline$_1$ measurements after day 5. If improvement was noted when an experimental procedure was employed, it would be difficult to determine whether the change was due to the technique the teacher was using

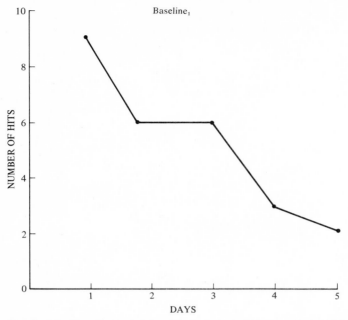

Figure 3-9 Hypothetical data of the number of times a student hit his classmates during a five-day Baseline₁ period.

or whether the improvement would have occurred without any special procedures. In such a case Baseline₁ measurements should be continued for more sessions. Similar considerations should be studied if it is desirable to increase the level of a behavior and the data already show an increasing trend during Baseline₁.

Broden (1968) pointed out that the length of Experimental Phase₁ also depends on the stability and trend of the data. Perhaps the best rule to follow is that Experimental Phase₁ should be carried on until the data demonstrate a clear improvement in the behavior. The Baseline₂ (or Reversal) phase should be conducted until it is demonstrated that the behavior has deteriorated from the Experimental Phase₁ level. It is often possible to have fewer Baseline₂ sessions than Baseline₁ sessions. There is no reason why each experimental condition should be conducted for the same number of sessions.

SUMMARY

Behavior modifiers are committed to the practice of obtaining an ongoing record of student performance. By measuring a child's behavior, a teacher can objectively determine whether the behavior should be modified and whether the procedures she is using are effective or not. The measurement techniques can often be carried out without interfering with the other chores facing a teacher.

The initial step in the measurement process is to *define* the behavior in units which are specific and observable. Some behaviors lend themselves to easy definition (for example, spelling words correctly), whereas other behaviors must be defined with great care (for example, disturbing others). After obtaining an acceptable definition of the behavior of interest, a teacher must decide on a measurement procedure. Her choice will depend on the type of behavior she is measuring and the amount of time she can devote to the measurement process. If the student's behavior leaves a tangible product, as is the case when he writes the answers to arithmetic, spelling, or reading comprehension questions, "measurement of lasting products" can be used. The teacher simply grades the paper as 75 percent correct or 50 percent complete. The measurement process takes place at a time which is convenient to the teacher.

Other behaviors, such as hand raising and talking out, are transitory and do not leave a tangible product. To obtain an accurate measure of such behaviors, a teacher must make an *observational record* of the behaviors soon after they occur. There are four types of observational recording. One type is known as *event* or *frequency* recording and consists of noting the number of times a certain behavior occurs. Thus, an event record might indicate that a student talked out thirteen times during a morning session. Event recording is appropriate for behaviors of short duration (for example, talking out) but not for long-duration behaviors (for example, out-of-seat behaviors). When the amount of time a behavior lasts is important, "duration recording" can be used. A duration record might show that a student was twenty minutes tardy or that he gazed out the window for an hour. For some behaviors teachers will find duration recording too time-consuming, and alternative procedures must be sought. Another measurement operation that can be used when the duration of the behavior is important is known as "interval recording." The data sheet for such recording might appear as follows:

+	−	−	+

Seconds   15   30   45   60

The sheet is divided into fifteen-second intervals for a one-minute period. The observer records whether or not the behavior occurs during each interval. If "+" means in-seat behavior and "−" denotes out of seat, the recorder places a "+" in the interval if the student refrains from out-of-seat behavior for the entire interval. If he leaves his seat at any time during the interval, he receives a "−". As was the case with duration recording, interval recording often requires too much of a teacher's attention. A fourth procedure, which is usually easy to implement, is known as *time sampling*. Using the same data sheet as for interval recording, a teacher employing time-sampling measurement notes only what the student is doing at the end of the interval. Thus, if a student were in his seat at the fifteen-second mark, he would receive a "+"; if he were not in his seat at this moment, he would receive a "−". With as few as five measurements a day, time sampling can give an accurate measure of a student's behavior. The measurement process can be facilitated by having a timer sound when a measurement is due.

Behavior modifiers attempt to measure behavior as often as possible—usually on a daily basis. This is in contrast to other educational researchers who obtain only a pretest and a posttest, which are separated by many months. "Continuous measurement" gives a more accurate record of a student's performance because it eliminates problems such as students being ill or guessing well on the testing day. Such measurement also gives continual information to the teacher on the progress of her students and lets her know whether she should continue existing procedures or start new ones. In order to increase the probability of accurate measurement, many behavior modification studies employ "reliability checks." The process consists of having a second observer independently rate the behavior of the student, and then determining the degree to which the observers' records agree with each other. Reliability checks usually occur on about one out of every five sessions.

Behavioral investigators use experimental designs that differ from those employed in traditional educational research. The most common design used in educational studies is known as the *group design*. According to this design, a researcher who wishes to determine which of various methods produces superior learning will randomly assign the students to different groups. Each group will receive one of the learning procedures. If it is found, for example, that group A received significantly higher scores than the other groups, the procedure which group A received would be considered the best technique of those under investigation. In spite of the widespread use of the group design, behavioral researchers have generally rejected its use. This is so because the group design does not give information on individual performance and because of difficulties in obtaining adequate samples of students.

Behavioral researchers usually employ the "reversal design," in which each student receives every technique under investigation. Typically, the student's behavior is measured under normal or baseline conditions. Next the student receives a procedure which is intended to improve the behavior. If the technique is ineffective, he might receive a second procedure. Once a procedure improves the student's behavior, the researcher will usually revert to baseline conditions. If the behavior deteriorates, the researcher can be certain that the previously noted improvement in behavior did not result from uncontrolled factors.

When a behavior is unlikely to reverse, or when a reversal phase might prove dangerous, the "multiple-baseline" design can be employed. One type of multiple-baseline design involves taking separate measurements on two or more behaviors. A procedure is applied to one behavior, and if the behavior improves, the procedure is applied to the second behavior, and so on. If each behavior improves only after receiving the procedure, one can be confident that the procedure that was used accounted for the improvement in student performance. A second type of multiple-baseline design involves applying the procedure to the same behavior in different settings, and the third type consists of applying the procedure to different students at different points in time. Experience has shown that teachers with a minimal amount of training can conduct behavioral research and, thereby, participate in the development of their field.

After collecting data each day, teachers should plot the results on graph paper. By inspecting the graph, a teacher can make an appropriate decision on whether certain procedures are beneficial or not, whether a slow but definite improvement or regression is occurring, and whether she should cease one phase and begin another.

QUESTIONS AND ACTIVITIES

1 Have two neighboring teachers define the term "aggressive" and compare their definitions with yours.
2 Distinguish between interval and time-sampling measurement. Why is it usually easier for a teacher to use time-sampling rather than interval measurement?
3 Of what benefit is it to a teacher to use continuous measurement of student behavior?
4 Have someone else and yourself independently record a behavior, using at least two of the observational recording techniques described in Chapter 3. Determine the reliability of your observations.
5 What is the purpose of returning to baseline conditions when using the reversal design?
6 Show how you would use each of the multiple-baseline designs to investigate whether a certain procedure increased the rate of completing classroom assignments.
7 Take a behavior of your own and attempt to modify it, using a procedure of your choosing. Use a reversal design to determine whether your procedure is causing the change to take place. Graph the data from all phases of the study.
8 Do No. 7 but with another individual(s), and use a multiple-baseline design.

REFERENCES

Alley, S. J., and L. Cox: "Doing Dishes as a Contingency for Reducing a Husband's Rate of Leaving Clothes in the Living Room," in R. V. Hall (ed.), *Managing Behavior, Part III* (Lawrence, Kans.: H & H Enterprises, 1971), pp. 42–43.

Axelrod, S., and Piper, T. J. "Suitability of the Reversal and Multiple-Baseline Design for Research on Reading Behaviors." Paper presented at the meeting of the Association for the Advancement of Behavior Therapy, San Francisco, December, 1975.

Baer, D. M., M. M. Wolf, and T. R. Risley: "Some Current Dimensions of Applied Behavior Analysis," *Journal of Applied Behavior Analysis*, **1**, 91–97, 1968.

Broden, M.: "Notes on Recording and Conducting a Basic Study." Unpublished manuscript, University of Kansas, 1968.

Eaton, M. D., and T. C. Lovitt: "Achievement Tests versus Direct and Daily Measurement," in G. Semb, D. R. Green, R. P. Hawkins, J. Michael, E. L. Phillips,

J. A. Sherman, H. Sloane, and D. R. Thomas (eds.), *Behavior Analysis and Education—1972* (Lawrence, Kans.: Support and Development Center for Follow Through, Department of Human Development, University of Kansas, 1972), pp. 78–87.

Foxx, R. M., and P. L. Martin: "A Useful Portable Timer," *Journal of Applied Behavior Analysis*, **4**, 60, 1971.

Gaasholt, M.: "Precision Techniques in the Management of Teacher and Child Behaviors," *Exceptional Children*, **37**, 129–135, 1970.

Gallagher, P. A., S. I. Sulzbacher, and R. E. Shores: "A Group Contingency for Classroom Management of Emotionally Disturbed Children." Paper presented at the meeting of the Kansas Council for Exceptional Children, Wichita, March 1967.

Hall, R. V.: *Behavior Management Series: Part I—The Measurement of Behavior* (Lawrence, Kans.: H & H Enterprises, 1971).

———, S. Axelrod, M. Foundopoulos, J. Shellman, R. A. Campbell, and S. S. Cranston: "The Effective Use of Punishment to Modify Behavior in the Classroom," *Educational Technology*, **11**, 24–26, 1971.

———, C. Cristler, S. S. Cranston, and B. Tucker: "Teachers and Parents as Researchers Using Multiple-Baseline Designs," *Journal of Applied Behavior Analysis*, **3**, 247–255, 1970.

Hooper, W.: "The Effects of Teacher Attention and a Token Reinforcement Program on the Classroom Behavior of a First Grade Child." Unpublished manuscript, University of Kansas, 1970.

Kubany, E. S., and B. B. Sloggett: "Coding Procedure for Teachers," *Journal of Applied Behavior Analysis*, **6**, 339–344, 1973.

Kuypers, D. S., W. C. Becker, and K. D. O'Leary: "How to Make a Token System Fail," *Exceptional Children*, **35**, 101–109, 1968.

Leonardi, A., T. Duggan, J. Hoffheins, and S. Axelrod: "Use of Group Contingencies to Reduce Three Types of Inappropriate Classroom Behaviors." Paper presented at the meeting of the Council for Exceptional Children, Washington, D.C., March 1972.

Lindsley, O.: "Direct Measurement and Prosthesis of Retarded Behavior," rev. ed., *University of Oregon Curriculum Bulletin*, Eugene, Oreg., **25**, 1969.

O'Gorman, M., B. Schneider, and H. McKenzie: "P 12," in H. McKenzie (ed.), *1968–1969 Report of the Consulting Teacher Program*, Vol. II (Burlington, Vt.: Consulting Teacher Program, College of Education, University of Vermont, 1970).

Risley, T. R.: "Behavior Modification: An Experimental-Therapeutic Endeavor," in L. A. Hamerlynck, P. O. Davidson, and L. E. Acker (eds.), *Behavior Modification and Ideal Mental Health Services* (Calgary, Alberta, Canada: University of Calgary Press, 1970), pp. 103–127.

——— and D. M. Baer: "Operant Behavior Modification: The Deliberate Development of Child Behavior," in B. Caldwell and H. Ricciuti (eds.), *Review of Child Development Research, vol. III: Social Action* (Chicago, Ill.: University of Chicago Press, 1973), pp. 283–329.

Chapter 4

Typical School Problems and How Educators Have Solved Them

The information in the preceding chapters is the foundation on which teachers can build their own behavior modification programs. They should view the principles as being helpful not only to remediate problems but to prevent difficulties and accelerate the learning process. Initially, it is probably best for teachers to attempt to modify relatively minor problems than to attack major ones. (Shaping is important for adults as well as for children.) Thus, a teacher's first effort might be to increase the hand-raising rate of one child or to decrease the out-of-seat behavior of another youngster. Only after he has had a considerable amount of practical experience should he concern himself with a problem so grandiose as improving the reading comprehension skills of an entire class.

Although it is common practice for teachers to call upon outside help when they encounter problems, they should rely, as much as possible, on their own devices. Teachers have the advantage of observing students over long periods of time and, as a result, of learning the likes and dislikes of their students as well as the conditions under which desirable and undesirable behaviors tend to occur. Although the observations are informal, the information is worthwhile and can serve as the basis for an effective behavior modification program.

Before attempting to modify a behavior, a teacher must decide whether or not the behavior should be modified. In many cases the decision is an easy one: the behavior is occurring too often or too seldom, it is occurring in the wrong situations, or it is not developing quickly enough. In other cases, the decision is not so simple. A teacher should not attempt to modify every behavior that annoys him. Hence, if students are leaving their seats and talking out at a moderate rate, or if they make occasional reading errors, a teacher should not feel an immediate need to institute a behavior modification program. Teachers should be able to tolerate some level of student disruption and academic imperfection. Teachers who have difficulty achieving this state should give priority to modifying their own behavior rather than their students'.

As indicated in the previous chapter, once the decision to modify behavior is made, the teacher's first task is to define the behavior. This job can be easy or difficult, depending on the number of behaviors that appear to be problems and the degree to which each behavior lends itself to precise analysis. When a number of behaviors are of concern, the teacher is usually better off if he initially concentrates on modifying only one or two behaviors. Often, he will find that solving one management or academic problem will lead to a corresponding improvement in other behaviors. Also, trying to modify too many behaviors at once can prove too difficult a task for both the teacher and the students.

In order to derive a definition of an apparently diffuse behavior, it is sometimes helpful for a teacher to jot down a description of each occurrence of the behavior. It may be the case, for example, that Carl consistently "annoys" his classmates. Before the teacher attempts to modify the behavior, she should specify exactly what she means by "annoy." Hence, when she sees Carl jabbing a classmate in the ribs, she should make a note of this. Later, if she notices that Carl removes some material from another student's desk and hides it from view, she should also record this information. After a few days of obtaining such information, the teacher can peruse her notes and devise an adequate definition of the behavior. A teacher cannot be too precise in defining a behavior for herself or her students. The author can recall an early effort in which he attempted to modify out-of-seat behavior. The students were informed that if they left their seats without permission, they would lose free-play time. The students soon determined that they could avoid the penalty by moving the seats with them. Aghast, the author watched as children propelled themselves through the classroom with seats attached to their rear ends! Clearly, he needed a better definition of out-of-seat behavior.

Once a teacher has defined the target behavior he should decide on a measurement technique. When academic problems are of concern, there is usually a lasting product of the student's work, and the measurement process is generally easy to accomplish. At times, however, there may be too much work to grade, and teachers might consider grading only a portion of each student's work. When it is necessary to use observational recording, measurement problems can be more complex. A teacher should strive for a measurement technique which strikes a balance between yielding representative data and being feasible, given the myriad of tasks he must accomplish. Hence, if a student is calling out during the entire school day, he might make a frequency count for only fifteen to thirty minutes a day. If the calling-out activities occur occasionally but are of an extremely hostile nature, the teacher should find it practicable to keep a record of the talking-out activities throughout the school day.

When a teacher has devised a measurement technique which he feels comfortable with, he can take $Baseline_1$ measurements. He should view the data he obtains not merely as being necessary for scientific purposes, but as providing an information base for the ensuing behavioral technique which he intends to employ. Hence, if $Baseline_1$ data indicate that Helena usually makes ten to twelve reading errors per page, the teacher can set a criterion for reinforcement at eight or fewer errors. As Helena's reading performance improves, the teacher's data will so indicate, and the criterion for reinforcement can be set at a lower number of errors. Whatever the data indicate, the teacher should write a report of what he attempted and the results he attained and place the information with each student's permanent record card. In this manner future teachers will be aware of which procedures were effective and which were ineffective, and thus they can plan programs accordingly. Too often there is a lack of communication between successive teachers, with a resultant decrement in scholastic progress.

The technique a teacher implements in order to bring about behavioral improvement depends on such factors as the severity of the problem, the types of procedures that have been effective with the student in the past, and the amount of resources available to him or her. Teachers should not immediately turn to contingency operations to solve their problems. At times it is more profitable to determine whether children are receiving adequate nutrition at home, whether they might benefit from auditory and visual examinations, whether the heating or lighting conditions of the classroom could be improved, and whether seating arrangements should be changed. When the use of contingencies seems to be called for, teachers should first consider using positive reinforcement and extinction techniques. The initial types of positive reinforcement procedures might be various forms of praise for appropriate behavior. If social reinforcement does not seem reasonable, or if it proves ineffective, more complex systems, such as token reinforcement procedures, might be attempted. In these cases teachers should first consider back-up reinforcers intrinsic to the classroom, such as the privilege of being classroom messenger, before contemplating the use of reinforcers external to the classroom, such as candy, toys, and trips.

When punishment tactics appear to be necessary, teachers should proceed from the mild to the austere. Thus, response cost involving the loss of extra minutes of free play should be considered long before a time-out procedure is contemplated. Teachers should also make use of published studies in order to obtain ideas on effective methods. Whatever procedure a teacher decides upon, she should apply it consistently and for a long enough period of time to determine its effectiveness. If the procedure proves ineffective under these conditions, she should seek alternative methods.

In order to familiarize the reader with the behavior modification approach to solving problems, the fourth chapter has been devoted to a description of the variety of school difficulties and the remedial techniques educators have employed. The population of students ranges from preschool through elementary, junior high, and senior high school youngsters. The settings include regular and special education classes, as well as the lunchroom and the school bus. The number of individuals in the studies varies from 1 to 455. In the first eight studies, various types of management problems were the targets for modification. In the final seven studies an academic behavior was modified. In some of the studies both a management and an academic behavior were remediated. The procedure used for modification usually involved some type of contingency. The reader should take particular note of the variety of ways in which educators successfully employed social reinforcement techniques. The individuals responsible for carrying out the procedures include teachers, a principal, a counselor, and a bus driver. Although interobserver reliability was assessed in all studies, the information is not presented, in order to save space and prevent tedium.

The sources of studies consist of books, journals, and student reports. An effort was made to select studies which were carried out within the educational realities of personnel, cost, and time. The accounts which follow are my own summary of the original authors' reports. In addition to the implemented procedure, some alternative approaches that educators *might* have considered to solve the problems will be described. For one reason or another, these alternatives were unacceptable tactics but in many cases illustrate approaches that have typically been used in education. It is suggested that the reader examine the following studies for suggestions on procedures to use when problems occur or to prevent difficulties from arising. Of course, there is no guarantee that a procedure that works in one situation will work in another, but procedures with some history of success are probably a good starting point.

MANAGEMENT PROBLEMS

Situation 1: Wetting, Isolate Play, and Thumb Sucking in a Preschool Child

Background Preschool teachers are confronted with a variety of problems unlike those faced by teachers of older children. During the beginning of the school term, unwilling children are dragged kicking and screaming into class each morning, as their baffled parents try to calm the youngsters down. As the school year progresses, the teachers notice that some children refuse to play with their classmates, that other children are not completely toilet-trained, and that still others have temper tantrums when they are denied access to favored activities. Given the immaturity of the students and the high student-to-teacher ratio existing in many preschools, it is necessary that the teacher quickly remediate the difficulties, lest she or he face a year of frustration and chaos.

Problem   The study involved Kevin, a 4.8-year-old boy who was shy around other children but not with adults; he often wet his pants and he usually had his thumb in his mouth. In other respects Kevin appeared normal and he had average intelligence.

Rejected Remedial Alternatives

1   The teacher could read a book on child development to find out why young children behave as Kevin does.

2   The teacher could ask for a parent conference to determine whether there were any peculiarities in Kevin's early training that might account for his difficulties.

3   The teacher might suggest to the parents that they wait another year before enrolling Kevin in nursery school so that "he will have a chance to grow up."

Implemented Behavioral Solution   Ms. Paula Madakacherry, Kevin's teacher, did none of the above. Instead, she worked directly with Kevin's problems to see whether she could remediate them. First, she defined each of Kevin's problem behaviors as follows:

Definition of Behavior

Wetting: If Kevin was wet at the time a measurement was made, an instance of wetting was recorded. Any degree of wetness or dampness was counted, since he was provided with clean, dry clothes after each accident.

Isolate behavior: If Kevin was not interacting with at least one other child when a measurement was made, the teacher recorded an instance of isolate behavior. If Kevin was with the teacher, he also had to be with at least one other child. Social interaction included conversation and play, not just proximity to another child.

Thumb-sucking: Ms. Madakacherry recorded thumb sucking if any part of Kevin's thumb was in his mouth when a measurement was made.

Measurement of Behaviors   The teacher used a time-sampling procedure to measure each of the behaviors throughout the six-hour school day. She rated the behaviors with the aid of a memo timer (p. 85) which was covered with clay in order to mute the sound. The timer sounded on the average of once every twenty-four minutes, but the interval between rings varied from one measurement to the next. Hence, the first ring might occur three minutes after class began, the second one twenty-eight minutes later, and so on. The teacher noted fifteen times a day whether Kevin had his thumb in his mouth, whether he was involved in social activity, and whether his pants were wet.

Procedures and Results   Ms. Madakacherry conducted baseline for seven days on pants wetting, fifteen days on isolation behaviors, and twenty-three days on thumb sucking, according to a multiple-baseline design. Figure 4-1 indicates that Kevin's pants were wet a mean of 44 percent of the time, that he

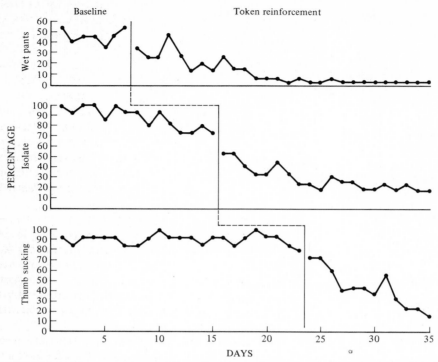

Figure 4-1 The percentage of time Kevin's pants were wet, he was engaged in isolate behavior, and he sucked his thumb. *(From P. Madakacherry, "Reducing Wetting, Isolate Play, and Thumbsucking by a Preschool Child." Unpublished manuscript, Temple University, 1974.)*

was isolated from his peers 87 percent of the time, and that he had his thumb in his mouth an average of 92 percent of the time. The teacher's remedial procedure consisted of a token reinforcement system in which she placed a star on Kevin's paper if he was behaving appropriately when a measurement was made.

Initially (day 8), Ms. Madakacherry concentrated only on Kevin's pants-wetting behavior. If his pants were dry when the timer rang, he received a red star; the stars were exchangeable for the opportunity to engage in a variety of activities which Kevin and his classmates enjoyed. If Kevin earned ten stars, *all* children could hear a storybook record; for twelve stars all students could have forty minutes of preferred play (for example, clay baking or finger painting); for fifteen stars they could have thirty extra minutes of playground time. They could also save their points to earn a circus day, a cooking party, or an outing for the entire class. The accompanying figure indicates that after five days of using the token procedure, wetting decreased until Kevin was almost always dry. On day 16, the teacher applied the procedure to social behavior.

She continued to give Kevin a red star if his pants were dry, but she also gave him a green star if he was interacting with another child. Since Kevin could now earn twice as many stars as were previously available, Ms. Madakacherry doubled the price of each of the reinforcing activities. Isolation behaviors decreased and reached a mean level of 30 percent (as compared with 87 percent during baseline). Finally, on day 24 the procedures included the awarding of blue stars if Kevin's thumb was out of his mouth; the price of each activity was increased to three times its original level. Thumb sucking decreased steadily throughout the remainder of the study.

Highlights

1　The teacher determined the reinforcers in the study by asking the students to describe favorite activities. In my experience children are an excellent source of suggestions for reinforcers.

2　By having all children engage in the reinforcing activities, Kevin's classmates encouraged the youngster, rather than being hostile to him and the procedure. They often reminded him to keep his thumb out of his mouth and to go to the bathroom; as he earned the reinforcers for the entire class, he became more popular with the children and formed many good friendships.

3　The teacher reported that Kevin's classmates showed greater enthusiasm for schoolwork when the reinforcing activities were available.

Reference　Madakacherry (1974).

Situation 2: Kindergarten Students Not Following Instructions

Background　When students inconsistently follow their teacher's instructions, classroom control becomes difficult to achieve. The problem is particularly common with preschool children, who seem to have a unique ability to ignore directions which do not appeal to them. If a teacher is unable to acquire instructional control over students' behavior, she will find herself putting away materials students are responsible for, repeating the same instructions several times, and wondering why she chose teaching as a profession. Although there may be many factors which affect the degree to which students will obey their teacher's requests, one important element is whether compliance is associated with positive consequences. Thus, if students behave in accordance with a teacher's directions and receive reinforcement, they are likely to follow teacher directions in the future. If they do not receive reinforcement, it should be expected that the students will tend *not* to follow teacher directions in the future.

Problem　The study involved five girls, 4.8 to 6 years of age, who were enrolled in a regular kindergarten classroom. The girls were generally well behaved but had a tendency not to follow many of their teacher's instructions.

Rejected Remedial Alternatives

1   The teacher could progressively raise the pitch and volume of her voice (that is, scream) each time a youngster failed to follow her instructions.

2   The teacher could send notes home to the girls' parents complaining about their lack of compliance with requests.

3   The teacher could give the girls a lecture on the importance of paying more attention to her.

Implemented Behavioral Solution   The initial step for the teacher was to devise ten instructions which she would give the girls each day. The instructions were, "Pick up the toys," "Sit down," "Come and get a pencil and paper," "Fold your paper," and so on. The behavior of concern was defined as follows:

Definition of Instruction Following   Every time a child complied with an instruction within fifteen seconds of the time the teacher spoke, she was considered to have followed the instruction.

Procedure and Results   During Baseline$_1$ the teacher gave each of the girls the ten instructions every afternoon. She responded to the girls in the same manner, whether or not they followed the instructions. Figure 4-2 indicates that the five girls followed the teacher's instructions an average of 60 percent of the time during Baseline$_1$. In the second phase of the study, the teacher continued to give the girls the ten instructions each day but also complimented the girls

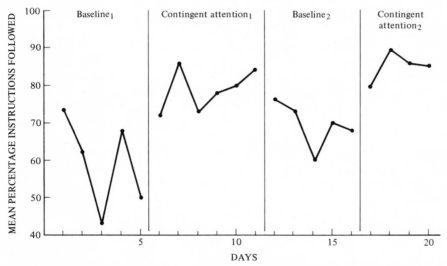

Figure 4-2   The mean percentage of teacher instructions five kindergarten girls followed each day. *(From R. C. Schutte and B. L. Hopkins, "The Effects of Teacher Attention on Following Instructions in a Kindergarten Class,"* Journal of Applied Behavior Analysis, **3**, *p. 120, 1970. By permission of the publishers.)*

each time they followed an instruction. She might say, "Thank you for doing what I asked, Shannon," or "You are so good today, Beth!" The effects of reinforcing the girls for complying with instructions were immediate. On the first day of Contingent Attention$_1$, the girls followed instructions 74 percent of the time and averaged 78 percent for the entire phase. When the teacher ceased complimenting the girls during Baseline$_2$, the percentage of instructions decreased to 69 percent but it increased to a higher level when compliments were reinstated during the final phase.

Highlights

1   When a teacher makes a request and a student obeys her instruction, there is a tendency for the teacher to be pleased with the student's behavior but to fail to express her appreciation to the student. If this sequence of events occurs a sufficient number of times, it is likely that students will eventually fail to follow teacher directions. If teachers can remember to compliment students for observing their directions, they will usually find that students will comply with their requests.

2   The study involved normal preschool youngsters who were basically well behaved. The fact that they sometimes failed to observe the teacher's directions was hardly a cause for alarm. Nevertheless, the study indicated that a teacher who is capable of applying reinforcement principles to mild behavioral problems is able to acquire a high degree of classroom control without resorting to aversive techniques. In so doing the teacher can achieve a more pleasant atmosphere for herself and her students.

Reference   Schutte and Hopkins (1970).

Situation 3: All Talk and No Work

Background   An age-old problem that teachers have faced through the years is a high rate of unauthorized jabbering among their students. In studies done by practicing teachers enrolled in sections of his behavior modification course during the past five years, the author found that 27 percent of them chose talking-out behavior as a target for modification. Talking out, of course, is not as serious a problem as aggressive behavior or an inability to read. Nevertheless, it interferes with the work habits of more cooperative students, is incompatible with completing academic assignments, and annoys the teachers terribly. When talking out is an annoying problem, teachers will generally find that behavior modification procedures are uniquely suited to remediate the difficulty effectively.

Problem   The present case involved twelve educable mentally retarded (EMR) youngsters who talked out in class at a high rate. The level of talking-out instances made it necessary for the teacher to repeat directions many times and to frequently demand the attention of the youngsters.

Rejected Remedial Alternatives

1   The teacher could try to outyell the students.
2   The teacher could attempt to embarrass the worst offenders by making them apologize to her before the entire class.
3   The teacher could ask the principal to "read the riot act" to her students.

Implemented Behavioral Solution   The teacher, Ms. Kathleen Bodnar, defined and measured the target behavior as follows:

Definition and Measurement of Behavior   "Talking-out" behavior consisted of any incident in which a student called out to the teacher, or answered one of her questions, without raising his hand and being recognized; it also included occasions in which a student called out to a classmate without teacher permission. The teacher used a golf wrist counter to keep track of the number of talking-out instances. Each time a student talked out without permission, Ms. Bodnar advanced the counter by one and thereby determined the total number of talking-out incidents for the entire class each day.

Procedure and Results   As depicted in Figure 4-3, Ms. Bodnar found that the students talked out an average of 135 times a day during the five-day Baseline$_1$ period. On day 6 she introduced a token reinforcement system to reduce the number of talking-out experiences. First, she posted a chart listing the twelve most desirable jobs in the classroom and the number of points each would cost. Washing the boards cost thirty-five points, cleaning the chalkboard erasers cost thirty points, taking the trash around was worth thirty points, emptying the trash can was twenty-five points, and general cleanup was twenty points. Next, Ms. Bodnar taped a 3×5 inch card to each student's desk. If a child raised his hand and waited to be acknowledged before speaking, Ms. Bodnar praised the child warmly and placed a star on his index card. Only reasonable responses were rewarded, thereby preventing the children from raising their hand for the sole purpose of attaining a star. Ms. Bodnar also rewarded the children for asking permission to talk with friends. At the end of each day, she permitted students to choose a job which corresponded to the number of points they had earned. If a child earned thirty-five points, for example, he could have the privilege of washing the boards.

The effect of the token procedure was immediate and marked. On the first day of the "Tokens for Hand Raises$_1$" phase, talking-out incidents decreased to fifty-two per day and averaged thirty-six during the ten-day phase (about 27 percent of the Baseline$_1$ rate). When the token procedure was discontinued during the five-day Baseline$_2$ phase, talking-out incidents increased to seventy-eight per day, but the number dropped substantially when the token system was reinstated.

Highlights

1   The study demonstrated that many events already available in the classroom can serve as effective reinforcers. <u>Teachers should seek ways to</u>

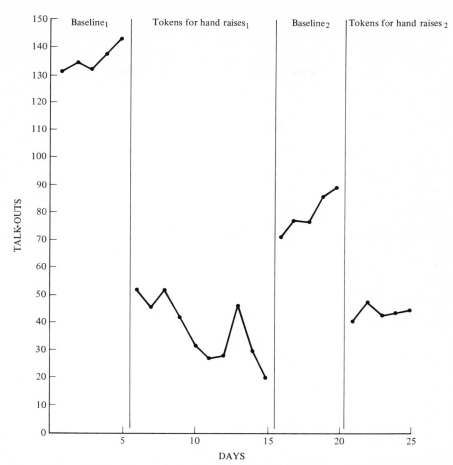

Figure 4-3 The number of talking-out instances by 12 EMR children. *(From K. Bodnar, "Reducing Talk Outs in an MR Class with a Token Reinforcement System." Unpublished manuscript, Temple University, 1974. By permission of the author.)*

administer the privileges in a contingent manner, rather than awarding them to students regardless of their behavior.

    2   The teacher anecdotally noted that the quality and quantity of the students' work increased when talking-out incidents decreased. This outcome is not surprising, of course, but more studies should keep track of the effect of reducing management problems on students' academic output.

    3   Most of the children in the present study were spending their first year in an EMR classroom. Although it might seem that placement in such classes would be determined by achievement tests and intellectual measures, research has shown that disruptive children are more likely to receive EMR placement than well-behaved youngsters, even though both groups might be at the same academic level. One can only wonder whether some of the children in the present study could have avoided special-class placement had their regular class teachers employed effective classroom management procedures during the previous school year.

Reference   Bodnar (1974).

Situation 4: Disruptive Behavior in the Cafeteria

Background   One of the settings in which it is most difficult to control disruptive behavior is the school cafeteria at lunchtime. In classroom situations there is a limited number of children; the teacher's responsibility for the behavior of each child in the class is clearly established; and a set of rules for classroom behavior is usually well defined. In the cafeteria the above conditions usually do not exist. The students of several classrooms gather together in one large room; the number of faculty members present for lunch duty is often insufficient for the number of students present; and it is not always easy to say exactly which behaviors are appropriate and which are inappropriate (for example, talking loudly, leaving the seat, and so on). The problems which result include fighting, the throwing and stealing of food, and running through the aisles. When the situation becomes sufficiently chaotic, teachers will often find themselves becoming both baffled and intimidated by the entire process.

Problem   The study took place in a combination elementary and middle school consisting of 455 students in grades one through eight. The children ate lunch at various intervals between 11:45 A.M. and 12:45 P.M. every day. Problems included running, loitering, and physical aggression. The cafeteria contained fourteen large tables seating ten children each, with the youngsters permitted to choose their own seats.

Rejected Remedial Alternatives

1   The school administration could require that the students eat their lunch in a classroom.
2   The administration could hire additional personnel to monitor the cafeteria.
3   The school could suspend children who violate specified lunchroom rules.

Implemented Behavior Solution
Definition and Measurement of Behaviors   "Loitering" was defined as any instance in which a student stayed in the cafeteria when he was not supposed to be there. "Physical aggression" included hitting, pushing, and kicking. Seventh- and eighth-grade students in the school were employed as observers and kept a frequency tally of each incident of running, loitering, and aggression. The students were also provided with a sound-level meter and recorded the number of times the sound in the cafeteria exceeded 80 decibels—a level considered appropriate for the cafeteria setting.

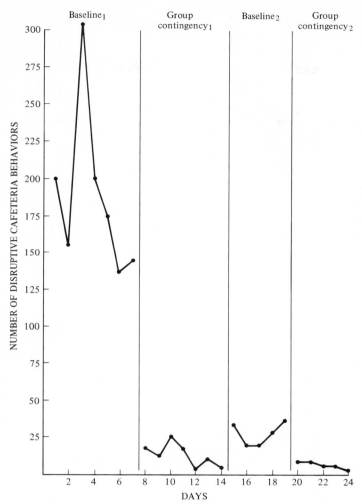

Figure 4-4 Total number of loitering, running in the school cafeteria, and aggressing incidents by 455 students in grades one through eight. *(From A. J. Muller, S. E. Hasazi, M. M. Pierce, and J. E. Hasazi, "Modification of Disruptive Behavior in a Large Group of Elementary School Students," in E. Ramp and G. Semb (eds.),* Behavior Analysis: Areas of Research and Application, *Englewood Cliffs, N.J.: Prenctice-Hall, 1975, p. 275. By permission of the publishers.)*

Procedure and Results The first seven days of the study constituted Baseline₁. The observers recorded each of the target behaviors, but no contingencies were placed on the students for performing any of the inappropriate behaviors. Figure 4-4 gives the total number of running, loitering, and aggressive behaviors that occurred each day in the cafeteria. Misbehaviors ranged from 135 to 304, with a mean of 188 for the one-hour lunch periods.

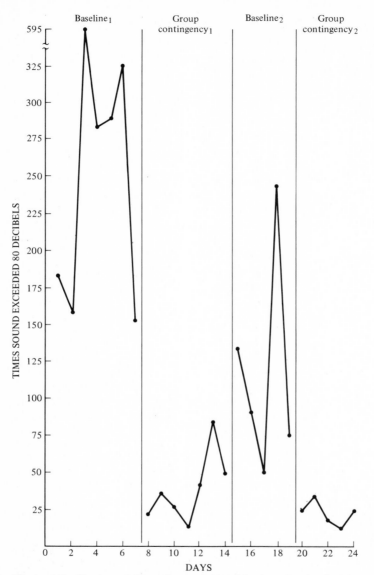

Figure 4-5 Number of times the sound level in the school cafeteria exceeded 80 decibels. *(From A. J. Muller, S. E. Hasazi, M. M. Pierce, and J. E. Hasazi, "Modification of Disruptive Behavior in a Large Group of Elementary School Students," in E. Ramp and G. Semb (eds.),* Behavior Analysis: Areas of Research and Application, *Englewood Cliffs, N.J.: Prenctice-Hall, 1975, p. 276. By permission of the publishers.)*

Figure 4-5 indicates the number of times the sound level exceeded 80 decibels. The mean number of times was 285, with a range of 155 to 595.

Before the initial day of Group Contingency$_1$, Mr. Adler Muller, the school principal, visited each classroom and told the students that a point system would be implemented. One point was to be awarded daily to each class that completely refrained from running, loitering, and aggression. When the total of points for the entire school reached twenty-five, Mr. Muller examined the data of all classes and awarded the members of the class with the highest total an extra thirty minutes of recess. The points were registered each afternoon on a large chart displayed in the main hall of the school, and the results were announced to the entire school over the public address system. The point system produced immediate and large decreases in each of the target behaviors. The mean number of disruptive acts diminished to fifteen (about 8 percent of the $Baseline_1$ level).

Although there was no contingency on making noise, the number of times the sound level exceeded 80 decibels decreased to an average of thirty-five times, which is approximately 12 percent of the $Baseline_1$ rate. When the group contingency procedure was discontinued during $Baseline_2$, disruptive behaviors increased only slightly, but they were virtually eliminated during the Group $Contingency_2$ phase. The noise level increased more substantially during $Baseline_2$, but it was still well below the $Baseline_1$ level, and it decreased to low levels during Group $Contingency_2$.

Highlights

1   An advantage in using a group contingency for inappropriate behavior is that it is not necessary to identify the individual(s) responsible for a particular transgression. This is particularly important for problems occurring in the cafeteria. When the problems consist of fights, litter on the floor, and intolerable amounts of noise, it is almost impossible to determine the students responsible. By using a group contingency, the problem is avoided, since consequences are applied to the entire group; a violation of the rules is a violation of the rules, and identification of a particular culprit is unnecessary.

2   The awarding of the free time was set up in such a manner that when the total number of points for all classes reached twenty-five, the principal of the school inspected the records of all classes and gave the class with the greatest number of points extra recess time. I feel that this procedure permits too few classes to receive the reinforcers; over a long period of time, classes that improve but do not receive the extra free time might eventually become disruptive again. My preference would be for a tactic that awarded each class its free time contingent upon that class reaching some predetermined number of points (for example, five points). In that manner, classes that showed improvement but were not the most outstanding would still be rewarded. (Remember shaping principles!)

3   It is gratifying to see the principal become actively involved in the solution to an important school problem. Given the great prestige of many principals, it is unfortunate that more of them don't take advantage of their reinforcing capacity to improve the performance of students and teachers alike.

Reference   Muller, Hasazi, Pierce, and Hasazi (1975).

Situation 5: Out-of-Seat Behavior on the School Bus

Background   The problems that occur in the school cafeteria are serious ones, but the difficulties that arise on the school bus are utterly dangerous. It is not unusual for the level of disruption on the bus to reach a point where the bus driver must reduce his concentration on operating his vehicle and instead direct his attention toward misbehaving youngsters. Also common are incidents in which students hurl objects from the bus, thus imperiling the safety of pedestrians and motorists.

It is not difficult to see why serious problems occur on the bus. One contributing element is the frequent absence of any school personnel to maintain discipline. A second problem is that the driver must direct attention toward operating the vehicle safely. In any event, the driver has difficulty seeing and addressing the children, because his back is turned toward them. Finally, when the bus ride is for relatively long periods of time, students become restless, particularly at the end of a school day. Thus, given the nature of a bus driver's duties and the fact that most operators are unfamiliar with behavioral principles, any procedure designed to reduce misbehaviors on the bus must be easy to implement and should have an immediate effect on the target behaviors.

Problem   The children in the study were fifty students in grades one to eight who rode the same bus to school every day. The youngsters had experienced several years of busing, changing schools, and community turbulence following court rulings on school integration. There were numerous incidents of running through aisles, climbing and standing on seats, and shouting.

Rejected Remedial Alternatives

1   Use more buses so that fewer children will be present on each bus.
2   Prohibit the most offensive children from using the bus. If this is not possible, place such children in special-education schools closer to their homes.

Implemented Behavioral Solution

Measurement of Behavior   It was surmised that the majority of the problems described above would be eliminated or reduced if the children remained in their seats. Out-of-seat behavior was, therefore, chosen as the target for modification. Each afternoon, the bus driver recorded the number of times the students left their seats during the ten-minute trip from school to the first stop. It was during this period of time that most disruptive behavior occurred. At the first stop, or shortly thereafter, most misbehaving children left the bus. The driver made use of his large rear-view mirror and a pencil and pad to count the number of children on each side of the bus who were out of their seats.

Procedure and Results   During the six day Baseline$_1$ phase, the bus driver recorded the out-of-seat behaviors of the fifty students and found that they left their seats an average of thirty-four times during the ten-minute period (see

Figure 4-6). On day 7 the driver told the students that the bus was to be divided into two groups by the aisle. The students on each side of the bus would receive a piece of candy at the end of the trip if the group members left their seats only three or fewer times. If the members of one group exceeded three out-of-seat behaviors, the members of the other group could still receive the prize by meeting their group criterion. The candy was given out by an eighth-grade girl who also praised the students when she gave them their treats. The effect of the procedure was immediate, with out-of-seat behaviors dropping to two on the first day of the "Candy for In Seat$_1$" phase. On eleven of the thirteen days of the phase, both groups received candy, and on six days there were no out-of-seat behaviors. The mean for the entire stage was 1.5 out-of-seat behaviors per day. In the Baseline$_2$ phase, the reinforcement procedure was discontinued, and out-of-seat behaviors occurred a mean number of fourteen times per day, with an increasing trend in the data. During the Candy for In Seat$_2$ phase, the contingency was reinstated. Beginning with day 27, however, candy was given out every other day and, ultimately, every third day, with the students not knowing on which days rewards were available. In spite of the less frequent reinforcement, out-of-seat behaviors returned to low levels, with a mean of 1.8 per day.

Highlights

1   The fact that the bus driver in the present study was willing and able to carry out the behavior modification procedures does not mean that such a

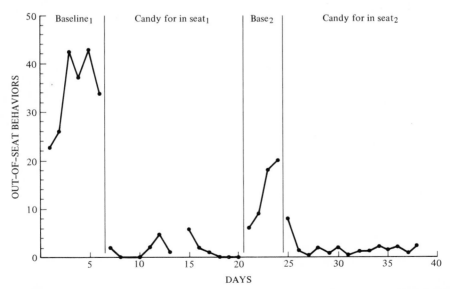

Figure 4-6   Number of times fifty students left their seats on the school bus during the first ten minutes of the trip. *(From J. W. Willis, T. R. Hobbs, D. G. Kirkpatrick, and K. W. Manley, "Training Counselors as Researchers in the Natural Environment," in E. Ramp and G. Semb (eds.), Behavior Analysis: Areas of Research and Application, Englewood Cliffs, N.J.: Prentice-Hall, 1975, p. 183. By permission of the publishers.)*

policy should typically be employed. On routes in which there have been serious problems, it would be better to have a teacher, an aide, or a bus matron available to carry out the desired technique. (Drive your bus and leave the behavior modification to us.)

2   A colleague of mine, Dr. Richard Otto (East Lyme Public Schools, East Lyme, Connecticut), used an interesting procedure to eliminate the disruptive behaviors of one child on the school bus. The youngster enjoyed school a great deal, so it became necessary for him to behave appropriately on the bus or else be excluded from school for the day. Dr. Otto worked out an arrangement with the boy's parents that involved having one of them follow the bus to school each morning. Upon the occurrence of any disruptive behavior, the bus driver signaled the parent, pulled off the road, and the child was removed from the bus and taken home. The procedure was effective but, of course, could not be used with a large number of acting-out children, lest there be a caravan of anxious parents following the bus to school each morning.

Reference   Willis, Hobbs, Kirkpatrick, and Manley (1975, Study 2).

Situation 6: Disruptive Behavior in a Junior High Special-Education Class

Background   The management problems encountered by elementary school teachers might seem minuscule compared with those facing secondary school teachers. A number of factors conspire to create difficulties for secondary school teachers. First, the physical size and strength of the students must be dealt with. Secondly, the application of behavior modification procedures is often hindered by problems in determining age-appropriate reinforcers. Third, the fact that most secondary school students have classes with many teachers sometimes makes the organization of remedial programs difficult. Unfortunately, secondary school teachers will receive only a limited amount of assistance from the published literature in behavior modification, which has dealt mainly with the problems of elementary school students.

The difficulties described above do not preclude the possibility of applying behavioral principles to the problems of secondary school youngsters. Instead, they mean that secondary school teachers must be imaginative and flexible enough to circumvent the problems they encounter. Hence, secondary-level teachers who are willing to explore their classrooms for appealing reinforcers and to perform the extra bookkeeping chores that are required will usually find that the long-range benefits outweigh the short-term burdens.

Problem   The case involved thirteen seventh and eighth graders in a special-education class. The students were several years behind in academic subject areas and had other problems, such as poor speech, reading disabilities, and episodes of delinquency. In-class management problems included profanity toward the teacher, refusal to obey teacher requests, and incidents of throwing school supplies, fighting, and chasing. The problems persisted for four months in spite of efforts to curtail the misconduct by praising appropriate behavior, reprimanding misdeeds, and sending children to the counselor's or principal's office.

Rejected Remedial Alternatives

1   Have the most delinquent of the students placed in special schools for delinquent children.

2   Have the least intelligent of the youngsters transferred to special schools or institutions for the retarded.

3   Hire additional counselors to see if they can find out "what is wrong with the youngsters."

Implemented Behavioral Solution

Definition and Measurement of Behavior   The study was conducted for six of the eight periods in which the students met each day. An observer used interval recording to obtain a measure of the time each of the thirteen youngsters was "on task." "On-task" behavior was recorded if a student was engaged in a teacher-assigned task, or if he was attending to the teacher or the appropriate pupil during class discussions.

Procedure and Results   During the ten-day Baseline₁ period, the teacher conducted class as she normally would. Figure 4-7 shows that the students were on task between 30 and 52 percent of the time, with a mean of 39 percent. In the second stage, the teacher implemented a token reinforcement system. Each pupil received a copy of the point system depicted in Table 4-1.

The "Earn Points" section indicates that students could acquire points for

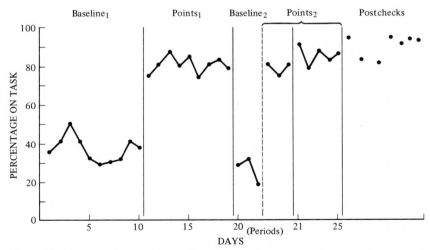

Figure 4-7   The percentage of time thirteen junior high students were on task during six periods of the day. *(From M. Broden, R. V. Hall, A. Dunlap, and R. Clark, "Effects of Teacher Attention and a Token Reinforcement System in a Junior High Special Education Class," Exceptional Children, **36**, p. 345, 1970. Reprinted with permission of The Council for Exceptional Children.)*

Table 4-1 Point System

Earn Points:
5	In seat
5	Quiet
5	Doing assignment
2	Extra credit (after regular assignment is complete)
3	"A" on assigned task
2	"B" on assigned task
1	"C" on assigned task

Minus Points:
15	Out of seat without permission
1	Talking out without permission
20	Out of room without permission
5	Incomplete assignment
3	Name calling, swearing
20	Throwing, hitting
20	Arguing with teacher
20	Teacher must tell you more than once

Spend Points:
50	Five-minute pass to rest room
50	Five minutes early to lunch
10	Leave seat for one minute
50	Move desk for one period
100	Move desk for one day
300	Move desk permanently
20	Pass to get a drink of water
10	Talk to another student for five minutes
50	Friday snack
400	Field trip
20	Nonacademic activities, such as knitting, puzzles, games, records

Source: M. Broden, R. V. Hall, A. Dunlap, and R. Clark, "Effects of Teacher Attention and a Token Reinforcement System in a Junior High Special Education Class," *Exceptional Children*, 1970, *36*, 341–349.

staying in their seats and remaining quiet for the entire period and for performing well on academic assignments. The distribution of points was set up so that students could earn twenty points during each class period with reasonably appropriate behaviors.

The "Minus Points" section depicts the number of points students lost if they behaved inappropriately. The distribution was such that the more serious the disruption, the greater the deduction of points.

The "Spend Points" portion of the table indicates the cost of each reinforcer; it deserves special attention. Each of the reinforcers except the Friday snack and the field trip were noncost activities. Presumably the teacher or the school could avoid the expense for the snack by having children bring one from home, and could do the same for the field trip by charging the parents a small fee. The price of the privileges was such that some reinforcers could be earned in one period whereas others were available by accumulating and saving points over several days. In devising the values in Table 4-1, an effort was made to strike a balance between the behaviors necessary to earn points and the appeal of each of the reinforcers.

The effect of the point system was sudden and great. On the first day of "Points₁," the class's on-task rate increased to 78 percent and reached a mean of 83 percent for the nine-day period (compared with 39 percent during Baseline₁). Before beginning the reversal phase, the teacher made an agreement with the authors that if the situation became too choatic, the token reinforcement system would be reinstated. The teacher apparently knew what she was talking about. Bedlam broke out during the first day of Baseline₂, and by the fourth period of the day the point system was again put into effect. Figure 4-7 indicates that the students were on task an average of 25 percent of the time during the three class periods of Baseline₂, but that order was quickly restored when the point system was reinstituted. The high level of on-task behavior was maintained during a six-week "Postchecks" period.

Highlights

1 The reaction of secondary school children to reinforcement programs is sometimes negative. In the present case, when the teacher first announced the point system, three pupils argued that it was childish, threatened to quit school, and stated that they would complain to the principal and counselor. The teacher ignored the comments. By the second day two of the three pupils were well behaved. The third student, Rob, however, became progressively more disruptive. He swore at the teacher, tore up materials, and stated that he would not be forced to do schoolwork. After four days other students were becoming more distracted by Rob's behavior and often laughed at his antics. The authors then decided to use a time-out procedure. The first time Rob refused to be quiet or to sit down, the teacher immediately sent him to the principal's office. The principal had screened off an area of his office so that Rob could not see the activity in the office. Rob spent the rest of the day in the office and the next day requested that he be returned to the classroom. From that time on, Rob presented no unusual problems to the teacher.

2 The comments of the teacher concerning the value of the program were interesting. She claimed that the system was helpful because it gave her a "black-and-white list of what is allowed in the classroom." She also stated that the pupils did more work and made better grades with the point system. During periods in which the students were working toward a highly valued prize, it became difficult for her to keep up with the extra-credit work. Finally she indicated that, with a specific list of rules in front of them, the students seldom complained about penalties.

Reference Broden, Hall, Dunlap, and Clark (1970).

Situation 7: The Counselor Intervenes

Background In my opinion two of the greatest sources of misused professional expertise are the school psychologist and the guidance counselor. The role of the school psychologist can often be defined as tester and report writer. The demands of the job are frequently so great that the psychologist cannot relate meaningfully to any particular situation. During my own tenure as a school psychologist, I can recall being told *not* to become involved in ongoing consultation with a few teachers, but to continually move on to new cases. Further detracting from the utility of school psychologists is the fact that their training often causes them to write psychological evaluations in terms that are difficult for the teacher to translate into concrete actions. As a result a teacher will often refer a student for psychological evaluation, have the child evaluated, receive and read the psychological report, but still not be able to solve the student's problems.

The role of the guidance counselor is somewhat different from that of the school psychologist in that counselors are expected to meet with and advise students for extended periods of time. A major complaint I have with counselors, however, is that most of the encounters they have with their students take place in the confines of their private offices. In a one-to-one situation almost any child will behave appropriately, and, as a result, the counselor often obtains a distorted picture of the problems the teacher must face. It is, therefore, unlikely that they will make helpful suggestions to the teacher. My position is that the school psychologist's and the guidance counselor's place is in the classroom, not in the office. I also believe that individuals occupying such positions should observe students in the classroom, make suggestions to teachers as to how problem behaviors should be measured and remediated, and conduct regular consultations with the teachers until the problems are solved. The study which follows provides an excellent example of how this approach may be implemented.

Problem The teacher in the present study was a junior high school mathematics teacher who reported that one class of twenty-seven seventh-grade students was so disruptive that learning was impossible. In spite of her threatening and punishing the youngsters, many students interrupted the class with loud, irrelevant comments and by freely wandering around the classroom. The teacher sought help from the guidance counselor.

Rejected Remedial Alternatives

1 The counselor could meet with the students and discuss their class-room deportment.

2 The counselor could refer the children to the school psychologist, who could test the children and confirm the observation that the children were disruptive.

3 The counselor could suggest to the teacher that since the youngsters were just entering junior high school, they were going through a difficult adjustment period and that they would eventually learn to "iron out" their problems for themselves.

Implemented Behavioral Solution

Definition and Measurement of Behaviors   A student teacher kept a record of the number of talking-out and out-of-seat behaviors for the entire class during the forty-five-minute mathematics period each day. A talking-out incident was noted whenever a student called out in class or spoke to a classmate at an inappropriate time. Out-of-seat behavior consisted of any incident in which a student left his desk without permission.

Procedure and Results   After the problem was referred to the counselor, the teacher and counselor met to discuss an in-class strategy to remediate the management problems. During the initial five days of the study, the teacher responded to misbehaviors in her usual manner. No special efforts were made to curtail the problem behaviors. Figure 4-8 indicates that during Baseline$_1$ there were between twenty-three and forty-four misbehaviors per period, with an average of thirty-three.

In the second phase of the study, the teacher implemented a procedure which she had jointly devised with the counselor. The teacher told the students

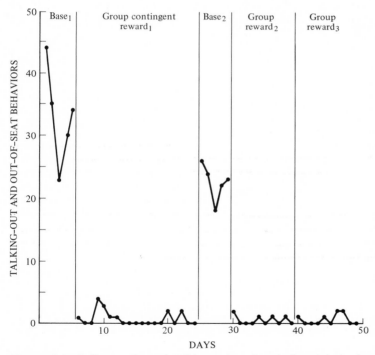

Figure 4-8 Daily number of talking-out and out-of-seat behaviors for twenty-seven seventh-grade students during mathematics period. *(From J. W. Willis, T. R. Hobbs, D. G. Kirkpatrick, and K. W. Manley, "Training Counselors as Researchers in the Natural Environment," in E. Ramp and G. Semb (eds.),* Behavior Analysis: Areas of Research and Application, *Englewood Cliffs, N.J.: Prentice-Hall, 1975, p. 180. By permission of the publishers.)*

that if the entire class refrained from talking-out and out-of-seat behaviors during the initial fifteen minutes of class, all students could have a five-minute break at the end of class. During this time they were free to talk, relax, and eat a snack if they wished. After one week, the amount of time that the children were required to behave properly was increased to twenty minutes, during the third week it was increased to thirty minutes, and during the fourth week to forty minutes. The amount of break time was always five minutes. Misbehaviors decreased immediately and drastically. On twelve of the twenty days of "Group Contingent Reward$_1$," there were no misbehaviors, and the average for the phase was less than one per period.

During a five-day Baseline$_2$ period, the children could no longer earn a break for behaving appropriately, and the number of misbehaviors increased to twenty-two per period. During "Group Contingent Reward$_2$," the students could again earn a five-minute break for refraining from talking-out and out-of-seat behaviors for forty minutes; inappropriate behaviors decreased to a mean of 0.8 per period. In the final stage of the study, the teacher told the students that they would receive a reward on only a portion of the days that they met their criterion. On a given day the teacher did not tell them whether they would be having a break until the final five minutes of class. On the average, reinforcement occurred about once a week, and the target behaviors remained at less than one per period.

Highlights

1   The authors pointed out that the approach that they used differed from that typically employed by guidance counselors. Traditionally, counselors have proceeded on the assumption that the remediation of management problems occurs when the counselor and client develop a warm, open, and trusting relationship. Although there is no reason to object to developing a warm relationship between counselor and student, there is also no reason to believe that such an occurrence will generally be functional in causing a favorable behavior change in the classroom. The approach used in the present study was to work directly with the problem in the classroom setting by devising a procedure that was likely to bring about behavior change. If the technique had been ineffective, it would have been the *joint* responsibility of the counselor and teacher to devise an appropriate alternative.

2   The authors also pointed out that a distinction between the present approach and the traditional one is that the counselor set objective criteria for determining whether her tactic was successful or not. If the children continued to misbehave at an unacceptable level, this fact would have been known to her and the teacher, and she could *not* have been satisfied with the results. This contrasts with the approach of the traditional counselor, who uses vague, subjective criteria such as the development of rapport between herself and the client to measure progress. The *absence* of objective data for assessment purposes permits a counselor to choose a procedure on the basis of personal preference rather than what is demonstrably beneficial to the student.

Reference   Willis, Hobbs, Kirkpatrick, and Manley (1975, Study 1).

Situation 8: Inappropriate Talking and Turning in a High School Class

Background   Walking into a classroom of high school students can be both an exciting and a frightening experience. High school youngsters tend to be enthusiastic when engaging in particular activities, suspicious of adults, and uncertain of their futures. Teachers of high school students will often modify their own behavior so as to be socially acceptable to the students. Thus, some teachers will conduct "rap" sessions with groups of youths in order to develop rapport with them. Others will join them in athletics during the lunch period or after school hours. Still others will spend a great deal of time counseling the youngsters on personal problems.

Developing good social relationships might be important in educating students effectively. Nevertheless, high school teachers should not lose sight of the fact that one of their primary responsibilities is to provide academic instruction in their classrooms. Thus, when they encounter classroom problems, the teachers should not dismiss the difficulties as irrelevant, nor should they assume that because of their ages, behavior modification procedures will be ineffective with high school youths.

Problem   The youngsters in the study were twenty-five students in a low-track, eleventh- and twelfth-grade English class. About 80 percent of them came from lower-class families, with the remainder coming from middle-class homes. The teacher reported that she had considerable difficulty in maintaining classroom control and that most students were doing poorly in their academic work.

Rejected Remedial Alternatives

1   The teacher could give the students a lecture, admonishing them to change their ways or else face a bleak future.
2   The teacher could consider the students' misbehaviors to be a natural result of their "insecurity" and make no direct attempt at remediation.
3   The teacher could attempt no intervention so as not to imperil her social acceptance by them.

Implemented Behavioral Solution
Definition and Measurement of the Behaviors   Talking-out behaviors and inappropriate turning behaviors were selected as targets for modification. "Talking out" consisted of vocal behavior by a student without teacher permission, except during group discussions. "Inappropriate turning" involved incidents in which a seated student turned more than 90° from the position of facing the front of the room. There were various situations in which turning was permitted and, in these cases, the behavior was *not* counted as inappropriate. The teacher kept a record of the behaviors by using interval recording, with

intervals of one minute. She was aided by a large wall clock whose minute hand moved in one-minute segments.

Procedure and Results During baseline the teacher kept a record of inappropriate talking and turning behaviors. The teacher did not receive any instructions on how to curtail the problem behaviors, nor were any restrictions placed on the types of management techniques she could use. The data in Figure 4-9 indicate that, for the twenty-seven days of baseline, talking-out

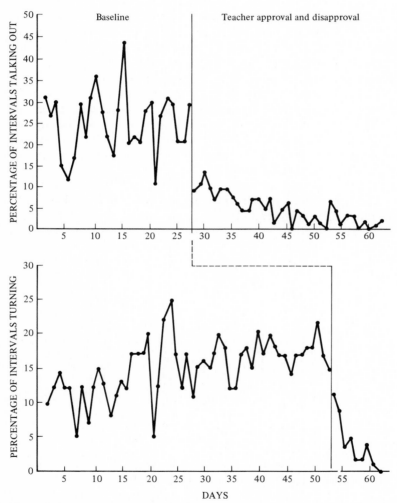

Figure 4-9 Percentage of intervals of talking out and inappropriate turning by twenty-five high school students in English class. *(Adapted from L. W. McAllister, J. G. Stachowiak, D. M. Baer, and L. Conderman, "The Application of Operant Conditioning Techniques in a Secondary School Classroom,"* Journal of Applied Behavior Analysis, **2***, p. 281, 1969. By permission of the publishers.)*

behaviors were occurring during a mean of 25 percent of the intervals, whereas inappropriate turning was occurring during a mean of 15 percent of the one-minute intervals.

On the first day of the "Teacher Approval and Disapproval" phase, the teacher used a combination of procedures to reduce talking-out behaviors. Whenever a student talked out, she made a direct verbal statement of reproof, in which the misbehaving student was identified. Typical comments were: "John, be quiet," "Jane, stop talking," "Phil, shut up!" When all students were quiet, the teacher made a statement praising the entire class. Examples of the comments were: "Thank you for not talking!" or "I'm delighted to see you so quiet today!" Since baseline data indicated that a large number of the misbehaviors occurred during the first two minutes of each class, the teacher praised the students very frequently during this period of time if they were well behaved. The teacher was instructed to refrain from threatening the students with consequences such as keeping them after school if they were disruptive.

The combination of procedures used during Teacher Approval and Disapproval reduced the level of talking-out behavior on the first day of the phase. The behavior decreased steadily during the remaining days of the phase and reached a mean level of 5 percent. The authors used a multiple-baseline design. After the Teacher Approval and Disapproval procedure was seen to be clearly effective with talking-out behavior, the teacher applied it to inappropriate turning behaviors. Beginning on day 53, the teacher complimented all students when they were not turned around and criticized individual students who were turned 90° or more. The procedure reduced the misbehavior until it reached a mean of 4 percent for the phase.

Highlights

1 There are probably no procedures that are more common than reprimanding individual students for misbehaving and praising a group of students for behaving well. Yet the present study showed that when a teacher systematically used these tactics with two isolated behaviors, she was able to bring about a high degree of control with one of the most difficult groups of all—a large class of rambunctious high school students.

2 The teacher used a combination of approval for appropriate behavior and disapproval for inappropriate behavior. Since the two procedures were used simultaneously, it is impossible to determine the contribution of each tactic in producing the desired effect. From a scientific point of view, it would have been better if the teacher had used each procedure separately and then, if necessary, had used both approval and disapproval.

3 There are two additional aspects of the procedure that are important. First, the teacher most often applied the social consequences during the first two minutes of the period. This was done because the authors had obtained objective data which indicated that during this interval most of the problems were occurring. Without such data this critical point might have been missed. Secondly, the teacher did not make threats that she could not carry out. When teachers commit this error, students quickly learn the meaninglessness of such statements and teacher effectiveness decreases.

Reference   McAllister, Stachowiak, Baer, and Conderman (1969).

ACADEMIC PROBLEMS

Situation 9: Poor Attention and Reading Performance

Background   Problems in developing adequate reading skills seem to occur regardless of geographic, socioeconomic, or intellectual factors. Black children, white children, urban children, suburban children, rural children, retarded children, and intellectually gifted children (for example, young Thomas Edison) all have representatives who exhibit reading difficulties. The fact that reading problems are widespread and have always existed, however, does not mean that teachers have a vast arsenal of techniques for dealing with such difficulties. Some reading journals are of little assistance because they concentrate on discussions of the correlates of reading difficulties or describe a variety of philosophical issues. In other cases, educational researchers have devised excellent procedures for dealing with reading problems, but teachers either are unaware of the discoveries or find the techniques difficult to implement. Thus, teachers who encounter youngsters with reading problems often find themselves in the position of having to devise their own procedures to remediate reading deficiences.

Problem   The youngster involved in the study was Danny, a nine-year-old, white, middle-class boy of average intelligence who was having considerable difficulty with reading. During the previous year and a half he received thirty minutes of one-to-one reading instruction each day in a special education class. In spite of the tutoring sessions, Danny had made only a three-month gain in reading level during the eighteen previous months, according to the Stanford Achievement Test (S.A.T.).

Ms. Mary D'Ippolito, Danny's teacher, reported that the youngster performed well when he was "in the mood." Unfortunately, he was seldom "in the mood." During a typical reading lesson, the child might argue with the teacher that the work was too hard, sit sullenly—refusing to read at all—or accuse other children of keeping him from doing his work. On such days Ms. D'Ippolito would try to cajole Danny into participating and often deprived him of such privileges as recess and movies when he did not cooperate. The youngster would also refuse to complete independent reading assignments, claiming that he did not understand what he was supposed to do. In contrast, when Danny was in a "good mood," he read well and completed independent assignments in a minimal amount of time.

Rejected Remedial Alternatives

1 The teacher could refer the child for psychological examination to determine whether emotional factors were interfering with Danny's learning progress.

2 The child could receive a neurological examination to determine whether a physiological factor such as brain damage was correlated with the reading problem.

3 The teacher could increase the amount of reading tutoring she gave to Danny.

Procedure and Results

Definition and Measurement of Behaviors Ms. D'Ippolito kept track of Danny's attending and reading behaviors. She measured attending behavior every five minutes, using a time-sampling procedure. "Attending behavior" was defined as orientation toward the reading lesson and included the following behaviors:

1 Looking at the blackboard when the teacher was illustrating a rule
2 Reading orally when requested
3 Looking at the workpad when Ms. D'Ippolito was pointing out mistakes or giving directions
4 Making workpad corrections
5 Correcting words he had misread in the text
6 Attempting to sound out words

Following each reading session, Ms. D'Ippolito asked Danny ten questions based on the content of the material he had just read. After Danny wrote the answers to the questions on his workpad, the teacher graded the paper and kept a record of the number of answers that were correct.

Procedure and Results Each day Danny read from six to ten pages in the *Palo Alto Reading Program: Sequential Steps in Reading* (1968). The reading materials are structured in such a manner that a student gradually builds up the skills requisite to being a competent reader. During Baseline$_1$, Ms. D'Ippolito reminded Danny to stay on task and to complete his written assignments but programmed no new contingencies for his reading performance. The top portion of Figure 4-10 indicates that during Baseline$_1$ Danny was attending to the reading assignment a mean of 42 percent of the time. The bottom section shows that he averaged 3.4 questions correct. On the seventh day of the study, Ms. D'Ippolito instituted a token reinforcement system in which Danny could earn tokens according to the following terms:

1 token for every sentence read without errors
1 token for sounding out a word without teacher assistance

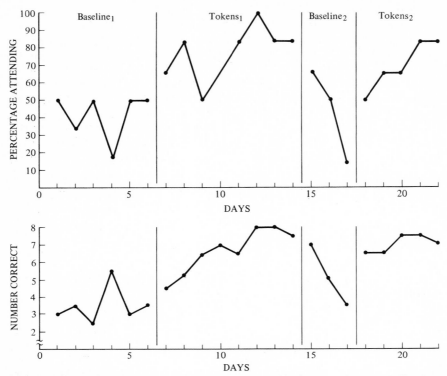

Figure 4-10 The top graph depicts the percentage of time Danny spent attending to reading assignments, whereas the bottom graph depicts the number of questions he answered correctly after reading six to ten pages. *(From M. Price and M. D'Ippolito, "The Effects and Side Effects of a Token Reinforcement System on Reading Behavior. Unpublished manuscript, Temple University, 1975. By permission of the authors.)*

2 tokens for every correctly written response on his workpad
5 tokens for completing the reading of each page in the textbook
10 tokens for answering correctly eight or more of the teacher's ten comprehension questions

The price of each of the back-up reinforcers was arranged in such a manner that Danny could spend the points he earned each day for a relatively small reward or save his points until a later date, at which time he could purchase a reinforcer of greater magnitude. The cost of each back-up reinforcer is listed below:

50 tokens for fifteen minutes of free time
100 tokens for a grab from a grab bag containing toys and trinkets
200 tokens for time to play any game of his choice with the teacher and two classmates
300 tokens for a Coke break with the teacher's aide in the cafeteria

> 400 tokens for a day without any reading seatwork
> 600 tokens for a day without any seatwork at all

The token reinforcement procedure produced an immediate and large increase in Danny's attending behavior and a more gradual but substantial improvement in his performance on the comprehension questions. During "Tokens$_1$," the mean rate of attending showed a gain of 25 percent over Baseline$_1$ levels. The number of questions answered correctly increased steadily for the eight-day Tokens$_1$ phase, reaching a mean which was 31 percent greater than Baseline$_1$.

When the reinforcement procedure was discontinued during Baseline$_2$, the levels of both attending behavior and comprehension questions correct decreased, but high levels were regained during the "Tokens$_2$" phase.

Highlights

1   In the present study Danny received reinforcement for a variety of reading behaviors, and substantial improvements occurred. It is interesting to note that a large increase in attending rate also took place, even though there was no consequence on attending behavior. In other words, when the token reinforcement procedure was in effect, Danny found it worthwhile to discontinue his arguments and off-task behavior and concentrated instead on performing the reading assignments.

2   Some readers might object to the fact that two of the privileges used as back-up reinforcers involved release from reading activities. It could be argued that Danny was, therefore, spending less time on reading than was necessary. Additional data from his performance on the S.A.T. argues against this concern. During the school year in which the study was conducted, Danny made slightly over a year's gain on the S.A.T.; this compares with the three-month gain during the previous eighteen months. Hence, it appeared that the amount of *effort* Danny made on the reading assignments was more important than the amount of *time* he spent on the activities (within certain limits, of course).

Reference   Price and D'Ippolito (1975).

Situation 10: Poor Creative Writing Skills

Background   Teachers have always accepted the notion that it was possible for them to intervene effectively when students created management problems, such as talking-out behavior, out-of-seat behavior, and aggressiveness toward others. Similarly, they have implemented techniques which were intended to correct certain academic problems, such as poor reading, spelling, and arithmetic. There are other student problems in which teachers have been less inclined to intervene. Thus, when a youngster has difficulty with artwork, musical skills, or other creative endeavors, including composition writing, teachers have often considered the problems to result from a lack of natural talent in the relevant areas. As a result, students with certain types of deficiencies have not always benefited from the remedial talents of their teachers because efforts in their behalf were regarded as futile. The present study, to the contrary, shows that with careful analysis of the target behavior, educators can lend their skills to enhancing the creative writing behaviors of students.

Problem   The students in the study were twenty-one second graders who were given a composition to write each afternoon. Teacher records indicated that the students tended to write sentences with few words and that the quality of their output was poor.

Rejected Remedial Alternatives

1   Conclude that good writers are born and not made.
2   Assume that as the children grow older and their language development increases, they will improve their creative writing abilities.
3   Hire an expert to give the teachers a workshop in training writing skills.

Implemented Behavioral Solution
Assignments and Measurements of Behavior   Before the study began, the teacher made a list of topics which she considered to be of approximately equal difficulty. The topics were then placed in random order and from them a theme was chosen for each day's assignment. At the beginning of the composition period, the teacher wrote the topic on the board and asked the children to write a composition on the designated subject. After ten minutes the teacher collected all papers.

Two types of student output were measured in the study. The first was the number of words the students wrote each day, with nonsensical or repetitive sentences excluded from the word count. An example of a repetitive sentence would be, "Bob ate. Mary ate. Mommy ate." The second behavior was the quality of the youngsters' compositions. The compositions were judged according to five criteria: (*a*) mechanical aspects, such as length, spelling, grammar, and punctuation; (*b*) vocabulary, variety, and word usage; (*c*) number of ideas; (*d*) development of ideas; (*e*) internal consistency of the composition. Students could receive from zero to five points for each component, with a maximum possible total of twenty-five points. The judge of the quality of the papers was a graduate language major. She was not aware of the fact that she was grading papers for an experiment, but was simply instructed to rate the quality of the papers according to the system described above.

Procedure and Results   During Baseline$_1$ the teacher gave the students a composition to write each afternoon. They were instructed to write as many words as they could and to try to avoid writing repetitious sentences. She then gave the students some examples of repetitive sentences. At the end of ten minutes the teacher informed the students that it was time to move on to other activities and that they should hand in their papers. The graduate student graded the papers but did not return them to the students.

Figure 4-11 indicates that during the five-day Baseline₁ phase, the students averaged about thirty words per ten-minute session. The quality ratings (not shown) averaged about six out of a possible total of twenty-five. On the first day of the second phase of the study, the teacher showed the children a chart displaying the maximum number of words each of them had written on all compositions during the previous five days. She also informed the students that she would be timing them for ten minutes on future compositions. The teacher stated that the object of this would be to see if they could beat their own previous high score. After the composition period had expired, the teacher counted each student's words and placed the total at the top of his paper. On the following day and for all succeeding days, the scores on the chart were changed whenever a student exceeded his previous high score. Hence, if a student's previous high had been seventy-two words, and on a given day he wrote a composition of seventy-eight words, the number next to his name on the chart would be changed from a "72" to a "78."

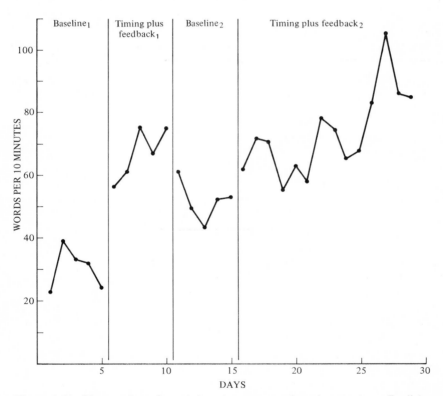

Figure 4-11   The number of words twenty-one second graders wrote on English composition assignments. *(From R. Van Houten, E. Morrison, R. Jarvis, and M. McDonald, "The Effects of Explicit Timing and Feedback on Compositional Response Rate in Elementary School Children,"* Journal of Applied Behavior Analysis, **7**, *p. 551, 1974. By permission of the publishers.)*

The prospect of exceeding their own scores apparently motivated the students to greater heights. On the first day of "Timing and Feedback$_1$," the youngsters more than doubled their Baseline$_1$ average for words written per minute, with the scores increasing during the remaining days of the phase. The quality of the students' work was two times as great as the Baseline$_1$ rate. When the procedure was discontinued during Baseline$_2$, the number of words written and the quality of the compositions decreased somewhat, but these again increased during the "Timing and Feedback$_2$" phase.

Highlights

1 An important aspect of the investigation was the demonstration that, with careful analysis, behavioral procedures can be applied to behaviors which are difficult to define and which some have considered *not* amenable to modification.

2 A second important element of the study is the actual procedure the authors employed. Unlike many of the other studies to which I have referred, the motivation for improvement was *not* a tangible reward or a desired privilege. Rather, it was the goal of beating one's own previous performances and the immediate feedback provided by the teacher. It is my opinion that too many behavior modifiers (including myself) are apt to employ goodies and privileges as reinforcers before determining whether easily programmed factors such as immediate feedback are effective. Of course, if a feedback procedure is ineffective, alternative procedures, such as the use of tangible reinforcers, should be considered.

3 In the present study students received feedback on the number of words they used in each composition. As the *quantity* of words increased, the *quality* of the compositions improved. Had this not been the case, it might have been necessary to make the quality of the students' work a target for modification.

4 Some additional aspects of the study are worth mentioning. The teacher of the class reported an improved "attitude" toward composition writing on the part of the students and a decrease in disruptiveness during the "timing and feedback" stages. Also observed was increased social interaction by the students just before and after the assignment. The interactions appeared to center around the posted scores. The teacher further noted that the students made enthusiastic comments, such as, "Hey, I beat my score!" and "Look what I got!"

Reference   Van Houten, Morrison, Jarvis, and McDonald (1974).

Situation 11: Digit Reversal Behavior

Background   It is not unusual to discover schoolchildren who reverse the formation of letters (for example, "p" for "q" or "b" for "d") or the order of multiple-digit numbers (for example, "21" for "12"). Children who consistently reverse letters or digits will often be referred for psychological examination and receive the classification of "learning disabled." The diagnosis implies the existence of a neurological irregularity resulting in perceptual disorders. Many such children will then receive perceptual-motor exercises in the hope that the activities will remediate their perceptual problems and that the reversal behaviors will be eliminated. In other cases the children will be placed in a resource room where a special-education teacher provides the students with individualized tutoring and encourages them to write the letters or numbers correctly.

Both of the above approaches are commendable in their intention to help children overcome their difficulties. It should be understood, however, that the youngsters are receiving extra help after making academic errors. If the children enjoy the special attention, it is possible that their errors are being reinforced with the extra attention, thereby making it likely that they will continue to make the errors in the future. The feasiblity of such an occurrence is well illustrated in the present study.

Problem   The youngster in the study was Bob, an eight-year-old boy considered academically capable by his teacher and parents. His problem was that he almost invariably reversed the order of digits when adding numbers, resulting in a two-digit sum (for example, he would write: $18 + 7 = 52$). As a result, Bob received a great deal of extra help, but the extra attention failed to correct the problem.

Rejected Remedial Alternatives

1   As indicated above, the student could receive a psychological examination to determine whether he should be labeled "learning disabled."
2   The teacher could refer Bob for neurological and visual examinations.
3   The youngster could be placed in a class for learning-disabled children.

Implemented Behavioral Solution
Assignments   Each day the teacher gave Bob twenty addition problems in which the correct answer consisted of a two-digit sum (for example, $47 + 39$). Numbers resulting in a sum of 10 or composed of two identical digits (for example, $33 + 66$) were not used. The twenty problems that Bob received varied from one day to the next.

Procedure and Results   Each day Bob would raise his hand when he finished his twenty arithmetic problems, and his teacher would grade his paper. During the seven-day Baseline$_1$ phase, the teacher placed a "C" on all correct answers. She marked an "X" on all digit-reversals and told him, "This one is incorrect. You see (*pointing*), you reversed the numbers in the answer." After grading all answers, the teacher gave Bob "extra help" with the answers he had reversed. The "extra help" consisted of going through the adding process with all reversals and using verbal hints and physical prompts to assist Bob in obtaining the correct answers. In spite of the teacher's efforts, Figure 4-12

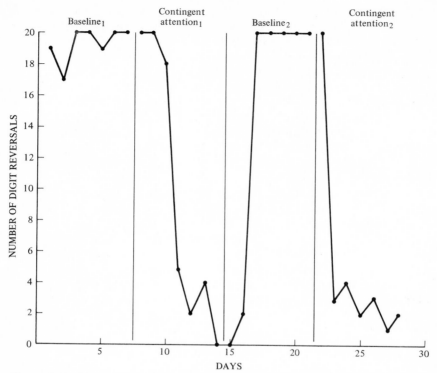

Figure 4-12 The number of two-digit numbers an eight-year-old boy reversed on daily twenty-problem addition assignments. *(From J. E. Hasazi and S. E. Hasazi, "Effects of Teacher Attention on Digit-Reversal Behavior in an Elementary-School Child,"* Journal of Applied Behavior Analysis, **5,** *p. 160, 1972. By permission of the publishers.)*

reveals that Bob reversed the order of numbers at an extremely high rate. During four of the seven Baseline₁ days, he reversed all twenty answers; on two days he reversed nineteen answers and on one day he reversed eighteen answers.

The authors suspected that the extra attention that Bob received for reversing numbers amounted to a reward for making errors. They even conjectured that placing "X" on the reversed digits was reinforcing to Bob because it let him know that he would be receiving special help. The teacher, therefore, ceased using "X's" and instead placed a "C" on all answers, *even if they were reversed.* When the answer was correct, however, the teacher smiled at Bob, patted him on the back, and made a comment such as, "This one is very good." The teacher said nothing to Bob if the answer was reversed and discontinued all forms of "extra help." During the first three days of "Contigent Attention₁," Bob continued to reverse almost all of his answers. On the fourth day of the phase, however, the number of reversals decreased to five and went down to lower levels during the remaining three days of the stage.

The number of errors Bob made increased when the teacher again gave him "extra help" for making mistakes, but rapidly decreased when she returned to giving him attention only for the correct answers.

Highlights

1   The results of the present study should not be interpreted as a condemnation of the practice of providing students with individualized attention when they experience academic difficulties. Undoubtedly, many specialized programs have been of great benefit to handicapped children. Rather, as the authors pointed out, teachers must be careful not to accidentally reinforce academically inappropriate behavior by giving children attention only after they make mistakes.

2   The teacher in the present study had several hints that Bob was capable of writing the digits in the correct order. First, he could easily discriminate numbers such as 27 and 72. Second, he often pointed to reversed answers on his paper, when the teacher failed to detect them. Finally, on several occasions the teacher observed Bob erasing correctly ordered sums and reversing the order of the digits. Hence, there was much evidence before the study began that Bob was capable of performing the correct behavior, but that he could attain a greater amount of attention by making mistakes.

Reference   Hasazi and Hasazi (1972).

Situation 12: Poor Spelling Performance

Background   Teaching spelling to children can be a frustrating task for teachers. The English language is replete with silent consonants, silent vowels, and letters that sound one way in one word and another way in a different word. Hence, teachers who attempt to teach spelling with sets of rules will feel as if there are as many rules as there are words to teach. Another problem in teaching spelling is the fact that children often find the task a boring one. Teachers will sometimes strain to conduct a spelling lesson while their students yawn at them or become distracted with other tasks.

It is, therefore, not unusual for people to go through their entire adult lives repeatedly making the same spelling errors, to the amazement, annoyance, or amusement of other adults. Nevertheless, my opinion is that, with certain populations, spelling is a relatively easy behavior to improve. Correct and incorrect responses are easily defined and it is usually not necessary to use a complicated procedure, such as fading or chaining, with children of normal intelligence who are at the third-grade level or above. My experience indicates that what is usually needed with such populations is an effective motivational system that will encourage the children to work harder on their spelling assignments. The present study is in support of this notion.

Problem   The case involved twenty-four fourth-grade children, most of whom were doing poorly in spelling. Seven of the students had repeated one grade and the group as a whole had a median IQ of 99. Once each week the students took a spelling test during a thirty-minute period. The teacher used eighteen-word spelling lists taken from *Spelling Growth, Grade 4* (Mason & Hudson, 1967).

Rejected Remedial Alternatives

1   The teacher could be complacent about the problem on the assumption that "Spelling is not really as important as other academic subjects."

2   The teacher could require the children to repeatedly write the words they spelled incorrectly on the weekly spelling tests.

3   The teacher could send notes home asking the parents to make certain that their youngsters learned their spelling words.

Procedure and Results   Each Tuesday the teacher gave the students a new eighteen-word spelling list and tested the children on the words the next week. Following the test the teacher announced the names of all the students who received a 100 percent score on the test. During the four-week $Baseline_1$ period, an average of 24 percent of the children had perfect papers. In the second phase of the study, the teacher made a list of the childrens' favorite jobs and privileges. These included washing the chalkboards, emptying the waste baskets, being captain of the gym teams, and so on. The teacher informed the students that any child who received 100 percent on a test would be able to perform one of his favorite jobs that afternoon. During the five-week "Jobs $Contingent_1$" stage, 65 percent of the children received 100 percent on their weekly spelling tests—an increase of 40 percent over $Baseline_1$. When the jobs contingency was removed during the three-week $Baseline_2$ phase, the number of children with perfect papers decreased to 30 percent, but it went up to 60 percent when the positive reinforcement procedure was reinstated.

Highlights

1   The fact that the teacher in the present study was able to bring about such great gains in spelling, with a relatively simple behavior modification program, should encourage other teachers to attempt similar procedures.

2   I have one major reservation concerning the procedure used in the present study. Setting a criterion of 100 percent accuracy for reinforcement may be too difficult for some children. As a result, if a youngster is initially spelling 50 percent of the words accurately and increases his weekly scores without reaching 100 percent, he may eventually cease his efforts to improve spelling performance because he does not receive the reinforcers. I believe that a better system would be to set individual criteria according to $Baseline_1$ scores. Hence, a student with a $Baseline_1$ average of 75 percent might have a criterion of 90 percent, whereas a child with a $Baseline_1$ mean of 40 percent might have a 50 or 55 percent criterion. If the children consistently meet their individual criteria, the teacher can gradually increase the accuracy level required for attaining reinforcement. (Shape! Shape! Shape!)

Reference   Christie (1971).

Situation 13: Decreasing Disruptiveness by Increasing Academics

Background   There are at least two behavioral approaches to remediating classroom discipline problems. The more common one has been illustrated numerous times earlier in the book. It involves directly attaching a consequence to a behavior such that the inappropriate behavior decreases in rate. Thus, a teacher might punish a student's talking-out behaviors or, alternatively, reinforce him when he does not talk out. Although the direct approach is undoubtedly effective, there are some who object to the tactic. Winett and Winkler (1972) claim, for example, that such a strategy does not necessarily lead to an enhancement in academic performance but instead produces orderly and docile children. Thus, the job of the teacher becomes easier, without always producing a corresponding increase in the student's learning level. Other educators will claim that it is difficult to teach academic subject matter to misbehaving students, and that when inappropriate behavior is reduced, good academic behavior is likely to follow.

The question remains an unresolved one. Meanwhile, teachers who prefer not to directly modify inappropriate behavior might adopt the alternative tactic of modifying academic behavior in such a manner that incompatible discipline problems are likely to diminish. This strategy was used by Price and D'Ippolito (1975; Situation 9 in this chapter), who found that when a reinforcement procedure improved a youngster's reading performance, off-task and complaining behaviors decreased. The present study demonstrates how a similar strategy can be applied to an entire class of students.

Problem   The class consisted of thirty-eight youngsters in a regular fifth-grade classroom. The school was located in an urban area inhabited mainly by upper-middle-class families. Two months after the beginning of the school year, disruption was so severe that a second full-time teacher was added to the classroom. Nevertheless, discipline problems persisted for the next three months, at which point the study began.

Rejected Remedial Alternatives

1   Add a third full-time teacher to the classroom.
2   Place a direct contingency on the inappropriate behaviors.
3   Add a fourth full-time teacher to the classroom.

Implemented Behavioral Solution

Definition and Measurement of the Behavior   In order to simplify the measurement of disruptive behavior, the authors recorded only the behavior of the five children whose behavior was most often inappropriate. The modification procedures, however, were applied to all thirty-eight students. Disruptive behavior consisted of leaving the seat without teacher permission, talking out at times when students were supposed to be working or listening, and physical contact with another student, his desk, or his possessions. The students were rated by means of interval recording, with intervals of ten-second duration. The authors also kept a record of the students' reading performance. The measure of reading performance was the percentage of questions the students answered correctly on daily reading assignments. The test material came from a standard reading workbook and consisted of comprehension, vocabulary, and other reading skills items.

Procedure and Results   During an eight-day Baseline$_1$ stage, the teachers gave the students their daily reading assignments. The students had fifteen minutes to provide written answers to the assignments, with the length of each assignment varying between one and two pages. During this period the students averaged about 48 percent accuracy in reading performance and were disruptive about 40 percent of the time. In the second stage of the study, the teacher used a point (that is, a token) system to improve reading performance. Each student who received a score of 80 percent or greater on his daily reading assignment received two points. Students with 100 percent accuracy were awarded five points. The students could exchange their points according to the following prices:

	Points
Access to game room (15 minutes)	2
Extra recess time (10 minutes)	2
Buy a ditto master	2
Have ditto copies run off (per copy)	1
Review grades in teacher's book	5
Reduce detention (10 minutes)	10
Change cafeteria table	15
Have the lowest test grade removed	20
Become an assistant teacher	Auction
See a movie	6
Have a good-work letter sent to parents	15
Become classroom helper for one week	Auction
Become ball captain for one week	Auction
Do bulletin board	Auction

For the seventeen days in which the point system was in effect, reading accuracy increased to 70 percent—22 percent higher than the Baseline$_1$ level of 48 percent. The return to baseline conditions led to a decrease in reading accuracy and an increase in inappropriate behavior. When the point system was reinstated during the final stage of the study, reading accuracy continually increased, whereas disruptiveness was almost completely eliminated.

Highlights

1   The study reconfirmed the notion that increasing academic performance will sometimes decrease misbehaviors, even if no contingency is directly placed on disruptive behavior. Such a demonstration should not be taken as a blanket endorsement of the practice of reinforcing academic behavior under the assumption that inappropriate behaviors will always decrease to acceptable levels. My supposition is that the more disruptive a classroom is, the more necessary it will be to make direct efforts to eliminate the inappropriate behavior. In some situations the best tactic might be to make direct efforts to increase both academic and on-task behaviors.

2   The reader should again take note of the excellent back-up reinforcers used in the present study. The list consisted of a sufficiently large variety of reinforcers to make it likely that each student would find several of them appealing over a long period of time. In addition, each of the reinforcers was an activity that would involve no financial expenditure on the part of the teacher or the school system.

Reference   Ayllon and Roberts (1974).

Situation 14: Poor Mathematics Performance

Background   Mention the word "math" and 70 percent of the adult population cringes. College students will use distorted logic and make impassioned pleas to their advisors to convince them that mathematics courses are an unnecessary part of their curricula. Secondary school students who have had difficulty with no other courses will struggle fruitlessly with mathematics assignments. Adults who are intelligent in other respects are sometimes observed using their fingers to add single-digit numbers. Somewhere along the line, many people have come to fear and avoid the learning of mathematical operations. It is impossible for me to explain the origin of such problems. Perhaps mathematics teachers have not made sufficient use of shaping principles, or possibly the problem is that human beings receive more practice with verbal tasks than with mathematical tasks. Regardless of the origin(s) of the problem, mathematics is an academic subject that can be learned in much the same manner as other subjects, and teachers will often find that behavioral principles will facilitate the process.

Problem   The pupil in the study was Tom, a thirteen-year-old, seventh-grade boy of average intelligence. Tom's teacher indicated that the youngster frequently failed to attend to his assignments and that he was doing poorly in mathematics. When the teacher gave Tom an academic assignment, it was necessary for her to remind him to do the work, and even after reminders he would work on the assignments for only a few minutes. On the rare occasions when he completed a mathematics assignment, he tended to make numerous errors.

Rejected Remedial Alternatives

1   Abandon efforts to teach the youngster mathematics, on the premise that "Some people have it, and some people don't."

2   Send Tom to a resource-room teacher for additional mathematics training.

3   Work on other academic areas on the assumption that most people "get by" in life with minimal proficiency in mathematics.

Implemented Behavioral Solution

Assignments and Measurement of Behaviors   The teacher set aside a twenty-minute block each day to help Tom with arithmetic achievement. During this period Tom received a worksheet containing twenty randomly selected multiplication problems. The complexity of the problems varied from a one-digit number times a one-digit number (for example, 3×7) to a three-digit number times a three-digit number (for example, 119×541), with every level of complexity in between (for example, 29×7, 173×12, and so on). The authors kept a record of the number of problems Tom answered correctly per minute.

In the initial stage of the study, Tom received his twenty arithmetic problems each day and was instructed to complete as many problems as possible in a twenty-minute period. The teacher corrected the problems and returned them the next day but did not praise Tom if he did well. Figure 4-13 indicates that during Baseline$_1$, Tom averaged less than one-half a problem correct per minute.

In the second phase, the teacher continued to give Tom twenty arithmetic problems but informed him that she would grade them as soon as he was finished or after twenty minutes had expired. When Tom handed in a paper, the teacher immediately graded it and praised Tom for his correct answers. Examples of the praise comments are:

1   "Good work."
2   "Excellent job."
3   "Great! You got fourteen right today."
4   "Since you did so well today, it won't be necessary to have your work checked as often tomorrow."

On the first two days of "Praise + Immediate Feedback$_1$" (days 6 and 7), the teacher graded Tom's paper and praised him according to an FR 2 schedule, that is, after every two problems. On days 8 and 9, the schedule was increased

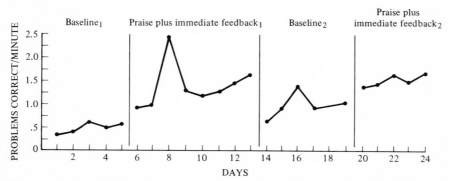

Figure 4-13   The number of problems a seventh-grade boy answered correctly per minute on daily twenty-problem multiplication assignments. *(From F. D. Kirby and F. Shields, "Modification of Arithmetic Response Rate and Attending Behavior in a Seventh-Grade Student,"* Journal of Applied Behavior Analysis, *5, p. 82, 1972. By permission of the publishers.)*

to FR 4. On days 10 and 11 it was FR 8, and on the final two days of the phase it was FR 16. The results indicated that with social reinforcement Tom's rate of correct answers increased to almost three times the Baseline$_1$ rate.

Highlights

1   In the present study, praise was used as a reinforcer for a junior high school boy. When a secondary school teacher employs social reinforcement, she must be careful not to use comments that will embarrass the youngsters in front of their peers. The manner in which social reinforcement is delivered is also critical, and some secondary school teachers might find that an affectionate poke in the ribs or a soft punch on the arm is a more effective reinforcer than a verbal compliment.

2   The authors admitted that in the early stages of Praise + Immediate Feedback$_1$, the teacher had to be in frequent contact with Tom. They pointed out, however, that in the later stages little effort was required of the teacher, since she was reinforcing only one out of every sixteen problems.

3   The reader should note that, although the teacher thinned the schedule of reinforcement from FR 2 to FR 16, there was an increasing trend in Tom's mathematics performance.

Reference   Kirby and Shields (1972).

Situation 15: Poor Spelling Performance

Background   It is a common practice for teachers of spelling to present students with fifteen to twenty-five new words at the beginning of each week. After copying the words in their lesson books, the students are often given homework assignments in which they are required to write a sentence containing each new word. During the week the teachers will usually review the words with the students and conduct additional exercises designed to help the youngsters learn to spell the new words. At the end of the week, the students take a test on all words.

This system has been widespread for many years. Nevertheless, there are at least two aspects of the procedure that may be questioned. First, there is no reason to assume that the students should receive all words at once. When describing the shaping process, the author stressed the importance of increasing the difficulty of the task in small steps. Hence, it is possible that student performance would be better if the youngsters received only a few words a day and concentrated on learning these words before proceeding to new ones. Secondly, giving the students feedback on their spelling performance weekly may not be often enough. Several studies have demonstrated the importance of frequent and immediate feedback in the learning process. Therefore, a system in which students take daily tests might be better than one using weekly tests. The present study examined the weekly spelling test performance of a junior high girl who initially learned spelling words in the traditional manner and then experienced a system in which she received a portion of the words each day and had a daily test on the words.

Problem   The student in the study was Delena, a thirteen-year-old, seventh-grade girl who had a history of poor performance on weekly spelling tests. Her performance on the Wide Range Achievement Test (Jastak, Bijou, and Jastak, 1965) placed her at the third-grade level in spelling. The study was conducted in a junior high language arts classroom.

Rejected Remedial Alternatives   In addition to the alternatives described in Situation 12, the authors rejected the tactic of placing a contingency on spelling improvement.

Implemented Behavioral Solution

Assignment and Measurement of Spelling Performance   The behavior being measured throughout the study was the number of words Delena spelled correctly on weekly twenty-two-word review tests. The words were selected from the seventh-grade *Basic Goals in Spelling* book (Kottmeyer and Claus, 1968).

Procedure and Results   During the initial six weeks of the study, the teacher, Ms. Fran Hathaway, presented twenty-two words to Delena at the beginning of each week. Delena received the words in the same order that they appeared in the back of the spelling book. During the week Delena performed workbook assignments involving the spelling words. At the end of the week, Ms. Hathaway tested Delena on the twenty-two words she received at the beginning of the week. Figure 4-14 indicates that during the six weeks of the "22 Words$_1$" phase, Delena spelled an average of seven words correctly, with a range of one to twelve. In the second stage, Ms. Hathaway divided the twenty-two weekly words into four lists of five and six words. She gave Delena a list of five or six new words each day and tested her on the words the next day. Delena continued to complete assignments from the workbook each day. On the final day of the week, Delena took a review test on all twenty-two words she had received during the week. During the six weeks of the "5 or 6 Words$_1$" phase, Delena averaged nineteen words correct on the weekly review tests. During the two-week "22 Words$_2$" stage, Ms. Hathaway returned to the traditional practice of giving Delena all words at the beginning of the week and testing her at the end of the week. On both occasions the youngster spelled eight words correctly. In the final two-week period of the study, Delena again received five or six new words a day and had a daily test. Her scores on the two tests were twenty-two and twenty words correct.

Highlights

1   The present study did not indicate whether the improvement in spelling during the second and fourth phases was due to the fact that Delena was receiving shorter word lists or that she had more frequent testing. The authors, however, conducted another study with a group of eight fourth graders. The investigation compared giving the students twenty words at the beginning of the week with giving the students five words each day with daily testing and

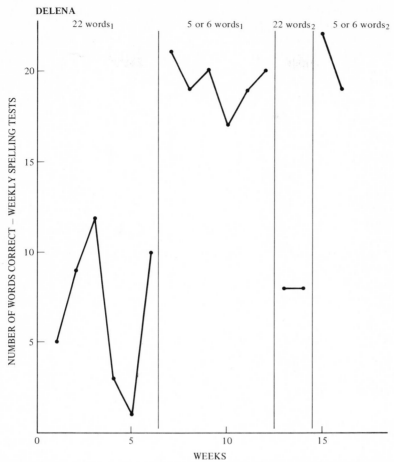

Figure 4-14 The number of words a seventh-grade girl spelled correctly on weekly twenty-two-word spelling tests. *(From H. Rieth, S. Axelrod, R. Anderson, F. Hathaway, K. Wood, and C. Fitzgerald, "Influence of Distributed Practice and Daily Testing on Weekly Spelling Tests,"* Journal of Educational Research, **68**, p. 74, 1974. By permission of the publishers.)*

with giving the students five words a day without daily testing. It was found that the poorest procedure was to give all twenty words at the beginning of the week, and that it was best to give shorter word lists with daily tests.

   2   The reader should note that the study did not make use of any type of contingency. Nevertheless, it was possible to use continuous measurement and a reversal design for the investigation. Such a methodology is usually associated with studies in which contingencies are programmed, but it can also be used to study the effects of a variety of other variables. I previously pointed out how continuous measurement and the reversal design were used to compare different types of seating arrangements. The methodology can also be used to compare the effects of different kinds of reading drills on word recognition (Haupt, Magee, Axelrod, and Cobden, in press), to compare the effects of different types of play materials on cooperative play (Quilitch and Risley, 1973), and to investigate almost any other variable of educational relevance.

Reference   Rieth, Axelrod, Anderson, Hathaway, Wood, and Fitzgerald (1974).

REFERENCES

Ayllon, T., and M. D. Roberts: "Eliminating Discipline Problems by Strengthening Academic Performance," *Journal of Applied Behavior Analysis*, **7**, 71–76, 1974.

Bodnar, K.: "Reducing Talk Outs in an MR Class with a Token Reinforcement System." Unpublished manuscript, Temple University, 1974.

Broden, M., R. V. Hall, A. Dunlap, and R. Clark: "Effects of Teacher Attention and a Token Reinforcement System in a Junior High Special Education Class," *Exceptional Children*, **36**, 341–349, 1970.

Christie, L. S.: "Improving Spelling Accuracy for a Fourth-Grade Class," in. E. A. Ramp and B. L. Hopkins (eds.), *A New Direction for Education: Behavior Analysis—1971* (Lawrence, Kans.: Support and Development Center for Follow Through, Department of Human Development, University of Kansas, 1971), pp. 164–166.

Hasazi, J. E., and S. E. Hasazi: "Effects of Teacher Attention on Digit-Reversal Behavior in an Elementary School Child," *Journal of Applied Behavior Analysis*, **5**, 157–162, 1972.

Haupt, E. J., J. W. Magee, S. Axelrod, and M. Cobden: "Rapid Reduction of Graphically Similar Substitution Errors in Oral Reading with a Drill Procedure." In press.

Jastak, J. F., S. W. Bijou, and S. R. Jastak: *Wide Range Achievement Test* (Wilmington, Del.: Guidance Associates, 1965).

Kirby, F. D., and F. Shields: "Modification of Arithmetic Response Rate and Attending Behavior in a Seventh-Grade Student," *Journal of Applied Behavior Analysis*, **5**, 79–84, 1972.

Kottmeyer, W., and A. Claus: *Basic Goals in Spelling* (New York: McGraw-Hill, 1968).

Madakacherry, P.: "Reducing Wetting, Isolate Play, and Thumbsucking by a Preschool Child." Unpublished manuscript, Temple University, 1974.

Mason, C., and J. Hudson: *Spelling Growth—Grade 4* (Oklahoma City, Okla.: Economy Co., 1967).

McAllister, L. W., J. G. Stachowiak, D. M. Baer, and L. Conderman: "The Application of Operant Conditioning Techniques in a Secondary School Classroom," *Journal of Applied Behavior Analysis*, **2**, 277–285, 1969.

Muller, A. J., S. E. Hasazi, M. M. Pierce, and J. E. Hasazi: "Modification of Disruptive Behavior in a Large Group of Elementary School Students," in E. Ramp and G. Semb (eds.), *Behavior Analysis: Areas of Research and Application* (Englewood Cliffs, N.J.: Prentice-Hall, 1975), pp. 269–276.

Palo Alto Reading Program: Sequential Steps in Reading (New York: Harcourt, Brace, and World, 1968).

Price, M., and M. D'Ippolito: "The Effects and Side Effects of a Token Reinforcement System on Reading Behavior." Unpublished manuscript, Temple University, 1975.

Quilitch, H. R., and T. R. Risley: "The Effects of Play Materials on Social Play," *Journal of Applied Behavior Analysis*, **6**, 573–578, 1973.

Rieth, H., S. Axelrod, R. Anderson, R. Hathaway, K. Wood, and C. Fitzgerald: "Influence of Distributed Practice and Daily Testing on Weekly Spelling Tests," *Journal of Educational Research*, **68**, 73–77, 1974.

Schutte, R. C., and B. L. Hopkins: "The Effects of Teacher Attention on Following Instructions in a Kindergarten Class," *Journal of Applied Behavior Analysis*, **3**, 117–122, 1970.

Van Houten, R., E. Morrison, R. Jarvis, and M. McDonald: "The Effects of Explicit Timing and Feedback on Compositional Response Rate in Elementary School Children," *Journal of Applied Behavior Analysis*, **7**, 547–555, 1974.

Willis, J. W., T. R. Hobbs, D. G. Kirkpatrick, and K. W. Manley: "Training Counselors as Researchers in the Natural Environment," in E. Ramp and G. Semb (eds.), *Behavior Analysis: Areas of Research and Application* (Englewood Cliffs, N.J.: Prentice-Hall, 1975), pp. 175–186.

Winett, R. A., and R. C. Winkler: "Current Behavior Modification in the Classroom: Be Still, Be Quiet, Be Docile," *Journal of Applied Behavior Analysis*, **5**, 499–504, 1972.

Chapter 5

Commonly Asked Questions About Behavior Modification and One Person's Answers

Prospective and practicing teachers often feel uncomfortable about the idea of using behavior modification procedures in their classrooms. This is hardly surprising since most teachers attend or have graduated from programs in which the doctrines of theorists such as Freud, Dewey, and Piaget were emphasized. As a result some teachers hesitate or refuse to use behavior modification procedures because they feel these are treating a surface problem rather than the real one; or they feel that they are bribing children who should be inherently motivated toward success; or they feel that they are being manipulative, when a more natural course would likely solve an existing problem. These concerns are understandable, and during my early exposure to behavioral principles I have experienced many of the same doubts and anxieties. This final chapter presents eleven questions commonly asked about behavior modification and provides the author's response to each question. The reader should note that the author is expressing his own opinion on each of the subjects, although he has made use of the comments of other authors in the field.

ISN'T REINFORCING CHILDREN THE SAME THING AS BRIBING THEM?

If I had kept track of the number of times I have been asked this question, I would have worn out three wrist counters by now. The problem is that many teachers (and other adults) do not feel comfortable reinforcing children "for what they're supposed to do." They feel that learning should be a self-satisfying process and that children should behave properly because it is expected of them. Some educators believe that when teachers reward students, they are artificially motivating them to engage in behaviors for which they should be intrinsically (that is, naturally) motivated. The use of rewards is then seen as a bribe to children for fulfilling their expected roles.

I have several reactions to this criticism, but it is first necessary to determine whether the practice of reinforcement conforms to dictionary definitions of bribery. Webster's (1970) primary definition of bribery is the giving or promising of anything, especially money, "to induce a person to do something illegal or wrong [p. 176]." Other dictionary definitions of bribery also contain the notion that an individual's behavior is being influenced in such a manner that he will perform an immoral act. Clearly, the examples of the reinforcement process presented in this book do not involve immoral behavior. The goals of teaching children to read, spell, perform arithmetic operations, and refrain from aggression are hardly behaviors that can be considered immoral.

Even if the practice of reinforcement does not conform to dictionary definitions of bribery, many teachers still find the process of rewarding children abrasive to their teaching philosophy. They should realize, however, that they themselves work under a reinforcement system. Teachers readily accept their paychecks as payment for their duties and would cease teaching if their checks were not forthcoming. Similarly, teachers are delighted when they receive merit increases, and they enter into collective bargaining with school districts to establish higher pay scales. Teachers are expected to educate effectively, but still they want to be reinforced for their efforts; and they wish to be reinforced, not merely at a subsistence level, but at a level that will afford them the pleasures of life (that is, their M&M's). Risley and Baer (1973) point out that what has developed is a double standard in which adults insist on pay for their work but criticize children for behaving in the same manner. Since children will ultimately have to function under the same capitalist reinforcement system as adults do, one can only wonder what value there is in enforcing the double standard.

Homme (1969) indicates that some adults find it "immoral to reward today's child for doing assignments that earlier generations had to do 'or else' [p. 20]." He points out, however, that youngsters learn better and more willingly if reinforcers are provided for academic achievement; they are enthusiastic about learning and delight in achieving a task and receiving reinforcement; they are not characterized by timidity and aggressiveness as are children being coerced by the "do it or else" standard, nor do they demonstrate the "spoiled" traits of youngsters who receive privileges and treats independently of their behavior. Admittedly, many adults adequately learned academic tasks without the benefit of programmed reinforcement procedures. That does not mean, however, that modern children should be denied superior teaching methods when they become available any more than it means that they should be denied improved dental and medical developments just because their parents survived without them.

It would be a happy state of affairs if all children were naturally motivated to perform academic assignments and to refrain from inappropriate behavior. Unfortunately, experience has shown that often this is not the case. This does not mean that we should abandon our efforts to educate such children. To do so would be to forsake a large segment of our student population. It would also ignore the fact that some academic tasks become self-satisfying only after a reinforcement program has motivated the children to engage in the tasks. It has been found, for example, that some poor readers must initially be motivated by a reinforcement procedure to engage in reading activities. Once accomplished, the reinforcement procedure can often be removed without a decrement in student performance (Axelrod and Piper, 1975).

Horowitz (1975) points out that if children are learning in a classroom using reinforcement procedures, and one criticizes such a practice as a matter of principle and advocates its discontinuation, one should offer alternative techniques which are at least as effective; "Otherwise, one is saying here is something that works, but I don't like it for philosophical reasons, so stop doing it—I don't have anything to substitute for it right now, but when I do I am sure it will be better and will not be philosophically objectionable [pp. 8–9]." She further states that such a position is socially irresponsible and that it is ironic that only those individuals who have greatly benefited from "adequate education have the luxury of opposing educational techniques on theoretical grounds [p. 9]."

WHAT GIVES TEACHERS THE RIGHT TO MODIFY STUDENT BEHAVIOR? BY DOING SO ARE THEY NOT DEPRIVING CHILDREN OF FREEDOM OF CHOICE?

By accepting a position as a teacher, a person has not only a right but an *obligation* to modify student behavior. Children enter the schools without the necessary social and academic skills to function independently and productively in adult society. Since the schools have been entrusted with a large portion of the responsibility for training students in the requisite skills, teachers who do not bring about suitable changes in student behavior are failing to live up to the responsibilities of their profession.

To some teachers the problem of modifying behavior is a semantic one with the term "behavior modification" conjuring up the notion of arbitrarily manipulating other human beings. Such a concern is understandable, but educators should realize that just because they use words such as "guide," "counsel," "enlighten," and "edify," it does not follow that they are not interested in changing behavior. Regardless of the process a guidance counsel-or uses in an attempt to get a youngster to be less pugnacious, he wants to see the pupil's behavior change from hitting other students to not hitting other students. Similarly, a civics teacher who is concerned about the racially bigoted comments of one of her students hopes that her influence will be such that bigoted comments will cease. Again, the teacher is interested in behavior change and in the means of bringing about that change.

Society in general and educators in particular long ago decided to modify the behavior of children; the schools themselves are an enormous behavior modification enterprise (Risley and Baer, 1973). Given that educators accept the appropriateness of modifying student behavior, certain ethical problems must still be dealt with; but these are the same ethical problems that all educators must confront (Morrow and Gochros, 1970). The tasks include decisions on which behaviors should be modified and on the means that teachers will permit themselves to use to bring about behavior change. These decisions should be based on a determination of which behaviors are critical to the present and future well-being of the student and society and an analysis of the most effective procedures for bringing about behavior change.

On the surface it might appear that behavior modification programs have deprived children of certain freedoms, and in one sense they have. Successful behavior modification techniques have deprived children of the freedom to hit their classmates, to destroy their property, and to sit placidly in class without participating in academic activities. In a larger sense, however, effective behavior modification procedures have given children an increased amount of freedom. As children are taught to respect the rights and possessions of other youngsters, many of them become capable of developing friendships that were previously impossible. Self-controlled, the youngsters can choose to spend their free time alone or with other children. Physically destructive children have no choice but to spend most of their free time without playmates.

Similarly, Cohen (1969) points out that illiterate people do not have the freedom to make choices that literate people have. People who can read and write have job opportunities, educational opportunities, and many pleasures of life available to them because of their skills. Illiterate people will find their choices in these areas more limited. Even if successful behavior modification procedures initially deprive children of some freedoms, their ultimate effect is to increase the individual's social and academic choices. The ideal of giving children freedom should not be seen as giving them license of their actions to do "their own thing" at the extreme, without regard to the consequences. Children who fail to meet certain standards of conformity have a great chance of finding themselves in such freedom-depriving establishments as institutions and jails. As adults and teachers we should be aware of these possibilities, and should program short-term contingencies for those behaviors which will ultimately grant children long-term rewards and the freedoms associated with such rewards.

It is important to distinguish freedom from a lack of planning and structure. Kagan (1971) indicates that critics of traditional schools have blamed educational failure on the rigidity of the school system and have proposed that, "If the child were left completely free he would seek the proper intellectual diet. . . . In one class [in which all rules were relaxed] that stands out clearly, almost half a fourth-grade class of middle-class children was seriously behind normal grade level in reading competence. This would not be a tragedy if the students had developed an exciting proficiency in poetry or gymnastics. But they had not. . . . The result was a quiet, almost apathetic classroom [p. 146; cited by Haskett and Lenfestey, 1974]."

In a similar vein, Salzberg (1972) discusses a school system which opposed authoritarian classrooms and adopted the "free-school" model as an alternative. Classes were voluntary, and children had a free run of the school. There were numerous daily and long-term field trips. Children were not coerced into participating in any activities. As the school year progressed, the students did less and less academic work. The children were rude and inconsiderate toward each other and their teachers. There was abuse both to work projects and to the physical well-being of students. The children had acquired one type of freedom at the expense of another. In planning for the next school year, the staff reconsidered the notion of freedom and decided that certain freedoms could exist only if they were accompanied by responsible student behaviors. They also expanded their definition of freedom to include freedom to leave a project without returning to find it decimated or stolen; the freedom to work in the absence of constant interruptions; the freedom to come to school without fear for one's safety; and so on. The staff then instituted a program limited to mathematics classes.

Since the youngsters had had no systematic mathematics instruction for the previous two years, they were far behind in this area. They then experienced various experimental conditions which permitted them to engage in free time as soon as they finished their mathematics assignments, *as long as they did not disturb other students.* By the end of the school year the children were completing their mathematics assignments at four times the normative rate of their school-age peers. They frequently came to school early and volunteered to take work home. There were also improvements in self-help skills, promptness, and social behavior. Finally, a questionnaire filled out by the students indicated their strong preference for the structured school format as compared with the free-school arrangement of the prior two school years. Plans for the ensuing year were to extend the system to all classes.

The reader should understand that behavior modifiers did not invent the principles which influence human behavior—they merely discovered them (perhaps "rediscovered" is a better description). The principles were always there, and they have always affected the behavior of humans. Risley and Baer (1973) point out that the contribution of behavior modifiers is that, rather than letting the principles operate randomly, they have systematically employed the principles in such a manner as to produce desirable behaviors. Educators may reject the notion of programming behavioral principles, but they should not do so under the assumption that somehow the principles will disappear and that some mysterious process will take place and automatically make children into freer, more independent human beings.

AREN'T YOU AFRAID THAT UNETHICAL PEOPLE WILL USE OPERANT CONDITIONING TECHNIQUES?

Almost any time that a useful invention or discovery is made, certain dangers are present. Few would deny that insulin has been a great boon to diabetes patients. Yet difficulties in regulating dosage levels have sometimes resulted in serious problems. Aspirin kills pain; sometimes it also kills human beings. Automobiles permit people to enjoy vacations, live in areas remote from their places of work, and shop in convenience. Nevertheless, automobiles are a major source of air pollution, reduce the amount of exercise many people receive, and are involved in accidents resulting in serious injury or death. Likewise, operant conditioning techniques can benefit children and adults at the same time that they can be abused. The problems concomitant with operant conditioning procedures do not mean that the techniques should be abolished any more than the use of insulin, aspirin, or automobiles should be prohibited. What is necessary instead is a means for regulating the use of operant conditioning operations.

Hively (1971) points out that although the danger of exploitation is a serious one, its solution is reasonably simple. He suggests that individuals employing operant conditioning procedures be required to make public the techniques they will use, the behaviors they wish to alter, and the intended long-term benefits for the students. The system would thus be subject to public scrutiny and pressure for change. This recommendation should be relatively easy to implement since behavior modifiers are already oriented toward clearly defining target behaviors and specifying remedial procedures. Hively states that in cases in which the benefit to the student is dubious, the community served by the teacher can decide whether or not it is desirable to maintain, alter, or eliminate the techniques.

Making public one's procedures and goals would not only benefit the community but should also provide some much needed assistance for the public relations aspect of behavioral research. Consider the example of behavior modification projects directed toward teaching inner-city black children the speech of white middle-class America. Baer (1971) points out that critics of these programs argue that altering the language patterns of a black child deprives him of his heritage and forces him to conform to the standards of a white society. If a public forum for debate is established, a behavioral researcher can counter with Baer's argument that language skills are only one part of a black child's repertoire, and that in many other ways he can continue to live according to his culture. The behaviorist could also point out that by developing white middle-class language skills, black children would have greater access to good-salaried jobs and thereby derive a greater number of the reinforcers available in the black culture. Parents and the black community in general can accept or reject the arguments of behavioral researchers. Meanwhile, with public disclosure of procedures and goals, the view of behavior modification techniques as dictatorial and surreptitious should dissipate.

It might be argued that the greatest danger posed by behavior modifiers is that they develop punishment procedures that can be adopted by unethical people. Indeed, the license to use punishment can be abused by both ethical and unethical people. I once noticed an excellent teacher using a behavior modification procedure for serious offenses such as destroying other's property and hitting classmates. Once the critical problems were eliminated, the teacher extended her procedure to include less and less serious misbehaviors until the children were penalized for "dirty looks" and for speaking in harsh tones. Certainly, such behaviors do not call for a punishment tactic; but once a teacher discovers an effective technique, there is always a danger that she will apply it to any behavior that annoys her. More extreme examples of the ways in which punishment can be abused are all too evident in the history of mankind.

Nevertheless, categorically prohibiting the use of punishment could have negative repercussions in a variety of situations. Consider the case histories of numerous institutionalized retardates who continually bang their heads and bite and pinch themselves. Many such people are kept under restraint in order to prevent serious injury. Attempts to modify self-abusive behaviors with positive reinforcement and extinction have often met with failure. To the contrary, punishment procedures have frequently led to quick and permanent elimination of the deviant behaviors, thus freeing the person from a life of restraint. This does not mean that people should be quick to use a punishment procedure when alternatives are available. As Morrow and Gochros (1970) point out, however, "If a carefully controlled aversive technique can eliminate severely disruptive, handicapping behavior when other procedures have proved ineffectual, it seems unethical not to use the aversive technique [p. 303]." Again, by requiring public disclosure of procedures and goals, one should be able to derive the advantages and avoid some of the difficulties associated with a punishment tactic.

The fear that unethical people might use behavior procedures is understandable. What I fear more is that *ethical* people will not use them. At a time when inner-city schools are reporting high rates of illiteracy and violence, when retarded children are unjustifiably kept in restraints, and when malingerers are being pitied, the well-intentioned but unskilled teacher who fails to employ effective behavioral procedures might be causing more harm through the acts of omission than the immoral person does through acts of commission.

IT SEEMS THAT IF TEACHERS USE BEHAVIOR MODIFICATION PROCEDURES, THEY WILL BE COLD AND MECHANICAL

I believe that the problem here is that people sometimes confuse the process of being systematic with being cold and mechanical. As an example, take the case of a teacher who uses a social reinforcement procedure to increase a student's on-task behavior. The teacher is being systematic in that she consistently ignores inappropriate behavior while waiting for a student to behave appropriately. When he is behaving appropriately, the teacher gives him social reinforcement. This takes the form of smiling at the student, patting him on the back, hugging him, and complimenting him. Certainly, these are social actions which are compatible with the notion of human warmth, as opposed to being cold and mechanical. The teacher may have been systematic, but she was not cold.

When a teacher discovers an effective behavior modification procedure, she often finds it possible to relate more warmly to her students. I refer to a story about a special-education teacher I once knew. She was in her first year of teaching and had sixteen extraordinarily rowdy children in her class. During the initial period in which I observed her, I found her to be unsociable toward the children. I was unable to recall one incident in which she made warm physical contact with a student; in addition, she seldom smiled at or praised the children. After a baseline period, the teacher employed a response-cost procedure to reduce out-of-seat and disturbing-others behaviors. Misbehaviors immediately decreased to low levels. At the same time, I noticed that the teacher tickled a few children, that she smiled more frequently, and that she sometimes complimented individual youngsters. As the students improved, the teacher became friendlier and warmer to them.

The actions of the teacher in the previous paragraph were verbalized by another teacher in a study by Otto (1975) in which various behavior modification techniques were used to decrease inappropriate behavior. "I do think that in some ways it was [a] warmer class too. As I think about the class, I felt much better about the overall behavior and felt warmer towards the children during the experimental conditions. I think I wasn't yelling as much for one thing. . . . I felt more relaxed at the end of each half hour because the room was quiet and because there was some control [pp. 282–283]."

The point to both of these stories is that many teachers find it difficult to be warm and kind to students who are behaving inappropriately. Teachers are as human as anyone else, and it is understandable that they become frustrated, irritated, and unsociable toward children when their teaching efforts continually fail. When effective procedures are discovered, however, many of these feelings are reversed and teachers find it easier to demonstrate human warmth toward their students.

Some teachers object to the practice of giving social reinforcement to children because they feel that they are being dishonest or insincere in the process. I can sympathize with this feeling because I have experienced it myself. To such teachers I say, "Do it anyway!" Initially there is awkwardness; but as academic behaviors increase and management problems decrease, teachers find themselves becoming more comfortable with the social reinforcement process. The enthusiasm that a teacher initially feigns will become genuine as her students improve.

Even if social reinforcement procedures are not considered cold and mechanical, one might raise the question as to whether *other* behavior modification techniques, such as token reinforcement tactics, can be so characterized. A study by Mandelker, Brigham, and Bushell (1970) showed, however, that when appropriately arranged, a token reinforcement procedure can increase the amount of social contact between a teacher and her students. There were six kindergarden children in the study, who had a twenty-minute handwriting lesson each day. During the reinforcement phases, the teacher gave the students tokens for correct writing responses. The tokens were placed in a cup in front of the children and were exchangeable for a variety of classroom privileges. The major finding of the study was that the token reinforcement procedure led to an increase in the amount of verbal and physical contact that the teacher had with her students.

In summary, I believe that teachers are most likely to be warm and kind to their students when their students are reinforcing them, and there are few events that can reinforce teachers as much as the accomplishments of their students. If behavior modification procedures bring about student success, I believe that they will also bring about teacher warmth and sincerity.

MUST TEACHERS AND OTHER EDUCATORS USE SCIENTIFIC PROCEDURES?

Educators who have read the third chapter might shrug their shoulders and say, "All that scientific stuff is fine, but what has it got to do with me? I am only interested in what works, and besides, who has time to go around measuring behavior and using reversal designs?"

In response to such questions, I would first like to state that all *I* am interested in is what works. The problem is that unless a teacher is systematic and objective, she cannot be certain whether a particular procedure or philosophy is worthwhile or not. In the absence of adequate evaluative techniques, a teacher must make important decisions on the basis of "what seems right." Decisions made according to such a standard may be inaccurate as the result of a variety of factors. It is possible, for example, that a teacher will be enthusiastic about the prospects of a certain technique producing an improvement in her students' academic performance. Without objective data, her enthusiasm may convince her that her students have made gains when, in fact, they have not. Hence, she will continue to use ineffective procedures. Conversely, it is feasible that a teacher will implement a technique that produces a gradual but definite improvement in behavior. In the absence of accurate data, the teacher might not realize that gains have been made and might abandon a procedure which she should maintain. In any event, the problem of persuading teachers to use behavior modification procedures is an important and difficult one.

As mentioned earlier, most practicing teachers received their training from education departments that did not teach, or were opposed to, behavior modification procedures. In order for such teachers to become convinced of the value of behavior modification techniques, they will need definite evidence of the effectiveness of these techniques. This can be achieved by measuring behavior and by using a reversal design in which gains deteriorate after behavior modification procedures are withdrawn.

Hall, Hawkins, and Axelrod (1975) describe some direct benefits to a teacher who employs scientific methods. First, in the process of measuring behavior, the teacher is required to precisely define the behavior of interest. In so doing, the teacher focuses on a specific behavior and is thereby more likely to bring about a desirable change in the behavior. Secondly, measurement of behavior serves diagnostic purposes. A gradual decline in a student's perform-ance over days, for example, lets a teacher know that the child might be satiating on the available reinforcers or that he is bored with his assignments. Also, by receiving constant feedback on student progress, the teacher can make minor adjustments in her procedures until the final procedure is more effective than the original one. Finally, at a time when there is a growing trend toward accountability in education, a teacher using scientific techniques can confidently demonstrate to her supervisor, the principal, or parents that her techniques are suitable. When asked to demonstrate the effectiveness of a certain procedure, she can show that the level of a particular behavior is better under Reinforcement$_1$ condition than it was during Baseline$_1$. When asked how she can be certain that other factors were not responsible for the improvement, she need only point to the deterioration of the behavior during Baseline$_2$. (Touché!)

Teachers with a scientific orientation are able to participate in the development of the field of education. By using appropriate experimental methods, teachers can provide convincing evidence that they have devised effective procedures. They can transmit the relevant information by word of mouth or by publishing the results in school newsletters, journals, or books such as the present one. Teachers can test their own ideas, and the field can benefit from the insights of educators who spend their days in classrooms rather than depending on professional researchers who spend relatively small periods of time in classrooms.

In the absence of adopting a scientific methodology, the field of education has been characterized by a continuous stream of cycles and fads. Risley (1970) points out that a particular approach is proposed, accepted, and applied. Later the approach is dropped and another one replaces it. The earlier approach might have had much merit, whereas the latter one might be detrimental; nevertheless, new fads continue to rise and fall independently of their worth. Risley also indicates that modern-day behavior modifiers are using procedures remarkably similar to those employed in the eighteenth and nineteenth century by educators such as Rousseau, Itard, and Sequin. One might be tempted to laud the efforts and foresight of the early educators, but perhaps this would be a mistake. In the absence of provision of convincing evidence of the value of their work to the educational communitites of their times, these initial efforts were not continued by succeeding educators. Instead, other philosophies prevailed, and it became necessary to rediscover the same principles a century and a half later.

The evaluative methodology proposed by behavior modifiers is not science for the sake of science. It is science for the sake of making better teachers. Nevertheless, it would be naïve of me to think that teachers and other educators will suddenly embrace scientific techniques on a daily basis. Teacher education programs have a long history of ignoring or disdaining the notion of a scientific approach toward teaching. Until teacher education programs develop a more scientific orientation, and until the idea of using scientific methodology in the study of human behavior is introduced into elementary and secondary school curricula (as it is in chemistry, for example), the teacher who employs scientific techniques will probably be the exception rather than the rule. I will make one plea, however, to the teacher who wishes to use behavior modification procedures but is not committed to scientific practices. I would ask that he make at least some measurements and perform some experimental manipulations. He might, for example, take two or three days of Baseline$_1$ data, measure the behavior once or twice a week during the intervention phase, and later withdraw his procedures for a few days. Such a practice is inferior to careful scientific investigation, but it will still provide the teacher with some relevant information.

IF YOU ELIMINATE ONE INAPPROPRIATE BEHAVIOR, ISN'T IT POSSIBLE THAT A WORSE ONE WILL REPLACE IT?

The concern expressed in this question probably emanates from the medical model of human behavior proposed by Freud and other proponents of the psychoanalytic school. One of the basic tenets of that school of thought is that human behavior can be explained in terms analogous to physical medicine. Just as germs and viruses operating within an individual lead to a disease and its associated symptoms, aberrant human behavior is seen as a symptom of an underlying psychological disease. Being only a symptom of a deeper disorder, it is claimed that one should not attempt to directly alter the behavior which is manifested but should probe further for the underlying cause of the problem. Psychoanalytic psychologists claim that the maladaptive behavior that is exhibited is the most economical and least harmful one the individual could have adopted under unfavorable conditions. They further propose the "hypothesis of symptom substitution," which states that if one maladaptive behavior is improperly removed, a more pathological one will replace it. It is, therefore, contended that, if parents use a procedure to eliminate thumb sucking, problems such as bed wetting and temper tantrums might substitute for the original disorder. The Freudians claim that in order to achieve the appropriate kind of change, there must be cognitive and emotional growth, and that an individual must have increased insight into the original cause of his problems.

The notion of symptom substitution has a certain amount of common-sense appeal. The main argument against it, however, is that there is little or no research evidence to support it (Ullmann and Krasner, 1965). Baer (1971) noted, for example, "Behavior modifiers eliminated a few thousand tantrums in children who did not subsequently explode into psychopathology. Instead, they looked very much like children they had been previously, but without tantrums. Many of them, shorn of their one weapon of parent abuse, began to seem like children again to those parents, and pleasant, family-like things often happened subsequently [p. 359]." Morrow and Gochros (1970) and Yates (1958) also noted that there is little evidence for the symptom substitution hypothesis. Nevertheless, numerous psychoanalytic psychologists still propose the hypothesis as if it were true—a phenomenon that is likely to occur when one is oriented toward armchair philosophizing rather than the careful collection of data.

Behavior modifiers not only reject the hypothesis of symptom substitution but resent the very term itself. One difficulty is that the term "symptom substitution" implies that behavioral disorders have an underlying medical origin—a notion which lacks experimental validation. Another problem is that the hypothesis states that the new behavior will necessarily be worse than the one it replaces. In fact, in those cases in which novel behaviors have emerged, they have sometimes been found to be desirable behaviors. The term preferred by behavior modifiers is "side effects," which refers to changes which take place in behaviors other than the target of modification. The term does not state the origin of the behavior change, nor does it imply that the change is necessarily favorable or unfavorable.

Some behavior modification studies have been directed toward determining whether any unusual side effects are associated with the implementation of behavioral procedures. Risley (1968), for example, thoroughly investigated the effects and side effects of reducing a variety of serious misbehaviors performed by an autistic girl. He found that when a punishment procedure led to a decrease in climbing on bookcases, the child made increased eye contact with him and she began to climb on chairs. The increased eye contact was desirable, of course, but climbing on chairs was not. As a result, eye contact was not modified but the punishment procedure was effectively applied to chair climbing. The decrease in chair climbing was not associated with further adverse side effects. Similarly, Sajwaj, Twardosz, and Burke (1972) found that an extinction procedure reduced the rate of excessive conversations a retarded child initiated with his teacher. Simultaneously, social behavior with children increased, as did disruptions during group activity. Later, the disruptions were easily eliminated by the use of a time-out procedure.

When behavior modification procedures are applied in classrooms, a number of beneficial and easily explained side effects may emerge. Implementing a procedure to increase the in-seat behavior of hyperactive children will often be associated with an improvement in the academic performance of the youngsters. Similarly, when a behavioral procedure reduces the destructive behavior of a student, an improvement in his relations with both peers and adults will often occur. Such results are to be expected, of course, and are, therefore, at marked variance with the aura of mystery surrounding the hypothesis of symptom substitution.

In summary, the hypothesis of symptom substitution should be taken seriously but, in the opinion of behavior modifiers, should be replaced with the term "side effects." Overall, there are few instances in which behavior modification procedures have been associated with unexpected side effects. When side effects have been noted, however, the behaviors were often desirable. When undesirable side effects occurred, these problem behaviors could also be modified in the same manner as other behaviors (adapted from Risley, 1968).

DOES BEHAVIOR MODIFICATION STIFLE CREATIVITY?

This question is difficult to answer, partly because of problems in obtaining an acceptable definition of "creativity." Elizabeth Goetz, who has done several studies involving the application of behavior modification procedures to teaching creativity, points out (Goetz and Salmonson, 1972) that definitions of creativity include reference to such diverse areas as mental processes, personality, verbal behavior, and physical behavior. She states, however, that it is only the products of verbal and physical behavior that can be analyzed as creative or noncreative. One common element in the judgment of a product as creative is the notion of novelty. Goetz and Baer (1973), for example, indicate that prior researchers define creativity as behavior which the individual or his group has not previously displayed in a given setting. Similarly, Maloney and Hopkins (1973) define creative behavior as different responses to the same situation.

With such definitions one can begin to teach (and, therefore, not stifle) creativity. The first step is to define creativity for the situation of interest. Next, a teacher can apply reinforcement procedures to the occurrence of the target behavior in the same manner as one would reinforce other behaviors. Goetz and Salmonson (1972), for example, were interested in teaching three preschool girls to be more creative in easel painting. They had found that all three youngsters tended to use a low number of forms in their painting. The authors identified and defined twenty-five types of painting forms. These included "blended color" (any hue formed by mixing two or more colors on paper), "diagonal line" (a straight line at least three inches long, forming a 10° to 80° angle), and so on. After a baseline period, the teacher praised a student each time the student painted a form she had not previously made during the period. If a student blended colors for the first time in a period, the teacher might say, "That is very nice; I like the way you mix colors." The next time the student blended colors, the teacher would not make a comment; she would praise the child, however, if she made a diagonal line for the first time. For all three girls the social reinforcement procedure produced increased diversity of painting forms as compared with baseline rates.

Goetz and Baer (1973) showed how behavior modification procedures can be used to teach creative block building. The authors first described twenty commonly seen block forms in which two or more blocks were used to produce a specified shape or function. A "story," for example, was defined as two or more blocks placed on top of each other, with the upper block resting completely on the lower. An "arch" consisted of the placement of one block on two lower blocks which were not touching each other. Using a procedure similar to that employed by Goetz and Salmonson (1972), the teacher complimented each of three preschool girls the first time she constructed a new form during a session. The initial time the girl constructed an arch, the teacher might say, "Oh, that's nice—that's different!" There resulted an increase in form diversity in block building for all three children from the praise procedure.

The authors of the previous studies should be complimented for their original work in defining and teaching creativity. Nevertheless, pioneering efforts are almost necessarily limited in scope, and many readers will still find behavior modification techniques contrary to the concept of creativity. This is not surprising, since the practices of measuring behavior, specifying rules, and rewarding children for their adherence to the rules would seem to be more compatible with the ideas of conformity rather than of creativity. Still, I believe that if one considers skill development important in creativity, behavior modification has a role in teaching creativity.

I refer to the story of an artist I know who became interested in fine arts after she received her undergraduate degree. Initially, her work was considered to be of limited quality. As a result of hard work and the instruction and feedback of her professors in graduate school, she mastered the elements of line, mass, space, light, color, and texture and the principles of unity, variety, contrast, balance, rhythm, and emphasis. Gradually her artwork improved until, presently, she is well recognized for her artistic creations. My point is that this person did not suddenly become creative. She became creative partly because she learned the skills which were critical to her being able to express herself. To the degree to which such skills can be taught, behavior modification can provide an important function.

There are people who prefer to regard creativity as a natural, mysterious process that can come about through the absence of structure. I am not one of them. If teachers can help to guide students to become more creative, all of us—not just a select few—can experience the joy of being creative. There is nothing to be lost by teaching creativity, except for the mystery surrounding the process.

WHAT HAPPENS TO CHILDREN WHEN BEHAVIOR MODIFICATION PROCEDURES ARE WITHDRAWN?

The present question is raised with respect to two different concerns. The first is whether children who have previously experienced a reinforcement procedure will refuse to work in the future unless they receive rewards for their efforts. The second issue is whether a child's behavior, having improved as the result of a behavior modification procedure, will persist when the procedure is discontinued and will generalize to other situations. The initial question will be addressed first.

A number of behavioral researchers have provided their observations as to whether children who have been exposed to programmed reinforcement will later refuse to work without it. Homme (1969) states that he initially had this concern, but that experiences to the contrary relieved him of his apprehensions. He indicated that the students who participated in his behavior modification programs became happy, eager children for whom learning itself became a rewarding experience. Rather than becoming more dependent on programmed reinforcers, they became less so.

Mosier and Vaal (1971) describe a case involving an emotionally disturbed boy, Keith, whose problems included poor work habits and frequent incidents of crying, complaining, staring off into space, and making irrelevant comments. When he was in the second grade, Keith was placed in an adjustment class in which the goal was to successfully return the children to the regular classroom. The special-class teacher made use of a variety of behavior modification techniques, such as social and token reinforcement. After four years Keith made considerable progress and was spending most of his time in a regular sixth-grade classroom. Keith then approached his adjustment-class teacher and told her that, since he would soon be entering junior high school, a setting in which token reinforcement procedures would not be employed, he no longer wished to work for tokens, and he returned all those that he had earned to the teacher. His teacher, of course, was delighted and gave Keith a "maturity party" to which all regular-classroom children were invited. Frequent checks on his progress indicated that Keith made a successful adjustment to his new environment without the use of tokens.

Although anecdotes such as those presented above may be interesting, they are also inconclusive, particularly since they were reported by individuals already committed to the use of behavioral procedures. What is better is to have a systematic investigation of the question, as was provided by Feingold and Mahoney (1975). The authors were concerned with the claim that some children who begin to receive material rewards for behaviors which they previously performed without reward will refuse to work if the rewards are discontinued. Five second-grade students from a range of academic and socioeconomic levels took part in the study. During Baseline$_1$ the students completed exercises in follow-the-dots books in which a picture resulted if the dots were correctly connected. In the reinforcement phase, the students earned points exchangeable for a variety of prizes for the pictures they completed, and the productivity of all students increased. In the final baseline phase, the students could no longer earn points for connecting the dots, but the performance of each of the students remained at rates considerably higher than Baseline$_1$ levels. Hence, exposure to reinforcement did not lead to a refusal to perform the task when reward was withdrawn but actually facilitated it.

The second concern deals not so much with the refusal of students to work following discontinuation of reinforcement as with whether some of the gains made during the reinforcement stage are maintained when rewards are no longer available, and whether gains made in one situation will generalize to other situations. The study by Feingold and Mahoney is relevant to the question of maintenance of gains, but, in fairness, the experiment dealt with only five children and, therefore, the results may not be true in general. Indeed, there are cases in which performance during the final baseline phase is inferior to that which occurred during the initial baseline. There are also numerous cases in which the gains made in one setting did not generalize to other settings. There are several factors and procedures which influence the maintenance of gains (following a behavior modification operation) and the generalization of behavior from one setting to another. I have summarized some of these factors and procedures below:

1. Behavior which is self-reinforcing (that is, enjoyable in and of itself) will probably be maintained and generalize. Hence, if a socially withdrawn child is induced to join in cooperative play through a behavior modification procedure and finds such play enjoyable, the behavior modification procedure can probably be withdrawn without a decrement in social behavior.

2. Behaviors which are likely to be reinforced by the natural environment should continue and generalize. Behaviors such as walking, talking, and reading are reinforced in a variety of ways by the natural environment and, therefore, tend to endure outside of, and following, training sessions.

3. In programs in which tangible reinforcers are used to improve behavior, praise should precede the administering of the tangibles, thus establishing praise as a conditioned reinforcer. This practice increases the probability of the maintenance and generalization of the behavior, since praise is likely to occur outside the environment in which training occurs.

4. Gradually decreasing the amount of reinforcement that is available or gradually increasing the amount of time between the desired behavior and the consequence, or both, is often helpful in preventing deterioration of gains. This process is known as "thinning the schedule of reinforcement" and was described earlier (pp. 46–48).

5. The best way to ensure maintenance and generalization of behavior is to plan for it. In certain cases this will mean implementing some of the procedures above. In other cases it will mean training a variety of people in a child's environment, such as parents, siblings, neighbors, classmates, and teachers, to carry out effective procedures. Whatever is required, it is best to keep in mind Baer, Wolf, and Risley's (1968) admonition, stated previously (pp. 35), that "Generalization should be programmed, rather than expected or lamented [p. 97].

SO WHAT IF A BEHAVIOR MODIFICATION PROCEDURE KEEPS CHILDREN QUIET AND IN THEIR SEATS— DOES THAT MEAN THAT THEY WILL LEARN MORE?

The question has been raised by a variety of sources, including teachers, administrators, parents, and both proponents and opponents of behavior modification practices. As indicated in the previous chapter (Ayllon and Roberts,

1974, Situation 13) the concern is that some teachers will effectively use behavior procedures to eliminate disruptive behavior and, thereby, make their jobs easier. The question is whether the teachers have merely established "law and order [Winett and Winkler, 1972, p. 499]" or whether students who are becoming more cooperative will also make academic gains in the process. Research on the question has produced conflicting results. Fox, Copeland, and Hall (1971), for example, found that when a social reinforcement procedure increased the on-task rate of a ten-year-old child, there was a corresponding increase in the number of arithmetic problems the youngster completed. A study by Ferritor, Buckholdt, Hamblin, and Smith (1972), on the other hand, found no correlation between an increase in on-task behavior and arithmetic performance. Given the ambiguous results of the studies, it is probably safest to conclude that reducing inappropriate behavior will sometimes be associated with an improvement in academic performance, and that sometimes it will not be.

There are many factors which are likely to determine whether an increase in on-task behavior will also result in an improvement in academic output. Presumably, these factors include the nature of the academic task, the student's ability to perform the task, and the degree to which the teacher reinforces successful academic performance. In cases in which there is an improvement in scholastic output corresponding with the implementation of a behavior modification procedure for disruptive behavior, there can be no doubt about the value of the behavioral tactic. But what about situations in which a teacher uses a behavior modification procedure to reduce a management problem and there is no immediate corresponding improvement in academic performance? Is there any value to such a procedure, given that the purpose of schools is to educate rather than contain children?

I believe there often is. There are certain situations in which the youngsters are so disruptive that a teacher just cannot proceed with academic assignments until classroom order is achieved. Once the disruptiveness that interfered with academic success is reduced, the teacher can concern herself with means of improving the scholarly performance of her students. Some of the studies presented in the previous chapter (for example, Price and D'Ippolito, 1975, Situation 9; Ayllon and Roberts, 1974, Situation 13; Kirby and Shields, 1972, Situation 14) supported the idea of reinforcing academic behavior in such a manner that incompatible, disruptive behavior will drop out. This is a worthy goal, but I maintain that in certain cases the teacher's first task must be to gain classroom control. I have yet to see a situation in which a teacher successfully reinforced a child's arithmetic or spelling behavior when he was dancing on desk tops.

A teacher should see her job as only partly completed when her children become less disruptive. Behavior modification procedures should not be viewed as a means of establishing control for control's sake alone. As educators, we should always question whose welfare has been served when we implement change in the classroom (O'Leary, 1972). One of the main purposes of the schools is to teach children academic skills. As such, teachers who use behavior modification procedures to reduce disruptive behavior should simultaneously attain records of the academic performance of their students in order to determine whether the students are making scholarly gains. If there is no evidence of academic progress, the teacher should consider using a behavior modification technique to improve academic output. It would be an abuse of behavior modification tactics to have a teacher use the procedures simply to produce quiet, compliant children. Therefore, when a teacher brings about classroom control, it becomes her burden to provide students with appropriate academic materials and to shape the youngsters through the learning process.

I once observed a teacher successfully employ a behavior modification procedure to reduce discipline problems in her classroom. Rather than take advantage of the improved deportment of her students to encourage scholarly gains, she seemed content to let her students sit quietly in the absence of stimulating activities. She often ignored the raised hands of students seeking assistance, apparently believing that the behavior modification tactic would keep them from becoming disruptive. Eventually, however, the bored, angry students ignored the classroom rules, and the teacher lost control of her class. Fortunately, such cases are the exception to the rule, and most teachers who achieve classroom control will eagerly approach the prospect of teaching academic tasks to cooperative children.

WHEN A TEACHER APPLIES A BEHAVIOR MODIFICATION PROCEDURE TO ONE STUDENT, HOW DO THE OTHER STUDENTS REACT?

Educators often express two concerns with respect to the above question. First, some educators fear that when a misbehaving student is singled out for a behavior modification program, other students will imitate his misbehaviors so that they too will be placed on a program offering special rewards. The second concern is that students who observe a classmate obtaining special rewards will object to the arrangement and refuse to work unless they are also included in the program. Although I have never encountered the initial problem, I have had to contend with the latter one several times, and below I have enumerated some suggestions for avoiding the difficulties. Several of the suggestions were adapted from an article by O'Leary, Poulos, and Devine (1972):

1 The teacher can explain to all students, *in advance*, that a youngster in the class has a particular problem and that a special program will be implemented in his behalf. She should also point out that the student will be receiving special rewards and that she would appreciate the help of all students in conducting the program. Although this solution might appear somewhat naïve, I have seen it work remarkably well with children at a variety of grade levels. The teacher can also offer the children group rewards for their cooperation.

2   In cases in which the first suggestion is largely effective but a small number of children continually voice objections, the teacher should ignore the complaints. Ignoring is effective with a variety of other behaviors and will often reduce complaining behaviors. I would *not* implement the ignoring procedure until I was certain that the students understood why a particular child was involved in the behavior modification program; but, once accomplished, I believe that ignoring the grumbles is in order.

3   The teacher can have all youngsters share or participate in the rewards earned by the student of concern. This arrangement has been used in several studies previously described in this book (for example, Tribble and Hall, 1972, p. 5 and can take the form of providing each child in the class with a special privilege contingent upon a particular student meeting the behavioral criterion for reinforcement. In one situation that I am familiar with, a student refused to wear his eyeglasses, presumably because his classmates taunted him with derogatory names such as "four eyes," "goofy," and "professor." The teacher instituted a behavior modification procedure in which she periodically checked to see if the youngster was wearing his glasses. If he was, all students received extra free time. Immediately after the tactic was implemented, the students ceased the name-calling and instead complimented their breadwinner with comments such as, "You're really looking cool today with your specs on." Hence, the students lent their support to the procedure rather than undermining it or being hostile to it.

4   The child can receive his rewards in a setting outside the classroom, such as the home. Children will usually not object to having a classmate receive the special attention associated, for example, with the awarding of points. They are more likely to object to a classmate who sticks his tongue out at them while he skips out of class with a new game under his arms. Teachers might provide cooperative parents with a report on the number of points their child has earned each day. The parents can then translate the points into an allowance or a special privilege without the knowledge of their child's classmates.

5   Whenever feasible, the teacher should use social rather than tangible reinforcement. Children object less to having a classmate receive social reinforcement than they do to the sight of one child receiving tangible reinforcers or special privileges. Also, even though one child may be a particular problem, there is no reason why the teacher cannot grant social reinforcement to other children who are well behaved. This can be done by reinforcing individual children or by complimenting the entire group.

6   If several children perform the same misbehavior, a group contingency procedure might be in order. Since the same rules apply to all children, no particular child is singled out for rewards. The teacher might be specifically concerned about the problems of one child, but this fact will usually not be noticed by the students when a group contingency procedure is in operation.

There is at least one other matter with which a teacher must concern herself if she singles out one child for a behavior modification program—not neglecting other students in the class. There is no doubt that a teacher's attention can be reinforcing to a child, and that the time she spends with a student can assist him in the learning process. But what happens to the rest of the class when this occurs? A study by Scott and Bushell (1974) was concerned with the relationship between the amount of time a teacher spent with one student and the on-task rate of the other students during mathematics class. The authors found that contacts of long duration with one child caused a substantial decrease in the on-task rate of his classmates. With contacts of shorter duration, the on-task rate of the classmates was much higher. A major conclusion of the study was that the duration of a teacher's contact should be long enough to help a particular student, but not so long that the teacher neglects the responses (e.g., hand raises) of the other students.

WHEN A CHILD DOES NOT LEARN, BEHAVIOR MODIFIERS PLACE THE BURDEN ON THE TEACHER TO DEVISE ALTERNATIVE PROCEDURES THAT WILL BE EFFECTIVE. DON'T THEY EVER TAKE INTO ACCOUNT THAT CULTURAL AND PHYSIOLOGICAL FACTORS MIGHT BE INTERFERING WITH A YOUNGSTER'S ABILITY TO LEARN?

Certainly physiological and cultural factors are important in the learning process of any child. The difficulty is that such factors are not under the control of educators. Educators cannot modify the genetic makeup of a child, nor can they prescribe medicine for ailments that might affect a student's academic performance. Similarly, educators cannot alter the family size of students, nor can they expect to have much effect on the manner in which some parents encourage or discourage scholastic achievement. Educators must begin their work where physiological and cultural factors leave off. Nevertheless, their efforts are often fruitful. With appropriate teaching, culturally different children learn to read; blind children develop mobility skills; and withdrawn children become more sociable. My opinion is that teachers who claim that students are not making progress because the youngsters come from "bad homes" or because "they're too dumb to learn" are evading their responsibility as educators. If all students were naturally intelligent and came from homes that supported academic excellence, one wonders how necessary schools and teachers would be.

Perhaps because of the pervasive influence of Freud, many parents, educators, and psychologists are bothered by the fact that behavior modifiers do not probe into an individual's past before attempting to remediate his difficulties. There are several reasons for this. First, the problems in correctly reconstructing one's past are immense. Accuracy depends on the individual's ability to precisely recall the past as well as the degree to which he reports the events truthfully. Accuracy also depends on the actions of his "therapist." Some therapists expect clients to report or interpret events in certain ways and will reinforce them with smiles and nods when they do; they will also withdraw reinforcement when the client does not make the expected report. The fact that a therapist does not approve of behavioral procedures does not mean that he is not applying them—knowingly or unknowingly.

Another objection that behavior modifiers have to probing a child's past is that the factors that originally *caused* a problem are not necessarily the same as the ones that are *maintaining* the problem. A one-year-old child, for example, might start crying at night because he is ill. After a few nights, his illness might be cured. Nevertheless, he continues to cry because he has learned that crying brings his anxious parents running into his bedroom. His illness was the original cause of his crying, but his parents' attention is maintaining the problem; it is his parents' attention, rather than the illness, that must now be remediated.

Cultural and physiological processes might make the job of the behaviorally oriented teacher easier or more difficult. Regardless, she enthusiastically and optimistically attacks every school problem as if it can be solved. In her efforts to educate children, she finds that she is now always successful. In such cases she blames herself and not the student's culture or genetics. As Homme (1969) points out, "A student fails in the classroom because the motivational system fails, not because the student is 'stupid' or 'bad' [p. 111]." When the behaviorally oriented teacher is unsuccessful, she is obligated to try to find another solution to the problem. I can recall a situation in which I was hired as a consultant for a case involving a retarded woman who was continually disrobing. Initially I suggested ignoring her. After that failed, I suggested a combination of social reinforcement and ignoring. Later, a variety of time-out procedures was attempted, but the problem persisted. By the end of the year I had suggested eight different procedures, but the woman continued to remove her clothes. I was never able to find an adequate solution to the problem. Still, I believe that the problem could have been remediated had I been clever enough. Perhaps I am wrong, but I would rather make the error of believing a problem can be solved and find out that it cannot, than to assume a problem cannot be solved when in fact it can be.

CONCLUSIONS AND A LOOK AHEAD

The ability of behavioral processes to improve the academic and social development of children is well documented. Nevertheless, the road ahead will not be an easy one. Presently, there is a growing schism between professional and public acceptance of behavior modification principles. At a time when disciplines such as nursing, counseling, and occupational therapy (to mention a few) are showing greater interest in behavioral methods, there are increasing signs of public discomfort. The latter takes the form of regulations restricting the use of behavior modification practices and unfavorable newspaper and magazine articles.

Thus, behavior modification proponents must make greater efforts to improve the public relations component of their field. Rather than waiting until parents, community leaders, and reporters *find out* about behavior modification activities, advocates of the principles should *seek out* the concerned public and make all relevant information known. Parents, school administrators, and social workers who are aware of prospective programs can participate in the development and conduct of the programs. They can also observe, firsthand, the benefits of such programs and help to publicize the advantages of the approach.

Behavior modification supporters should realize that processes such as positive reinforcement and time out strike a sensitive nerve in many people. It then becomes their responsibility to convince doubters that rewarding children is comparable to processes that all adults experience and accept; that behavior modification procedures are no more manipulative than other effective techniques; and that the long-range benefits of procedures such as time out usually outweigh the immediate distress. Advocates can also invite reporters and public officals to scrutinize their programs and can help such people to write newspaper articles and legislation. It would be a disaster if the final chapter on behavior modification were written by legislators and judges with little basic knowledge of the field, who were reacting to misconstrued public outrage. This danger becomes more imminent if behaviorists consider that their only job is to modify children's behavior without modifying adult acceptance of their practices as well.

In addition to increasing public relations efforts, behavior modifiers must attend to developing programs that demonstrate the lifelong effects of their procedures. This is important both in terms of remediating and in preventing problems. It is not sufficient to demonstrate repeatedly that certain techniques are effective in alleviating existing problems. It is more important to show that children who experience a certain teaching philosophy will lead better lives. Hence, future research can concentrate on the effect of having students receive intensive behavior modification programs for three, six, or even twelve or more years.

In summary, a number of problems face a teacher who adopts a behavioral orientation. Nevertheless, the difficulties can be overcome by educators who *confront* the issues rather than *react* to them. The worst outcome would be for teachers to allow prospective problems to paralyze them into inactivity. A technology now exists for improving the educational lot of students, and it should be used. A public that has been forced to live with numerous ineffective educational systems will eventually embrace an effective one. Teachers must carry the message to the schools and to the public.

REFERENCES

Axelrod, S., and T. J. Piper: "Suitability of the Reversal and Multiple-Baseline Designs for Research on Reading Behaviors." Paper presented at the meeting of the Association for the Advancement of Behavior Therapy, San Francisco, December 1975.

Ayllon, T., and M. D. Roberts: "Eliminating Discipline Problems by Strengthening Academic Performance," *Journal of Applied Behavior Analysis*, 7, 71–76, 1974.

Baer, D. M.: "Behavior Modification: You Shouldn't," in E. Ramp and B. L. Hopkins (eds.), *A New Direction for Education: Behavior Analysis, 1971* (Lawrence, Kans.: Support and Development Center for Follow Through, Department of Human Development, University of Kansas, 1971), pp. 358–369.

———, M. M. Wolf, and T. R. Risley: "Some Current Dimensions of Applied Behavior Analysis," *Journal of Applied Behavior Analysis*, 1, 91–97, 1968.

Cohen, S. A.: *Teach Them All to Read: Theory, Methods, and Materials for Teaching the Disadvantaged* (New York: Random House, 1969).

Feingold, B. D., and M. J. Mahoney: "Reinforcement Effects on Intrinsic Interest: Undermining the Overjustification Hypothesis," *Behavior Therapy*, **6**, 367–377, 1975.

Ferritor, D. E., D. Buckholdt, R. L. Hamblin, and L. Smith: "The Noneffects of Contingent Reinforcement for Attending Behavior on Work Accomplished," *Journal of Applied Behavior Analysis*, **5**, 7–17, 1972.

Fox, R., R. Copeland, and R. V. Hall: "An Analysis of the Interaction between Attending Behavior and Academic Production in a Behaviorally Disordered Boy." Paper presented at the meeting of the Council for Exceptional Children, Miami Beach, April 1971.

Goetz, E. M., and D. M. Baer: "Social Control of Form Diversity and the Emergence of New Forms in Children's Blockbuilding," *Journal of Applied Behavior Analysis*, **6**, 209–217, 1973.

―――― and M. M. Salmonson: "The Effect of General and Descriptive Reinforcement on 'Creativity' in Easel Painting," in G. Semb, D. R. Green, R. P. Hawkins, J. Michael, E. L. Phillips, J. A. Sherman, H. Sloane, and D. R. Thomas (eds.), *Behavior Analysis and Education—1972* (Lawrence, Kans.: Support and Development Center for Follow Through, Department of Human Development, University of Kansas, 1972), pp. 53–61.

Hall, R. V., R. P. Hawkins, and S. Axelrod: "Measuring and Recording Student Behavior: A Behavior Analysis Approach," in R. A. Weinberg and F. H. Wood (eds.), *Observation of Pupils and Teachers in Mainstream and Special Education Settings: Alternative Strategies* (Minneapolis, Minn.: Leadership Training Institute, 1975), pp. 193–217.

Haskett, G. J., and W. Lenfestey: "Reading-Related Behavior in an Open Classroom: Effects of Novelty and Modeling on Preschoolers," *Journal of Applied Behavior Analysis*, **7**, 233–241, 1974.

Hiveley, W.: "What Next?" in E. Ramp and B. L. Hopkins (eds.), *A New Direction for Education: Behavior Analysis, 1971* (Lawrence, Kans.: Support and Development Center for Follow Through, Department of Human Development, University of Kansas, 1971), pp. 311–322.

Homme, L.: *How to Use Contingency Contracting in the Classroom* (Champaign, Ill.: Research Press, 1969).

Horowitz, F. D.: "Living among the ABAs: Retrospect and Prospect," in E. Ramp and G. Semb (eds.), *Behavior Analysis: Areas of Research and Application* (Englewood Cliffs, N.J.: Prentice-Hall, 1975), pp. 3–15.

Kagan, J.: *Understanding Children: Behavior, Motives, and Thought* (New York: Harcourt Brace Jovanovich, 1971).

Kirby, F. D., and F. Shields: "Modification of Arithmetic Response Rate and Attending Behavior in a Seventh-Grade Student," *Journal of Applied Behavior Analysis*, **5**, 79–84, 1972.

Maloney, K. B., and B. L. Hopkins: "The Modification of Sentence Structure and Its Relationship to Subjective Judgements of Creativity in Writing," *Journal of Applied Behavior Analysis*, **6**, 425–433, 1973.

Mandelker, A. V., T. A. Brigham, and D. Bushell: "The Effects of Token Procedures on a Teacher's Contacts with Her Students," *Journal of Applied Behavior Analysis*, **3**, 169–174, 1970.

Morrow, W. R., and H. L. Gochros: "Misconceptions Regarding Behavior Modification," *The Social Service Review*, **44**, 293–307, 1970.

Mosier, D. B., and J. J. Vaal: "Dependency on Material Reinforcers: An Anecdote of One Child's Experience in the School Adjustment Program," *School Applications of Learning Theory*, **3**, 13–17, 1971.

O'Leary, K. D.: "Behavior Modification in the Classroom: A Rejoinder to Winett and Winkler," *Journal of Applied Behavior Analysis*, **5**, 505–511, 1972.

————, R. W. Poulos, and V. T. Devine: "Tangible Reinforcers: Bonuses or Bribes?" *Journal of Consulting and Clinical Psychology*, **38**, 1–8, 1972.

Otto, R. G.: "A Comparison of Positive Reinforcement and Punishment in Two Special Education Classes." Unpublished doctoral dissertation, University of Connecticut, 1975.

Price, M., and M. D'Ippolito: "The Effects and Side Effects of a Token Reinforcement System on Reading Behavior." Unpublished manuscript, Temple University, 1975.

Risley, T. R.: "Behavior Modification: An Experimental-Therapeutic Endeavor," in L. A. Hamerlynck, P. O. Davidson, and L. E. Acker (eds.), *Behavior Modification and Ideal Mental Health Services* (Calgary, Alberta, Canada: University of Calgary Press, 1970), pp. 103–127.

————: "The Effects and Side Effects of Punishing the Autistic Behaviors of a Deviant Child," *Journal of Applied Behavior Analysis*, **1**, 21–34, 1968.

————, and D. M. Baer: "Operant Behavior Modification: The Deliberate Development of Child Behavior," in B. Caldwell and H. Ricciuti (eds.), *Review of Child Development Research*, vol. III: *Social Action* (Chicago, Ill.: University of Chicago Press, 1973), pp. 283–329.

Sajwaj, T., S. Twardosz, and M. Burke: "Side Effects of Extinction Procedures in a Remedial Preschool," *Journal of Applied Behavior Analysis*, **5**, 163–175, 1972.

Salzberg, C. L.: "Freedom and Responsibility in an Elementary School, " in G. Semb, D. R. Green, R. P. Hawkins, J. Michael, E. L. Phillips, J. A. Sherman, H. Sloane, and D. R. Thomas (eds.), *Behavior Analysis and Education—1972* (Lawrence, Kans.: Support and Development Center for Follow Through, Department of Human Development, University of Kansas, 1972), pp. 62–77.

Scott, J. W., and D. Bushell: "The Length of Teacher Contacts and Students' Off-Task Behavior," *Journal of Applied Behavior Analysis*, **7**, 39–44, 1974.

Tribble, A., and R. V. Hall: "Effects of Peer Approval on Completion of Arithmetic Assignments," in F. W. Clark, D. R. Evans, and L. A. Hamerlynck (eds.), *Implementing Behavioral Programs for Schools and Clinics: Third Banff International Conference* (Champaign, Ill.: Research Press, 1972), pp. 139–140.

Ullmann, L. P., and L. Krasner: *Case Studies in Behavior Modification* (New York: Holt, Rinehart, & Winston, 1965).

Webster's New World Dictionary of the American Language, 2d college ed. (Englewood Cliffs, N.J.: Prentice-Hall, 1970).

Winnett, R. A., and R. C. Winkler: "Current Behavior Modification in the Classroom: Be Still, Be Quiet, Be Docile," *Journal of Applied Behavior Analysis*, **5**, 499–504, 1972.

Yates, A. J.: "Symptoms and Symptom Substitution," *Psychological Review*, **65**, 371–374, 1958.

Name Index

Subject Index